13 —

ADVENTURES ON THE WINE ROUTE

A Wine Buyer's Tour of France

R. Trollat, K. Lynch, G. Chave, E. Trollat

Adventures on the Wine Route

A WINE BUYER'S TOUR OF FRANCE

KERMIT LYNCH

Photographs by Gail Skoff

FARRAR, STRAUS AND GIROUX § *New York*

Copyright © 1988 by Kermit Lynch
Photographs copyright © 1988
by Gail Skoff
Introduction copyright ©
1988 by Richard Olney
All rights reserved
Printed in the United States of America
Published simultaneously in Canada by
Collins Publishers, Toronto
Designed by Jane Byers Bierhorst
First edition, 1988

Third printing, 1990

Library of Congress
Cataloging-in-Publication Data
Lynch, Kermit.
Adventures on the wine route: a wine
buyer's tour of France/by Kermit Lynch.—1st ed.
Includes index.
1. Wine and wine making—France. I. Title.
TP553.L96 1988   641.2′22′0944—dc19   88-10348

To my clients,
who make these adventures possible

CONTENTS

Kermit Lynch, when we first met some twelve years ago, described himself to me as a recently defected hippie. I had been in France since 1951, had never met a hippie and was not very clear about the definition of the species; I soon came to realize that Kermit was merely an old-fashioned bohemian who happened to possess a remarkable nose and palate.

Today Kermit rattles off French with impressive facility, while taking voluminous notes on each barrel or vat of wine as he swirls, sniffs, sucks, chews, and spits, but at that time his French was on the primitive side and, to ease the problems of communication, he had asked me to accompany him on a week's ferreting out of vineyards in the Côtes du Rhône and Burgundy.

Before we headed for Châteauneuf-du-Pape, the southernmost stop on the Côtes du Rhône itinerary, a visit to the Peyrauds at Domaine Tempier (Bandol) was inevitable. The instant spark of sympathy kindled between Kermit and the ebullient family of Peyrauds could be likened to spontaneous combustion. Today Kermit spends half the year in his recently acquired house in the back hills of Le Beausset, where part of the Bandol *appellation* is also cradled. He has been absorbed into the Peyraud family, and to Lucien Peyraud he is *mon fils.*

Among the other *vignerons* encountered on that trip, who are now cornerstones of Kermit's stable, were Gérard Chave in Hermitage, Auguste Clape in Cornas, Jean-Marie Ponsot in Morey-Saint-Denis . . . Still others, whose wines were beautiful then, have since faltered in their loyalty to common-sense methods of vinification; these have fallen by the wayside to be replaced by the constantly unfolding new discoveries, often *vignerons* whose wines were sold to *négociants* in the past, who have discovered that it is both more interesting and more profitable to raise and bottle their own wines.

This was not Kermit's first wine-tasting trip to France, but I think that it may have been the real beginning of his Adventures on the Wine Route. If it was my pleasure to be able to open a few doors on that trip, it has been Kermit's to open a great many more for me in the years that followed. I have, perhaps, been especially grateful for the discovery of certain wines from the less hallowed viticultural regions—inexpensive, clean, refreshing, and undemanding, ideal daily aperitif and summer luncheon wines; typical are Jean Berail's white, Roque Sestière, and Yves Laboucarie's *vin gris,* Domaine de Fontsainte, both from the southwest Corbières *appellation.*

Adventures on the Wine Route is an intensely personal book, permeated with an aura of intimacy between the author and the living, changing wines of which he writes, enhanced by the kind of knowledge born of experience. It is also generously truffled with opinions, tastes, beliefs, and attitudes, expressed with an impertinence which will delight most readers but which may trouble or outrage some members of the society that, in one of his brochures, Kermit has baptized the FWDP (Fine Wine-Drinking Public). His disdain for the contagious fad of blind and comparative tastings of unrelated wines will surely rub some furs the wrong way, as will his indifference to the New-Oak-Cabernet-Sauvignon global boom. *Tant mieux . . .*

Like father, like son. Kermit's father was a preacher and so is Kermit, but the sermons that Kermit delivers to his flock deal with things more worldly than brimstone fire; often invoked are the emasculating crime of filtering wines and the dangerous pitfalls open to the vintage-chart mentality.

Coupled with this amassment of information, messages, insights, and convictions is a gallery of portraits, some only sketches, others fully brushed in, of the people who make the wines, their dedication, their passions, their beliefs, their strengths . . . and their weaknesses.

No book on wine and the people who make it has ever been written that remotely resembles *Adventures on the Wine Route.*

Solliès-Toucas, March 30, 1988

Richard Olney

ADVENTURES ON THE WINE ROUTE

A Wine Buyer's Tour of France

We Americans with our New World innocence and democratic sensibilities tend to think that all wines are created equal, and that differences in quality are simply a matter of individual taste.

The French, with their aristocratic heritage, their experience and tradition, approach wine from another point of view. Just as France had its kings, noblemen, and commoners, French wine has its *grands crus, premiers crus,* and there is even an official niche for the commoners, the *vins de table.*

The wines produced by each nation are different, and the wine of each is well served by the two national viewpoints. One understands the style of California wines better when one understands the pioneer spirit, and one cannot appreciate French wine with any depth of understanding without knowing how the French themselves look at their wines, by going to the source, descending into their cold, humid cellars, tasting with them, and listening to the language they employ to describe their wines. It is not the vocabulary Californians employ, and often a precise translation of wine terms from one language to the other is impossible. I spend a third of the year tasting with the French winegrowers, and my book is about my experiences on the wine routes and in the wine cellars of France.

Some people think wine is a glamorous business. Witness the influx of big money into California's Napa Valley. It is not merely a decent glass of wine that motivates investors, nor do they want to see their manicured fingernails stained purple. It is the dream of a certain life-style that lures them. I have even noticed people respond with an enthusiastic glimmer of envy when they learn of my profession, wine buyer and importer. Once I enjoyed a confrontation with a platinum-blond wine groupie who told me how exciting my buying trips must be, traveling through France, the fancy restaurants, the posh hotels, the little old winemakers. The fine black fabric of her blouse might have been diaphanous, but a look long enough to say for sure would have been prying. "If you need someone to carry your suitcases, or whatever, let me know," she said. "I would love to go with you next time." A day or two of it might be glamorous, but I wonder what she would have thought after a few days on the road.

When I opened a wineshop in 1972, I envisioned some tastes of glamour myself. I did not start by importing my own selections. I sold domestic and imported wines purchased from distributors, but I had dreams of going to the source. The first time I did buy wine directly from a winery, I went to an Italian grower near Martinez, California. After I had made a couple of visits to taste and buy his Zinfandel, he telephoned and invited me to lunch. Now I'm getting to the heart of things, I thought, real winery cooking and some old treasures from his private cellar. And he did have a way with a tuna sandwich. He poured himself half a glass of red from an unlabeled bottle. I supposed he wanted me to guess the vintage. He passed the bottle to me, then grabbed a pitcher and filled his wineglass the rest of the way to the top with a murky-looking liquid. He offered the pitcher to me.

"What is it?" I asked.

"Iced tea," he said.

The most important event in my career after opening a wineshop occurred in 1973 when an importer invited me to accompany him on his annual buying trip to Burgundy.

This importer purchased his Burgundies from various *négociants*. In Burgundy, a *négociant* buys wine in bulk from the individual growers and bottles it himself. I was barely aware an alternative existed, and in fact there were not many growers in those days who did estate-bottle their wine.

We tasted all morning long, broke for lunch, then continued tasting and placing orders in the afternoon. The *négociants* wined and dined us until my digestive system clunked to a halt.

One evening we were invited out to dinner by a *négociant* who had that very year taken over the reins of the old family firm. We were to arrive at his estate outside Beaune to share an aperitif with him and his bride before going to Le Vieux Moulin, which was in those days the Côte d'Or's most starred restaurant.

The *négociant,* whom I shall call Gaston, was a short, uncertain, self-conscious fellow. He wore his mustache; it looked like a prop or a masquerade, an attempt at maturity. Alone, one had the impression, he probably peeled it off to be more comfortable with himself.

When the importer and I rang at the courtyard gate, there was no response. Is this the right night, we wondered. We rang again. The bells were loud enough for all the village to hear. When we were about to give up, the gate swung open and Gaston thrust out his hand for shaking. He seemed out of breath, agitated, and his pupils were dilated. I smelled an aniselike aroma coming from him amid a cataclysmic dose of after-shave lotion. I wondered how anyone who smelled so bad could make a good-smelling wine. He led us up worn stone steps into the salon, where we met his new wife, a charming young woman showing intelligence and apprehension in her eyes. At first I thought the glimmer of fear was a sign of her discomfort in her new role as wife of a wine *négociant* with its attendant social responsibilities, including receiving strangers into her home. As we sat and drank a Kir as aperitif (Gaston abstained), I began to notice that her husband was the object of her uneasiness. With each ponderous tick of the clock against the wall across from us, Gaston's over-excitation seemed to be changing to inebriation, yet he still was not drinking with us. His speech grew slurred and he began to tilt in his seat. It was the strangest thing, and it was happening right before our eyes.

Suddenly he sprang up and rushed over to me. "You come with me," he said, grabbing my arm and pulling me to my feet. I thought perhaps he was taking me down into the cellar to pick out some old Burgundies for dinner.

In the passageway to the courtyard he waved toward a bridle and saddle hanging up on the wall. "Bring those along," he commanded, as if I were his valet. When I ignored him, he yanked them down himself in a fury. He threw the bridle to me, hoisted the saddle onto his shoulder, and staggered off. "Follow me," he said, and I obeyed, not wanting to annoy a supplier, although in truth I would have preferred to go straight on out the gate.

We arrived at his stable. A beautiful chestnut-colored mare stood eyeing us warily as Gaston climbed through the wooden fence and I passed the saddle over to him. By then he could barely stand. He stumbled up to the horse and threw the saddle up and over her back. He stood mystified, as if the saddle had disappeared into the twilight zone. It had merely fallen to the ground on the other side of the mare. Gaston figured it out and tried again. And again. And again. He wore an expression of bewilderment worthy of Buster Keaton. With each toss of the saddle, the horse grew more appalled and began to shy away. Gaston kicked at the saddle in frustration and resorted to fitting the bridle over the horse's muzzle, hoping to hold her still with the reins. She was having no more of it and began loping around the stable, with Gaston following along behind, trying to dig in his heels to check her. He fell but still did not let go the reins. He slid dragging along the ground through the mud and horseshit.

I snuck back to the salon. "Let's get out of here," I whispered to my importer. "That guy is bonkers."

My importer politely asked Gaston's wife if her husband had overdone the tippling before our arrival.

No, she had not seen him take a drink all day. I thought of the bizarre smell of his breath. Had he chugalugged a fifth of some anise-flavored liquor while we were ringing at the gate?

Here he came then, lurching into the room, splotched and smeared from head to toe. He bounced off the walls into another room and came right back out clutching a good-sized revolver. He weaved and harangued and gestured wildly, giving each of us a chance to stare down the barrel of his pistol.

In a relatively calm voice his wife suggested that we postpone our dinner date. I stared at her. How could she achieve normalcy when I expected to die any second?

Gaston did not like her suggestion, so he bullied us until we all filed out to the car at gunpoint.

Ah, France, the great restaurants, the little old winemakers . . .

Gaston babbled in the backseat, toppling over into his wife on the curves. I awaited a bullet through the seat cushion. The car smelled like horseshit, anise, and after-shave.

When we pulled up outside the restaurant, I hopped out quickly. My companions joined forces to try to convince Gaston that we postpone our dinner. He struggled to get out of the car, but was really too far gone to stand up under his own power.

"We can't postpone," he whined. "My father wouldn't like it."

Finally my importer, who probably weighed 200 pounds to Gaston's 140, blocked the doorway and said, "You sit back there and shut up, or I'll shut you up!" I was impressed, and so, apparently, was Gaston, who sat back, keeled over in slow motion, and seemed to pass out. Not a peep from the tiger, even as we carried him up to his bathroom, dropped him on the floor, and left his poor wife to clean up the mess.

Later I learned from village gossip that Gaston had suffered all his life from a tyrannical father who belittled him at every turn. Gaston loved a local girl who tended his horses and stable, but his father threatened to disinherit him if he married her. The father then arranged a proper marriage to the woman I met, permitting Gaston to become lord of the manor. He was paying a certain price, however.

Tastings in the *négociants'* cellars were marathon events, so I had to learn to spit out each taste. It is not difficult, nor does it interfere with one's appreciation of a wine. You simply savor the wine, sucking it over your tongue, then aim it into the bucket, sink, or onto the floor if it is gravel. To be tipsy by ten o'clock in the morning is unprofessional, and each firm offered a huge range of *appellations* for tasting, from Burgundy to the Chalonnais, Beaujolais, and the Rhône. Some of them were available in several different vintages. At one cellar I purchased Burgundies from 1971, 1969, 1966, 1961, 1959, 1953, 1947, and 1945.

Strange as it seems, each *négociant's* wines showed a house style that influenced their taste more than each particular *appellation* or vintage character. For example, a 1970 Volnay from Gaston resembled his 1949 Nuits-Saint-Georges more than it resembled other Volnays or other 1970s. There was a disconcerting, nearly impenetrable sameness to the wines throughout these *négociant* tastings. I chalked up my difficulty sorting out differences to my own inexperience. I figured my uneducated palate could not handle the subtle nuances. Now I am not so sure that my palate was the culprit, thanks to incidents such as a conversation with a grower in Chambolle-Musigny. He told me he had sold off his

1977s to a *négociant* because he was not happy with them. The *négociant's* tanker truck arrived and into it went the Bonnes Mares (a *grand cru*), the Chambolle Les Amoureuses (a *premier cru*), and his Chambolle *villages*. All into the same tank. Yet the *négociant* also picked up the documents which would allow him to market bottles under the separate labels Bonnes Mares, Les Amoureuses, and Chambolle-Musigny. The repercussions of his little tale resound endlessly.

After a wine tour of France, Thomas Jefferson wrote advice to a friend about how one should go about buying French wine:

> The *vigneron* never adulterates his wine, but on the contrary gives it the most perfect and pure care possible. But when once a wine has been into a merchant's hands, it never comes out unmixed. This being the basis of their trade, no degree of honesty, of personal friendship or of kindred prevents it.

One "merchant," or *négociant,* poured us a lovely 1954 Bonnes Mares. My importer told him that Americans considered 1954 an off vintage. Although the wine itself was fine enough, it would be difficult to sell.

"What would you like?" asked the *négociant.* "I can label it 1953 or 1955, whichever you prefer."

If he would do that, I wondered, why would he have any compunction about sending me a different wine than what I had actually tasted and ordered? It made me nervous.

Gaston's wines were remarkably unlike the others I was tasting. They were unusually weighty and tannic for Burgundy. It was two years afterward that I recognized Gaston's house style in the Châteauneuf-du-Papes that I tasted during my first trip to the southern Rhône, the same weight and tannin, shockingly similar flavors.

However, on that initial visit to Burgundy I did not know better, and subsequently Gaston's "Burgundies" enjoyed quite a success because in those days the California palate (mine included) demanded big mouth-filling wines at the expense of any other virtues, including authenticity. For the most part *négociant*-bottled Burgundies enjoyed a near monopoly, so one lacked a point of reference. And of course the California palate had been formed by the big, gutsy, sun-drenched local wines. Burgundy is not sun-drenched.

Previous to that first trip, my only tasting training, if one can call it training, consisted of frequent blind tastings, with the labels masked to keep the tasters blind to each wine's identity. Supposedly blindness ensured objectivity. Winning wines were invariably the blockbusters, wines loaded with tannin and alcohol, the more the merrier. Such wines are overwhelmingly impressive, particularly the first sniff and sip, which is what counts in a blind tasting. However, tannin and alcohol overwhelm the taste buds. One's capacity to taste is physically impaired. For real-life drinking, at table where wine belongs, it is difficult to sustain one's interest in tannin and alcohol. "That's a BIG wine," was a common appreciation at those blind tastings when it came time to state the reason for one's preference. Therefore, on my first buying trip, I looked for BIG wines. A Corton might smell like Châteauneuf-du-Pape, but if it was a chewy wine I bought it, and if the wine did not bite back I dismissed it. Which is to say, regretfully, I preferred a big gutsy wine with vulgar flavors to a light wine with exquisite flavors.

My next trip to Burgundy changed all that. I returned in order to taste the *domaine*-bottled wines offered by Frank Schoonmaker Selections. Visiting small cellars up and down the Côte d'Or, I began to notice that each village—Fixin, Gevrey, Morey, and Chambolle, for example—produced wine with a character different from its neighbors'. After the *négociant* wines, it was as if I had been swimming underwater with my eyes open and suddenly someone presented me with a pair of goggles.

On the final day of the tour, one of the winemakers mentioned that in his opinion the most talented winemaker in Burgundy was Hubert de Montille in Volnay. I canceled my flight home and drove to Volnay.

De Montille stands out in a crowd because of his shaved head. His cranium is not smooth like a billiard ball; it looks as if a sculptor had left his marks on it. The bumps and indentations, contours and ripples, give an impression of intelligence, as if they were the outward manifestation of a labyrinthine mental process. At the same time, there is a country elegance to the man, heightened by his attire. His olive-green corduroy trousers show wear, but one could spend hours searching in the best men's shops of Paris trying to find such high-grade fabric.

He conducted a tasting. Conducted is the word, because the series of wines unfolded like a set of musical variations. De Montille is a lawyer as well. Perhaps he structured the tasting as a lawyer builds a case. Whichever, it was a performance.

We began with his new wines, vintage 1974, from barrel. They were light and fragrant, the Pinot Noir fruit pure and seductive. Where before a wine's body had been its most important quality, with de Montille's Volnays and Pommards the body was absolutely without significance. Some were light, some full-bodied, some ethereal and delicate, others powerful and mouth-filling. The size was a trait which in no way influenced one's positive or negative appreciation of the wine. But the aromas coming off those wines, the flavors and balance . . .

We considered the 1973s, '72s, '71s, '69s, '66s, '64s, and terminated the tasting with a half bottle of his 1959 Volnay "Taillepieds," which de Montille said was beginning to go over the hill. I wanted to go with it.

I was struggling to learn French, so we had to drive into Beaune to the Office de Tourisme to find a translator to help us negotiate the purchase.

I left France having made my first wine discovery, my first direct purchase from a French wine *domaine,* and totally dissatisfied with the other wines I was selling. On the plane, my thoughts were soaring. I wanted more de Montilles. I wanted a de Montille in Vosne, Nuits, Aloxe, Savigny, in each village of the Côte d'Or. I wanted the 747 to turn back so I could begin ferreting out growers. That one tasting was a revelation, and what had been an interesting business became a passion.

My enthusiasm must have been contagious, because most of de Montille's wines had been reserved by my clients by the time the first shipment arrived. When the ship was unloaded, I could not wait to pull a cork. I poured his 1972 Volnay "Champans" into a glass and raised it to my nose.

Where was that fabulous Pinot Noir quality? How had a wine so expressive turned dumb? The wine was not bad, but it bore no resemblance to what I had tasted in Volnay, so I telephoned France and asked Monsieur de Montille why had he not sent me exactly what I had sampled. He claimed that he had. He said that his was a natural wine, that perhaps it was not happy after its month-long voyage from Volnay to Berkeley. Put the wines in a cool cellar for six months to see if they recover.

They recovered, but when it was time to import another batch of de Montille's wine I decided to use a refrigerated container, just to see if the temperature during shipping made a difference. The shipping company thought I was crazy. "Reefers," as temperature-controlled containers are called, were used for foods like cheese and meat. Perishables. But I had reason to believe that de Montille's wine was perishable, too. My first shipment had not actually perished, but it had arrived with some sort of *maladie*.

Wine travels in metal containers that hold around twelve hundred cases. I asked myself, how hot does it become inside as it crosses the Atlantic, creeps through the Panama Canal, and steams up the Mexican coast to California? Would I survive the same trip in a metal container? It must be like an oven.

When the second shipment arrived, I uncorked a bottle right out of the reefer and there in my glass was the true de Montille in all its splendor. It tasted exactly as it had in his cellar. After that experience, I used nothing but reefers for all my wine shipments, be they rare, expensive Burgundies or cheap little country wines.

The difference between a wine shipped at cellar temperature and one shipped in a standard container is not subtle. One is alive, the other cooked. I can taste the difference. And one never knows exactly how much the wine will suffer, because the climate en route cannot be predicted. It might arrive dumb like those first de Montilles, or it might arrive dead. By reefer the shipping costs are higher, but the wine is not damaged.

Around the same period, I decided to stop taking part in blind tastings. They seemed such tomfoolery. Blind, yes, that does sum up the vision involved in this popular method of judging quality. The method is misguided, the results spurious and misleading. I realized that I could not trust my own judgment under such tasting conditions. A number of wines are set up side by side, tasted, compared, and ranked. A tally is taken. One wine wins. The others are losers. Democracy in action.

Such tasting conditions have nothing to do with the conditions under which the wines will presumably be drunk, which is at table, with food. When a woman chooses a hat, she does not put it on a goat's head to judge it; she puts it on her own. There is a vast difference, an insurmountable difference, between the taste of a wine next to another wine, and the same wine's taste with food.

Test it yourself. Take two impeccable wines, the Domaine Tempier Bandol rosé, which *The Wine Advocate* has called the finest rosé in France, and a bottle of Château Margaux, which many critics consider the finest Médoc of the day. Compare the two side by side. Award points. Do not be surprised if the Margaux wins handily. Now serve the same two wines with a boiled artichoke and rate them again. The Margaux is bitter and metallic-tasting, whereas the Bandol rosé stands up and dances like Baryshnikov.

Which is the better wine? Which *wins?*

Or compare a good Musigny with a good Monthelie. More likely than not, if the wines are well made, the Musigny will win, but your own pleasure at table would best be served by a light, spirited young Monthelie with, for example, fresh egg noodles and truffles, and an older, nobler Burgundy like Musigny afterward with the proper cheeses. There you see a sensible progression of two impeccable wines. Comparing them side by side, you will find one a winner, the other a loser. Served intelligently at table, neither wine loses, your pleasure crescendos, and you, finally, are the winner.

And those people who would always drink the Musigny over a Monthelie no matter what they have on their plate are not wine lovers. They are status seekers.

A wine can only be judged as it relates to the environment in which it is served. The Chardonnay that looks best in the context of a comparative tasting is not likely to win next to a platter of fresh oysters.

I began to notice that most of the blind-tasting champions in my own cellar remained untouched, because I had no desire to *drink* them. Just as they had overwhelmed the other wines to win a blind tasting, they overwhelm practically any cuisine. Drink with Stilton? lamb fat? enchiladas?

Those big rock-'em-sock-'em blockbusters perform one function admirably—they win tastings. (One score sheet at a comparative tasting allotted four points out of twenty for *BODY!*) Usually such wines give their all in the first whiff and sip, but great wine is about nuance, surprise, subtlety, expression, qualities that keep you coming back for yet another taste. Rejecting a wine because it is not big enough is like rejecting a book because it is not long enough, or a piece of music because it is not loud enough.

As those tasting champions aged in my cellar, I learned that body has little to do with aging potential. Many ripe, tannic monsters lost their fruit but remained tannic monsters. They assault the palate; it hurts to drink them.

Well-balanced wines of whatever size developed well. In 1985 I tasted a 1954 La Tâche. It was rosé-colored. In terms of body it was almost not there. However, its aromas and flavors were magical, and I will never forget that wine. Light as a snowflake, it was sublime at thirty-one years of age.

In 1983 I tasted a 1900 Château Rausan-Ségla. It was not old-tasting; it was vibrant, alive, *à point.* During its first forty or fifty years, how would it have fared in a comparative tasting? It must have been closed, chaste, tight, unyielding.

Of course a wine's size or body is important, but only as it relates to its service, its placement in the progression of the other wines to be served, and its alliance with the specific cuisine to be served.

Comparative tasting results can make front-page headlines. They have had such an impact that vinification practices have changed in order to produce wines that conform to the winning formula. Bordeaux wines of today are designed to seduce the journalists and "blind" tasters upon release, in order to provoke early consumer demand. A wine such as that 1900 Rausan-Ségla will not be produced in the present commercial climate.

Bordeaux, Burgundy, Beaujolais, almost all of France's wine regions are guilty of overchaptalization (adding too much sugar to the fermenting grape juice in order to boost the wine's alcoholic content), because the public demands BIG wines, and high alcohol equals full body. Beaujolais used to be a light, sharpish little quaffer. One could down a bottle of it at lunch without needing a nap. Today, that full-bodied Beaujolais you taste may have begun its existence at 10 degrees alcohol (light wine) and end up in bottle at 14 degrees alcohol (BIG wine). But, after all, the consumer has to decide: does the wine smell good and taste good, or does it simply pack a wallop? When the public taste changes away from size to aroma and flavor as the most important criteria, we will all be drinking finer wine.

In 1976 my limited French was still causing difficulties. A friend told me about an American who had lived more than two decades in France who might be persuaded to interpret for me in the cellars, who knew wine, and might also have a few addresses for me. His name, Richard Olney, meant nothing to me, but when I mentioned him to Alice Waters, who has Chez Panisse restaurant in Berkeley, her mouth dropped open. "Richard Olney! Don't even think about it. Pack your bags and get on the plane."

I remember waking up at Richard's hillside home in Provence the morning after my arrival, the morning of our departure for the wine country, jet lag and the November chill numbing my bones. Before his kitchen fireplace we warmed ourselves with coffee and toast while a mistral tried to raise the roof. By the time we were prepared to leave for Châteauneuf-du-Pape it was 11:30 a.m., and Richard suggested we have a bite of cheese in order to avoid an immediate stop at a restaurant. He brought out a platter of cheeses on a bed of autumn-colored grape leaves and uncorked a 1969 red from nearby Bandol. It sounds simple, but I was astonished by that marriage of wine and cheese (mostly mild *chèvres* of various ages). And by that wildly delicious red wine!

What is a Bandol, I wondered.

And when it was sipped *with* those cheeses, it became one of the most fantastically delicious wines I had ever tasted.

Two lessons in one simple snack: you find gold kicking around in the unlikeliest places (Bandol, for example), and something can be created by matching food with wine that surpasses either of them standing alone.

After one week Richard had introduced me to Hermitage, Cornas, Côte Rôtie, Condrieu, Muscat de Beaumes-de-Venise, Côtes de Brouilly, and Mercurey, in addition to Bandol.

Moreover, he changed the way I tasted, judged, and selected wine. He did not instruct me. I observed him tasting, observed him matching wine to food and food to wine in restaurants, listened to his appreciations in the cellars as he searched for whatever distinguished each wine. He did not taste with a fixed idea of "the perfect wine" in mind. He valued finesse, balance, personality, and originality. If a wine had something to say, he listened. If a wine was a cliché, he had little interest. If it was different, apart from the rest, he appreciated it more.

From one producer in the Beaujolais, Richard bought a twenty-five-liter barrel of a light, tart *nouveau* to bottle at home. I told him that it would be impossible to market such a wine in California. "It is too light, too green."

"But that's exactly what I like about it," he responded.

Together we bottled it, corked it, and sloshed down a happy quantity one afternoon. No, we did not discuss the pH, the oak, the body, the finish. But there was a gaiety to it; the tart fruit perfumed the palate and the brain; it seemed thirst-quenching, and yet our thirst was never so quenched that another purplish slurp seemed out of order.

Wine is, above all, pleasure. Those who would make it ponderous make it dull. People talk about the mystery of wine, yet most don't want anything to do with mystery. They want it all there in one sniff, one taste. If you keep an open mind and take each wine on its own terms, there is a world of magic to discover.

Casting a backward glance at my first trip to the Loire, I see a younger man who supported discomforts that sound torturous today. I flew from San Francisco to New York, changed planes, landed in Paris, rented a car, and drove to the Loire. Twenty-two hours all told, with a nine-hour time change. Those days the excitement, the novelty, and the thrill of the chase kept me going nonstop from one cellar to another. It was a period of discovery—discovering wines, wine-makers, discovering France—and the adrenaline flow kept my blood as warm as the Loire cellars were cold.

It was late fall, the hunting season, and I settled into a little one-star hotel. I collapsed into bed for a late-afternoon nap and two hours later struggled to emerge from that deep black hole of sleep familiar to all who have suffered jet lag.

The hotel dining room was animated and colorful, filled with hunters dressed to kill in their shiny black-leather boots and bright red coats. I shared the spirit that filled the room. I had my own hunting to do.

The Burgundies on the restaurant's wine list were *négociant* bottlings priced higher than I charged at my wineshop in California. The Bordeaux selections were too expensive *and* too young. However, there was an intriguing collection of little-known Loire Valley reds: Chinon, Bourgueil, Saint-Nicolas-de-Bourgueil, and Sancerre. Mixing research with supper, I asked the proprietor to bring up his best Loire red. He poured a Bourgueil. The price was painless, the color a promising bluish purple, the aroma loaded with berrylike fruit, the flavors original and delicious, so delicious that I asked him to prepare a few tenths to take along in the trunk of my car to share with friends and winemakers along the route. Thus began my love affair with the Cabernet Franc of Chinon and Bourgueil, wines which at their best have such a strong personality that novice tasters are often startled. After that initial taste, it will be love or hate. It is no different than one's reaction to an individual with a strong personality.

The hotel proprietor, seeing my appreciation of his Bourgueil, next recommended a Sancerre *rouge*. I had thought all Sancerre white. No, he said, there is a small proportion of Pinot Noir planted there. The wine was brilliantly vinified. Anyone who could produce an impressive Pinot Noir in an unlikely place like Sancerre deserved investigation, so I jotted down the name of the *domaine,* which I must call Domaine X for reasons which will soon be obvious.

A duet of hunting dogs and church bells woke me up early the next morning. There was a bright glitter of sunshine that did nothing to thaw the brittle chill in the air.

I had two days for Sancerre. Domaine X was one of several producers I visited, including a large *négociant* who appeared to own most of downtown Sancerre, and whose name was sarcastically mispronounced by certain proprietors so that it came out meaning "half-water." A disturbing number of wineries had decorative oak casks outside and stainless-steel tanks inside their cellars. But the visit to Domaine X deepened my understanding of wine and helped set me on a course which I follow to this day.

Truth be told, Monsieur X was a wry, crusty old fellow who wanted to talk about his absent son more than anything else, including wine. His son, who spoke several languages fluently, who had been around the world four times already, and who would one day take over the wine *domaine*—that is, if he was not elected president of the Republic first. "He's in Indonesia right now," Monsieur X said, checking his wristwatch.

One after another, all day long, each Sancerre *blanc* I had tasted had been drawn from either glass-lined or stainless-steel tanks. There was a pleasant, easy sameness to them. Some growers were preparing to bottle their wine a mere six weeks after the harvest! It is simple. You heat your cellar to speed up the fermentation, then you run your wine through a sterile filter before bottling it. Your worries are over. The Sancerres of Monsieur X were still leisurely bubbling along, fermenting in ancient gray oak barrels that had nurtured many a vintage. I came from California, where new oak was a sign of seriousness and quality. Why did Monsieur X use old barrels?

"New oak masks everything," he growled. "The virtues and the flaws. I have nothing to hide behind the taste of new oak. On the contrary."

I was struck by the fact that fermentation in barrel produced a wine with more depth, more dimensions to it, than those from stainless-steel tanks where the wine is boxed in tight as a knot. In barrel there is an exchange between the wine and the air. The wine breathes through the pores of the wood. And the air it breathes has certain aromas, the cellar smells, which, however

View of Sancerre

imperceptible, are soaked up by the wine. Perhaps that is why whites that see glass only, or stainless steel only, seem one-dimensional in comparison. Of course, if the winemaker is not fanatically attentive, the wine in barrel can breathe too much, and instead of a beneficial evolution, instead of this subtle seasoning, you will have an oxidized wine. It is work to keep an eye on each barrel, to keep all of them constantly filled up to the top to avoid oxidation. Thus, the predominance of stainless steel today. It is easier, safer, and the large tanks take up less space. Something is lost, however.

A second difference between X and the others: he had not one Sancerre *blanc,* but three. There are different *terroirs* or soils at Sancerre, he explained, and he had vines planted in three types of soil: limestone, flint, and clay. At the other *domaines,* it would have been a matter of selecting for purchase the cleanest, best-balanced Sauvignon Blanc, because the fruit dominated. At Domaine X, the Sauvignon character was evident, but only as one part of the taste impression. More important was the personality imparted by the soil in which the vine nourished itself, because the wine from each soil type was vinified and bottled separately with the specific vineyard name on the label. Here were wines from the same grape, the same cellar, vinification, and vintage, but tasting them side by side, one encountered three remarkably different personalities. And the wine from flinty soil, for example, consistently showed the same personality traits no matter which vintage we were tasting, being leaner, tighter, with a stronger mineral flavor than the other two. If only everyone could make such a comparative tasting, I thought, instead of those silly blind tastings that are such the rage. Here was a comparative tasting that deepened one's awareness of the mystery of wine.

The third striking aspect was the old winery itself, which had been constructed on different levels of the hillside in order to permit racking and bottling by gravity flow. By avoiding mechanical pumping, Monsieur X produced bottled wines which retained all their nerve and vigor. Subsequently I began to make inquiries about bottling methods a routine part of my visit to new wineries.

The point is, Monsieur X's wines were not one-dimensional quaffers like so many Sancerres. They were more serious, more exciting to taste, because observing and defining their personalities engaged the intellect and the imagination. Rather than leaving the impression that wine is simply another beverage, they inspired the notion that wine can communicate something.

For several years I imported the Sancerres of Domaine X. In certain vintages I would buy the wine from all three *terroirs*. I cannot say that they had a fabulous commercial success; wine with a pronounced personality appeals to a small part of the public. But I took great pride in selling them because I believed I was importing the best. Imagine my emotions when I showed up one fine spring morning and was received by the son. He had thrown up a new barnlike winery building and filled it with stainless-steel vats. The reflections shimmering off the tanks gave the impression of a circus hall of mirrors. My face appeared two feet long. There was a new centrifuge. There was a special tank for refrigerating the wine down below zero to eliminate the possibility of tartrate crystal deposits. There were various pumps and filtering devices. The place looked like a winery-equipment showroom. Even worse, it smelled like a sulfur-dioxide factory. Where were those solid, proven old casks gently bubbling along? Where were the beautiful wooden tools like the hand-carved mallet Old Man X had used to knock the stoppers loose from the bungs of the barrels?

I could not restrain myself. I asked why he needed to centrifuge, cold-stabilize, filter, *and* dose his wines with massive quantities of SO_2. This fellow was taking no chances! He led me into his office, strutting like a rooster, a cigar poked into his bushy beard, his head blown up into a big balloon of self-congratulation. He pointed to a map of the world tacked on the wall behind his desk. I was represented by a colored pushpin stabbed into California. England had one too, and Belgium, Denmark, Germany, and so on. He stabbed a finger at a lone pushpin lost in the middle of the African continent. "I sell fifty cases a year here," he said, "and there is no way to know what the shipping conditions will be. I have to protect my wine so it won't spoil." Here was a man willing to strip his wine of its character in order to protect fifty cases.

I tasted the sulfur-laden wines. They were all alike, poor things. I walked out without placing an order. I drove away swearing out loud. That horse's ass ruined my Sancerre!

Touring the wineries in France over the years, I began to see that my experience at Domaine X was representative of a general evolution in French winemaking, and finding the old-style wines in each region and educating my clients to the diversity and virtue of those wines became a kind of crusade to me.

After Sancerre I headed west into the Touraine to investigate their reds. I found a Chinon and Bourgueil that I imported and presented to my customers as little country wines because that is what they were, nothing more or less than pretty little quaffers fun to drink cool for their berrylike fruit. As is often the case, a first visit to a new region did not turn up the finest wines. It serves as a scouting trip, and hopefully I will stumble across something of interest, good wines to whet the appetite of my clients, or perhaps some leads for subsequent visits. The wines I bought were not monuments to the vintner's art but they were unlike the California reds of the day, which seemed to be the result of a contest to see who could turn out the biggest alcoholic monster. Open-minded tasters appreciated those Loire reds. One said they tasted like "Bordeaux Beaujolais" because of their Cabernet character and their youthful charm.

Then, on my next trip to Burgundy, Jacques Seysses at Domaine Dujac told me he had recently returned from a tour of the Loire vineyards with a small group of Burgundian winemakers. One wine stood apart from the rest, he said, the Chinon of Charles Joguet. I jotted down Joguet's name in my notebook and a few days later drove off to find him.

§ 24 §

There is no *autoroute* from Burgundy to Chinon unless one drives all the way up to Paris and south again to exit at Tours. I took country roads that zigzag aimlessly across the landscape from one small village to another: Varzy, Donzy, Cosne-sur-Loire, Vailly-sur-Sauldre, Aubigny-sur-Nère, and Souèsmes, villages in which anyone visible gazes intently at your license plate, trying to divine from the last two digits where you hail from. One has the impression that this is the high point of their day, and on the surface at least the villages seem deathly dull. After Sancerre, in the Sologne, the forests crowd up to line the route, and at that time of year the autumn leaves swirled behind my car as I sped along trying to keep up with the setting sun.

I arrived late at Joguet's village, Sazilly, near Chinon, and was later still because I could not find his house. There was no sign to indicate it. Little light remained. It was painfully cold. The ground crunched underfoot. As I poked my nose through the opening of a tall hedge, I came upon the eeriest-looking person I have ever seen, a twisted, gnomish, hunched creature who peered up at me with difficulty because he could not turn or bend his neck and had to lean his body sideways and down in order to meet my eyes. I would not have been more surprised had I seen a witch on a broomstick.

"Monsieur Joguet?" I inquired.

He tugged at my sleeve and led me to the side door of the simple bourgeois house. He knocked crisply and sidled off into the icy ash-colored twilight. I heard irregular footsteps within. The door swung open and there in the light I beheld a second warped figure whose head tilted at a weird angle. He offered his hand for shaking and there was a finger or two missing. My God, I thought, there is a whole colony of them. Oh well, anything for a decent bottle of wine. But I also noticed that the eyes were full of fire and intelligence and a dash of self-humor. It was Charles Joguet.

My gnomelike guide, I learned later, had assisted at the *domaine* all his life, working the vines, tending the goats, rabbits, and chickens. He was not a Joguet; it did not run in the family. No,

Charles had recently suffered an automobile accident. His tilt was temporary, due to the cast and metal brace he wore to help mend his broken vertebrae. The fingers? An old tractor accident. The magic? He has it.

We began tasting with his newly vinified 1976 out of barrel. The nose was thick with black currants and violets. It was sizable on the palate, too. Ripe, rich, and succulent, it felt as if it must be staining my tongue purple. A serious, extravagantly flavored wine, this was way beyond the little country wines of my first trip. Very simply, at that stage it was the finest 1976 red I had tasted from any of the French vineyards. A Chinon! And Charles had never laid eyes on an importer. I felt like Columbus discovering the New World.

From the winery we trudged through the dark across a field. Charles opened an old wooden door into the hillside. We entered a limestone cave with a dirt floor. It was furnished with hundreds of old bottles. I have never been colder than in that cave. My teeth chattered and my hand trembled when I held out my glass for a taste of 1975, followed by 1974, 1973, 1971, 1969 . . .

Have you ever seen someone in a back and neck brace pulling corks? But I could not taste a thing. The wines were close to freezing, but the corks kept popping as he moved onward, or rather backward in time: 1966, 1964, 1961. Finally we took his 1959 back to the house and resorted to swirling our glasses over a wood fire, trying to liberate a bit of the wine's icebound aroma.

Then Charles took me to dinner at a nearby truck stop, Sazilly's only restaurant. He left the bottles behind, all those old Chinons from which only a taste or two had been poured, and we served ourselves glasses of the same plonk the truckers were drinking. The bulk stuff. Plastic bottles. Barely wine.

"Too bad," I told Charles. "It's the first wine I can really taste."

"It's not shitty," he said. "It's ultra-shitty. Shit-*de-merde*!" he exclaimed, laughing as he pounded his glass on the table. "Shit-*de-merde*" must be the ultimate franglais. Charles is endlessly scatological and endlessly pronouncing maxims: "Everything is

Charles Joguet. Chinon

possible!" he might offer, then: "Nothing is possible! Wisdom is all; wisdom is shit. Everyone seeks love; love seeks no one."

"Why didn't you bring one of your own wines?" I wondered, taking another sniff of our plonk. It smelled like vinegar with a bit of complexity from the plastic.

"The proprietor would take it as an insult," Charles answered.

The food was good family-style cooking. Above all, it was hot. I stopped shivering. That winter of 1976 was a cold one as Mother Nature made up for the previous summer's blazing heat.

When I returned to Sazilly in the spring, Charles repeated the tasting, vintage by vintage, and I have been an enthusiastic believer ever since. His 1959 would convert even the most leaden palate to the charms of Chinon. And his 1976 continued to develop beautifully. The Dionysian new wine aromas had diminished; there was a more complex smell to it, an elusiveness, as different aromas came and went. I imported a special *cuvée* of old vines, pricey for a Chinon, and I finally managed to sell all of it even though most wine buyers at that time were preoccupied throwing their money after those hard, dry, tannic monsters that Burgundy produced in 1976. One restaurateur called me to say that he had always loved the Chinons that he tasted in France and that Joguet's 1976 was the finest he had ever tasted. When he heard the price he rang off, telling me Joguet's was too expensive. At six dollars. Meanwhile his wine list offered many a Burgundy and claret at over a hundred dollars per bottle. I sat mulling it over while Charles whispered "shit-*de-merde*" inside my head.

As a young man, Charles Joguet left Sazilly for the Ecole des Beaux-Arts in Paris and studied painting. Then his passion turned to sculpture. He traveled to Italy to study the Old Masters, then to America to experience New York for a few months. But he returned to the vine ("instinctively," he says) after the death of his father in 1957. He began to split his time between the bohemian life in Paris and the winegrower's life at Sazilly. The dual existence continues today, and his brilliant wines reflect his artist's temperament and his commitment to family tradition.

It is not only that Joguet makes good Chinon: it is that he is one of the rare vintners whose wines can be gripping aesthetically, spiritually, and intellectually, as well as sensuously. Of course, it is impossible to know how much my judgment is influenced by the fact that I know the man, as well as the wine. One has the impression that Charles is out there on the edge, willing to take risks and willing to accept losses in order to make magic. There are not many like him in the world of wine. Those who have seen a Judy Garland concert performance will understand, the way she would take over a song, the emotion, the commitment, and the risk with which she invested her performance. I see Charles as a performer, and his wine is his song or act. He refuses to play it safe. He might ruin a *cuvée* because an improvisation or inspiration during the vinification did not work as he hoped. With the next *cuvée,* for the same reasons, he succeeds beyond all expectations. It will express something to you, something you understand on a certain level but which cannot be translated into words. But then musical expression presents the same dilemma. When one tries to put what it says into words, it sounds ridiculous.

There is always some crisis threatening to engulf him and bring him down. He is perpetually on the verge of bankruptcy. Most people do not understand that it costs more to make a good wine than a mediocre wine. Right off the bat, there is the question of quantity, the yield per acre. If you allow your vines to produce twice as much juice, your wine will seem diluted but you will have twice as many bottles to sell. A great Chinon *should* cost more than an ordinary one. Charles does whatever he must for quality, and when he thinks of money, it is to wonder, "How am I going to get by for another year?"

He was swindled by the company that constructed four new fermentation vats for him. The lining on the inside of the vats was not stable. He sued. He won. Meanwhile, the contractor had gone bankrupt, so he lost after all. How was he going to raise money for another set of vats in time for the next harvest? He was under the impression that his bankers had already heard one lament too many.

Along came a further exercise in ecstasy and despair. A friend told Charles that he had something interesting to show him, a piece of land for sale called Le Chêne Vert, or "The Green Oak." "I had heard of it," Charles says. "The origin of the name is known. There had been an eight-hundred-year-old oak there which was cut down about four hundred years ago. So I went along to look at the property, the cellars, the soils, the vines. That afternoon there was a splendid sunset illuminating the old city of Chinon. I knew that Le Chêne Vert was one of the two parcels originally planted by the monks here in the eleventh century. They introduced the Cabernet Franc here, and they knew what they were doing because Le Chêne Vert is certainly the most extraordinary site for the vine at Chinon. But half of it was grown over wild, the other half with untended old vines which had to be ripped out. The terrain is steep and uneven, very difficult to work. What a job, I thought, to put it into shape for replanting. None of the other winemakers was interested in it. It was to be sold at auction. It is an old custom here, *une vente à la bougie*. There is a candle burning on a piece of wood, and when the flame burns out, the auction is over. It takes about two or three minutes. I was curious to see what the land would go for, so I went to the auction. The only serious bidder wanted it as pasture for his sheep! No one thought I would buy it, especially me. At the last moment I opened my mouth and *voilà*, the candle went out. I said to myself, '*Zut!* Where will I find the money?' It was cheap, but when you are broke nothing is cheap."

He survived it, walking the financial tightrope through several years, but now he says his gamble is going to pay off. Le Chêne Vert, once the vines are of sufficient age, will produce his finest wine. That is what Charles means by "pay off."

One evening after dinner together in Chinon, I invited Joguet to my hotel room to taste a couple of red Burgundies that had interested me. I like to taste with him because he always gets right to the heart of things, and those who shop for wine armed with those idiotic vintage charts would do well to pay attention to his appreciation of the two wines. Both were of extremely good quality, I like to think. Otherwise, I would not have bothered to cart them to Chinon in the trunk of my car. One was from a *grand cru* vineyard and it was from 1976, a red Burgundy vintage which had attracted a stampede of consumer interest in the United States. The second was a little Saint-Aubin, 1973. With that name and that vintage, it would make about as big a splash as a Pinot Noir grape falling into the Dead Sea.

Joguet held his glass up to the dim yellow light. French hotels do not waste bucks on bulbs. The 1976 was dark, big, powerful. The 1973 was pale and light-bodied. He tasted each.

"The 1976 has not yet come together," Charles said. "One must wait a few more years. But you know, it will be of a unit, of a whole piece, for a very short time. The different parts will align themselves into a harmonious unit and then pass very quickly out of harmony. You will have to jump on it and drink it up during a very short period of time.

"The 1973 will never be great wine, but it is fine, an intelligent wine, the most difficult to make. One sees all of it, the Pinot Noir fruit, the *terroir* of that particular site, the structure, the perfect harmony of all its constituent parts. In each aspect of the taste experience, from the aroma through to the aftertaste, there is nuance and surprise. It may not be a wine for everyone; it took intelligence to make it and it takes intelligence to appreciate it."

My job is not only to taste and buy wines; I must sell them, too. I imported a good supply of that 1976 *grand cru,* one of the better red Burgundies of the vintage, and watched it fly out of the shop by the carton. Wisely, I did not have the courage to buy more than a few cases of that exquisite little 1973, and they sat around forever. The customer reaction upon tasting it: "It's too light," as if, to be considered worthwhile, a wine must be black and powerful. Study the vintage charts, however, and you will see that the hot years, whose wines are dark-colored and full of alcohol, receive the highest ranking. Vintages of light-colored, light-bodied wines, no matter how aromatic or how fine the flavors, receive low marks. Such judgments are far from a serious appreciation of fine wine. I do not care whose vintage chart you choose, you could turn it sideways and upside down and it would still be no less helpful as a guide to buying a good bottle of wine. Vintage charts are the worst kind of generalization; great wine is the contradiction of generalization.

One day Joguet told me that I should meet an old *négociant* friend of his near Vouvray—René Loyau, or Père Loyau as he is called by those in the local wine trade. With a wrinkle of disgust, my anti-*négociant* bent expressed itself. "You'll see, this *négociant* is atypical," Charles said.

The first time I did see René Loyau he was in his icy chalk-walled cavern above the banks of the Loire River seated at his ancient Rube Goldberg-style, pedal-driven labeling contraption, dressing his bottles one by one. "I do everything by hand," he was to tell me later, "and no one ever lays a hand on the merchandise but me." A strange *négociant!* Loyau's is no factory operation with tanker trucks lined up outside, no rows of clerks to handle the paperwork, and no offensive glug-glug pumped out under the fanciest labels. He has no office other than the desk in his apartment—no secretary, no typewriter, no computer. In his *cave,* where the work is done, there is not even a telephone. "I need tranquillity here," he says.

Père Loyau was born August 26, 1896, nine decades ago. He is mystified that his son, who ran a *tabac* in Tours, retired before he has. Loyau is five foot four, wiry (I saw him lift two full cases of Vouvray at the same time), white-haired, and invariably appears in a dapper, tightly knotted necktie.

His *cave* is indeed a cave in the hillside: chalk walls, dirt floor, stone-cold. Once I met another old fellow, an octogenarian, who had worked all his life under refrigeration in a meat-packing plant, and like Loyau he had a delicate, rosy, remarkably wrinkle-free complexion. Is the icy cave also responsible for Loyau's incredible exuberance? Let us hope the wine of Vouvray contributed something, because we can all lay our hands on some of that.

Loyau is a man worth listening to. He speaks with the wisdom of nine decades. Unfortunately, repeating his words does not convey the wonderment and awe he expresses when he discusses just about anything. For René Loyau the real world is the most incredible thing one could possibly imagine. It is miraculous, mysterious, profound. He sometimes flashes a look of pure amazement, like a baby who has just discovered how to rattle a rattle. Beaming forth from the visage of a ninety-year-old, it is an unforgettable expression.

Loyau says that there are two qualities responsible for the worth of a man, "intellectual dexterity and physical vitality," and he has maintained both qualities despite his age and despite the cataclysmic events of two world wars. Twice he was ravaged and twice he came back. From the war of 1914–18 he returned with his lungs in ruin, thanks to poison gas. He spent three years in the hospital and one in a sanatorium. Upon his release, he worked in the wine business with his father until 1930, when he and his wife took over the Hôtel des Négociants in downtown Tours. On June 19, 1940, the German Army stopped on the banks of the Loire across from Tours. They blew up the bridge, which Balzac called "one of the finest monuments of French architecture," and with it went the water lines into the city. Then they attacked with incendiary bombs. There was no water to fight the blaze, so thirty acres of the old city burned to the ground, including Loyau's hotel.

"When I think about it I don't know how we started over again. We were completely ruined! Our hotel had eighty rooms, all furnished, plus the restaurant . . . But one has to go on. I had two sons in school. I had to hide them from the *boches*. They took my third son to Germany. We had to suffer ghastly horrors. My father had to be committed; he lost his mind. But my wife, she was extraordinary, very patriotic, very courageous. We survived. But, you know, all of that forms a man, it gives a man character. You have spirit, you resist, you fight, but you become more generous, nobler in a sense, because you have seen such misery. Truly, those were extraordinary times, educational, but alas, brutal.

"We started again with a little bar in a wooden hut near what is now the post office. We had no car, so I transported my wine in a little chariot behind my bicycle. To get to my *cave,* I had to cross the Loire by boat because the bridge was down."

Today, Loyau is an old master at what I do. He visits the growers, tastes, and selects. However, he buys wine by the barrel, then trucks it back to his *cave,* raises it, bottles it by hand, and sells it under his own distinctive label. After a visit to his cellar, after hearing him discourse upon the history and mystery of wine and the complexity of events that go into creating a good bottle, drinking an ordinary wine seems like sacrilege.

The fissure in the hillside that forms the entrance to his *cave* is too narrow for a vehicle to pass through. Once you are inside, the stone walls widen a bit and upon each side of the path that descends deeper into the *cave* one sees the finished product stacked ready for sale in bottles and cartons. The womblike *cave* is vaguely cross-shaped, and in the most spacious part, at the center, there is a wooden table with tasting glasses and a corkscrew. It smells like earth and wine and barrels.

When I arrive, we always begin with a tour of the bottled wines to see what is available for purchase. These lie in a little wing off to the right. There are no bins, simply piles of unlabeled bottles stacked on the dirt. A little dime-store chalkboard leaning against each pile names the wine's provenance. There is one pile of around two hundred bottles of Moulin-à-Vent from the Beaujolais, another consists of a few dozen Gevrey-Chambertin. Loyau points out this and that, commenting on some, ignoring others, so I check out each pile myself in case he skips something which might interest me.

"This is a Vouvray from selected grapes," he says, "the smallest, ripest bunches. That is what makes an extraordinary Vouvray. I have some 1976 from hand-selected grapes like this. It is 17.5 alcohol!

"This is a 1978 Vouvray. I don't know what has become of it because I haven't uncorked one in a long time. I bottled one barrel of it for aging."

As we descend farther away from the single light bulb that lights this wing, Loyau pats his coat pockets to find his glasses. "I don't see very well, you know, but for the past two years I see better than I did." He raises his eyebrows and peers up at me bright-eyed as if nothing could be more miraculous. "It is true, *monsieur*! At a certain age your sight comes back, rejuvenated."

He waves his hand at another pile of bottles. "Here is a Chinon, but it is nothing spectacular. You buy yours from Joguet, a good fellow, serious. You have chosen well.

"I just finished bottling this Châteauneuf-du-Pape. I have been buying from the same property for fifty years. Now I deal with the grandson."

When Loyau names the *domaine*, I recognize it. "I visited him last year," I say. "I tasted his own bottling, but it is nothing like the Châteauneuf I buy from you. In fact, I thought his bottling was rather ordinary."

"One has to select! I taste all his *cuvées*. He has eighteen hectares [forty-three acres], and most of his wines are on the flatlands. You see what I'm getting at? I select. The proprietor combines his *cuvées* to make a single wine of it. A generalization. What I take is from the hillside vines. Of course I must pay extra for it, but then I have something to my taste. I warn him to give me exactly the *cuvée* I selected, because if he sends me another I'll send it back."

He points to a row of four bottles. "That is a 1976 Charmes-Chambertin, but that is all that remains." Next to it is a stack of three hundred bottles. "That is another Chambertin, but it tastes completely different. The Charmes is feminine, a pretty young maiden, while this one is a man who has something in his pants. In Burgundy, you know, the finest wine is harvested in the middle of the slopes. At the top there are the trees, then all of a sudden the soil changes. It becomes poorer. The middle, that's it! After that, there is the plain, the flatlands. Zero! In the wine trade, one has to be aware of the differences. One time at Meursault, an old fellow sent me a Puligny *villages* instead of the Meursault-Perrières I had ordered. I told him, 'No way, I'm returning the barrel to you, and if you want the money, send me my Perrières.' He blamed his son for the mix-up. A Puligny, that is a flatlands wine. It is not at all the same as a Perrières from the slope. I caught him because I remember tastes.

"Some people call me *le vieux goûteur,* the old taster, because at tastings of old wines I always find the vintage. In France you never have the same year. Each year gives its own character. One has to be aware of these things in our profession. Once I arrived at the estate of a *grand monsieur* at Chinon. I shall always remember that splendid fifteenth-century house with its magnificent furnishings. He had a bottle for us to taste, a sort of contest, you know, to guess the vintage. There were local *négociants,* winemakers, agents, enologists, mayors . . . Some said 1933, some 1928. The *monsieur* said, looking at me, 'And you, you have not said anything.' I told him that I had written my guess on a piece of paper and placed it in my hat so the others would not accuse me of copying them. I took off my hat and gave him the piece of paper. 'You are right,' he said. 'No one else guessed it correctly. It is a Bourgueil 1906.' I went on to tell him that the taste reminded me of a wine I once bought three vintages in a row from a Monsieur Landry, from a little parcel of vines behind a church called Le Coudreau. He was astonished because his 1906 had been purchased by his father from the father of that same Monsieur Landry!"

How had he identified its origin so precisely?

"It is a memory for tastes. There is a certain aftertaste in which the character of a wine manifests itself. The 1906 still had a little taste of wild plum and a suggestion of hawthorn blossom that reminded me of the *cuvée* Le Coudreau that Monsieur Landry sold to me."

Wine can express extra-vinous qualities. Tasters often find

black currants, for example, or mint, or eucalyptus, and so forth. The Martha's Vineyard Cabernet from California's Heitz Cellars is a dramatic example. Where does that characteristic aroma come from? How can vinified grape juice smell like another fruit, a flower or a leaf? To Loyau there is a simple explanation and he has proven his theory to his own satisfaction time and time again.

For example, when he was tasting in the cellars of a grower in Gevrey-Chambertin: "All his older wines exhibited a strong smell of wild currants," Loyau begins, wide-eyed with the wonder of it all. "However, in his more recent vintages the same aroma was not to be found. *Mystère!*"

He draws out the word and lets it hang in the air. His eyes narrow with cunning as he leans toward my secretary and taps her four times on her left breast. For emphasis, I presume, the old fox.

"I inquired of the grower," he continued with satisfaction, "and asked when he had torn out the patch of wild currants near his vineyard. Of course I had never seen his vineyard. It was pure deduction. And wouldn't you know it? There *had* been wild currants growing right up to the stone wall that separated his land from his neighbor's until . . . his neighbor cleared the patch of currants in order to plant vines!"

Loyau broke into an absolutely devilish grin and chuckled deeply. Then the professor in him reappeared. "There is only one possible explanation for this mysterious transfer of aromatic quality from one type of vegetation to another. Bees! The bees gather nectar from blossoms—in this case, wild-currant blossoms—then they alight on the grape blossoms, their little legs fuzzy with pollen from the currants."

Cross-pollination? Or nature's own genetic tampering? I have not presented Loyau's theory to a biologist because I would hate to see his romantic notion dissected, but I always think of it when I am tasting in Bandol, where black-cherry trees are planted alongside the vines. Their flavor has a thick, ripe presence in the aroma of Bandol's wines. Or in Cornas, where orchards of apricot and peach grow at the bottom of the terraced slopes, or at Nuits-Saint-Georges, whose wine often displays such heady cassis overtones.

After collecting a dozen bottles in a straw basket, we return to the central *cave* to taste them. We begin with a series of Vouvrays. Vouvray has always been Loyau's home ground, and his Vouvrays his most exciting wines. After World War II, Vouvray enjoyed a vogue in the United States. Frank Schoonmaker thought Vouvray's popularity was due to the fact that the Allied headquarters was at nearby Tours, and the soldiers on duty there simply acquired a taste for the local white. But Vouvray has passed out of vogue, perhaps because it has become a lesson in frustration to locate a good one. Today, to most wine drinkers, Vouvray has come to mean a sulfury, insipid, slightly sweet white wine. However, a well-vinified Vouvray from one of the great vineyards is one of France's noblest whites.

Vouvray's wine is a product of what we call the Chenin Blanc grape, but I prefer the local name, Pineau de la Loire, and Loyau is of the opinion that the original plantings of Pineau were Pinot, the Chardonnay, imported to Vouvray from Burgundy. Over sixteen centuries or more, the plant evolved ever so slowly as it adapted to Vouvray's soil and climate. Even today, Loyau says, certain Vouvrays show a striking aromatic kinship to the Chardonnays of the Côte d'Or. I have no opinion beyond finding Loyau's theory intriguing; however, I can say that the aroma of a good Vouvray is more reminiscent of Meursault (minus the new oak) than it is of the California rendition of Chenin Blanc.

Although produced from this single grape variety, Vouvray yields more than a single type of wine. The fact that Vouvray appears in several different guises must render it difficult for the public to comprehend. But once sorted out, the multiple personalities of Vouvray become an attraction, a complete little cosmos of wines ranging from gay to profound.

Vouvray can be a sparkling wine with a froth like champagne's. Such bottles are labeled Vouvray Mousseux.

Or it can offer a more delicate bead, and these are labeled

Vouvray Pétillant, whose light sparkle might arise intentionally or not, because in the traditional cold chalk cellars, Vouvray exhibits a natural desire to *pétiller,* or sparkle. A generous dose of sulfur dioxide will suppress this desire, but that is a bit like whipping a dog for wagging its tail. Instead, one might regard Vouvray's tendency to *pétiller,* to revisit the ebullient days of its infancy, as an additional charm. What harm is there in a subtle effervescence, a liveliness on the palate, which also serves to propel and rejuvenate the aroma? For some reason, many tasters seem to be threatened by such a spirited display of energy, so most Vouvray producers resort to all sorts of technical shenanigans to keep their wine still. Vouvray Pétillant has practically disappeared from the marketplace. When I imported a few cases, customers returned it because they thought it was still fermenting. In the Vouvray cellars, however, the *pétillant* continues to be produced. It is poured for friends and downed with great pleasure.

As for still Vouvrays, they can be dry (*sec*), off-dry (*demi-sec*), or unctuous and botrytized like Sauternes (*moelleux*). They can be fresh, seductive wines that drink well right out of the barrel, or perfectly developed old masterpieces after several decades.

One must not make the mistake of saying "I don't like Vouvray" because one encounters a bad one. Vouvray can be many things, from gutter rinse to a work of art. But the same is true of the wine of any region.

Loyau begins the tasting with his Mousseux, a sparkling Vouvray that he makes by the *méthode champenoise.* It is his pride and joy. "I make one like no other," he says, gently twisting out the plump cork until a little whisper of sound and a curl of smoke escape from the bottle. "No one vinifies it like I do. They all want to hurry it along too much. Here is how I do it: I buy one hundred hectoliters of wine from three different cellars because I want the Mousseux to be from a blend of soils. That is important. From the three I make a single *cuvée.* If you don't blend from different soil types, you will end up with a *goût de terroir* amplified by the second fermentation, the fermentation in bottle, which produces the sparkle, and so the *goût de terroir* would have too great an influence on the taste. It would be disagreeable. But if you blend your soil types, there is a strange phenomenon, the same phenomenon that is produced by mixing colors of the rainbow. Blend the fundamental colors of the rainbow and you obtain white, *le blanc!* Strange, isn't it? And with Mousseux one observes the same phenomenon. I blend my soils until I find *le blanc.* That is how they do it in Champagne, only now they plant no matter where and they sell the wine within a year of the harvest. I hold mine for four years before selling it! When I find *le blanc* I put it into bottle, adding the yeast and sugar solution to induce the second fermentation. Then I lay the bottles down and I don't touch them for at least three years."

There are two Mousseux to taste, a 1978 and a 1976. Loyau remarks that the bead of the 1976 is quite fine. "You won't find such a fine bead in those champagnes that are disgorged too young. We are champagne's biggest competitors. Since they no longer make it as it should be made, the clients come here to buy. I have never sold so much Mousseux. Look at the *pellicule.*"

"One says *pellicule*—dandruff—for bead?" I ask.

"*Pellicule,* it means any very small particle. Like the *pellicule* on the skin of a grape, which is also called the bloom. If you rub a grape with your finger, you will see the powdery bloom. It is the source of a wine's breed. I am sort of a professor, you know. I receive students from the University of Tours here in my *cave.* One day there were several students here with their professor, and I explained to them the importance of the bloom. It is also the most important element in wine's fermentation. Afterward the professor said, 'But I didn't know that.' Imagine, a professor who does not understand wine."

When I express a preference for the 1978 because of its novel, exotic aroma, Loyau hesitates. "Perhaps . . . but that harshness in the aftertaste . . ."

It is Père Loyau's gentle way of telling me that the 1976 is a *finer* wine than the 1978. When I retaste the 1976, I can see that it has more finesse from start to finish, and that the 1978's violent aroma must seem a touch vulgar to him in comparison. Finesse is a word that does not have much meaning to American tasters, who use it when they are trying to find something positive to say about a light-bodied wine, but to a serious French wine-maker it is one of the most complimentary words in the vocabulary, and to appreciate the noblest French wines one must learn to recognize and appreciate finesse. Most important, finesse is not another word for "light."

"My Mousseux has this aroma because it rested *sur lie,*" Loyau continues. The *lie* is the natural sediment which falls from a wine during fermentation. "When you leave the wine *sur lie,* on its lees, you are beginning with a wine which has suffered certain violent manipulations, whose flavor bacteria are atrophied, neutralized. They are the living matter in a wine. They must be revived, renewed, if the wine is going to have any aroma. The lees restore the wine's taste and aroma." He raised a finger in the air, an exclamation point. "Very important!"

My thoughts turn to the cellars I have seen full of glittering instruments designed to remove any trace of living matter. When one tastes a wine that is alive, it can be a shock. Think of the difference between eating canned peas and those harvested in the morning dew. They could be two different species. Yet the wine world hurtles forward after a sort of canned-pea perfection, and we have reached the point at which wine drinkers confronted by a living wine are sometimes startled enough by the aromas coming off it that they decide the wine must be off.

"But my way takes time," Loyau says. "Three to four years. It is costly. Imagine, the others have sold three vintages and collected their money. But one cannot be guided by profit. If you are, you end up with nothing of value. No, you must do whatever has to be done. And look, look at what you have in the glass! Your clients should understand all this, monsieur. You must explain it to them."

I picture myself trying to convince a client to buy a sparkling Vouvray because of the dandruff on the grape, blending different soil types to achieve *le blanc,* and nourishing the flavor bacteria by leaving the wine three years on its lees. Mention bacteria and you have lost 99 percent of your clientele right there. No, most wine buyers are more interested in what their vintage charts have to say.

While Loyau uncorks a series of still Vouvrays, I ask him if he can find a barrel of a good Montlouis for me. Montlouis is also from the Pineau de la Loire, grown across the river on the Tours side.

"It is difficult to find anything decent at Montlouis," he replies, rinsing our glasses with a splash of the next wine in order to eliminate any trace of that wildly aromatic 1978 Mousseux. "Montlouis produces too much wine. No matter where you are, if your vines overproduce you cannot make great wine. Here, taste this, a 1981 Vouvray *sec*. The production was thirty-five hectoliters to the hectare. This year at Montlouis they brought in one hundred twenty hectoliters to the hectare! Need I say more?"

His 1981 dry Vouvray shows a crystalline sensuousness. There is a vibrant nervosity at the wine's core, while outwardly it seems tender and supple.

"In theory, our *sec* must not be *too* acidic," Loyau says. "All this is subtle, you know. There is a certain suppleness here, which is typical of the vineyard, which is called the Clos des Roches . . ."

He pours another 1981 *sec*.

". . . while this one, a Vouvray Clos du Petit Bois, shows above all a striking freshness, like freshly picked grapes."

Vineyard names rarely appear on Vouvray labels, but they should, because the vineyard site is the genesis of a wine's quality, whether you are in Burgundy, the Loire, or wherever. And Vouvray's vineyards have names, lovely names. Wine is subject to fad, and when Vouvray again rises to the position it merits, we will see the specific vineyard sites designated once more on the labels. Here are some of the highly regarded growths, with Loyau's comments on the origin of the names:

La Bourdonnerie. A wild site where bumblebees (*les bourdons*) seek shelter.

Bel Air. A well-situated site that has a pretty appearance.

Barguins. A vineyard created after much hesitation by the proprietors. They shilly-shallied (*barguigner*) for a long time before deciding to plant.

Bois Rideau (forest curtain). A forest rises above the vineyard sheltering it from frost and hail.

Gaimont. A knoll that receives lots of sunshine.

Paradis. Vines that produce the fruit of the Creator.

Les Gais d'Amant. A site preferred by lovers.

Les Madères. A vineyard near the village of Vernou whose wine in certain years has a flavor reminiscent of Madeira.

La Réveillerie. A vineyard with an eastern exposure that receives the earliest rays of the sun (*réveil* = awakening).

La Queue de Merluche. A parcel of vines that is shaped like a salted cod's tail, which we call *merluche* (*queue* = tail).

Pierre Brejoux's book *Les Vins de Loire* (1956, available so far in French only) names forty-six vineyards from an ancient classification of Vouvray's *terroirs,* and points out that many of the names have something to do with hillside locations: Gaimont and Moncontour, for example. Indeed, there is a Clos le Mont listed, as well as a Clos le Petit Mont, which Monsieur Loyau is pouring into our glasses.

"1976 *sec*," he announces respectfully. "Perhaps the most successful Vouvray vintage since 1947."

A rich, golden wine, well-structured, with plenty of sap and vigor, it is amazing how slowly and beautifully a fine Vouvray develops with age because normally one thinks of it as a rather feckless wine. The best vineyards, those chalky hillside sites, invest it with the backbone to support such an unexpected potential for aging.

Next Loyau pours from a mold-covered bottle that looks like a champagne bottle, but what fills the glass is not sparkling. The robe is deep gold with glints of green-tinged amber. I hold

René Loyau. Vouvray

up the old bottle. It must weigh three times today's wine bottle. "If you are pleased by this 1959 *sec,*" Loyau says, beaming, "I still have a little cache. It came from the same vineyard, Clos le Petit Mont."

When I say that no one in the States would believe that twenty-seven-year-old dry Vouvray could still be drinkable, Loyau leaps up with the agility of a man sixty years younger and grabs me by the arm. "But, monsieur, I have bottles over a hundred years old. Come here, look at this, the *cave du patron,*" and he leads me through a little iron gate into the smallest part of his *cave.* There are bottles in racks, others stacked in little piles in the dirt. All are of that dark, heavy glass that they once used to protect their precious Vouvrays.

Loyau stoops and picks up one of the bottles and cradles it in his arms. "This was harvested grape by grape like they do *chez* Lur-Saluces. It is a Vouvray Moelleux, 1945. Next to it, those are 1947s. One is a Clos du Bourg, which is a great growth like Petit Mont. This one is Fouinières. Here are the 1921s. This is from 1919, but it is not as good. I give it to my grandchildren. They like to add cassis to it, make Kir out of it, and it is delicious! There, look at the vintages: 1874, 1858, 1847. In all the world of wine, Vouvray and Sauternes are the two which age the longest."

He picks up a bottle of the Fouinières and Clos du Bourg and we return to the table and our wineglasses.

"In 1947 I bought the entire harvest of Les Fouinières, twenty-five barrels. The proprietor was Monsieur Gaston Martin, but he is dead now, and alas, he had no children to follow him. It is still distinguished by a certain freshness, isn't it? The Clos du Bourg is similar, but it has more scope, more length.

"I don't uncork these very often, you know. I keep them for my five grandchildren and their children. I want them to know the experience of tasting wines like these. I never open them alone, but it gives me great joy to offer them to people who appreciate them."

After rinsing our palates of those sweet 1947s with a taste of

Mousseux, we turn to Loyau's little collection of handpicked reds. There will be wines from the Rhône, Beaujolais, and Burgundy, and his passionate commentary will continue on into the late afternoon. My energy ebbs before his. What a man!

When I telephoned René Loyau to express my best wishes on the occasion of his ninetieth birthday, he told me he was considering retirement.

"I am here with my family," he said. "We have uncorked some old bottles. One of them is a little older than I am, an 1874. It was a wine given to my father for a service he rendered to the Château de Moncontour. It is showing well, but that is altogether normal because it comes from one of the best slopes. I still have some 1858, but I'm saving it for my hundredth birthday. You know, these Vouvrays, they hold up a long time."

Instead of pointed down into a glass of the local wine, tourists in the Loire usually have their noses aimed skyward as they gaze at one of the region's countless grand châteaux. These are not the stolid, bourgeois châteaux of Bordeaux. These are breathtaking monuments to the aristocratic splendor of another era, works of art in themselves, and much of French history transpired within their walls.

Joan of Arc was transformed from peasant girl to historical figure within the stone walls of the château at Chinon. Richard the Lion-Hearted died there. One of its proprietors was the sinister, ingenious Cardinal Richelieu.

Leonardo da Vinci is buried in the chapel of the château at Amboise. Louis XIV, the Sun King, used the same château as a prison.

Each château has its story, horrible and sublime, each its allure. However, all the treasures of the Loire are not aboveground, and a side trip to visit the wine cellars of Vouvray can be just as striking an experience for the wine-impassioned as a tour of Chenonceaux would be for the history or architecture enthusiast. Not only wine cellars burrow into the chalk cliffs overlooking the Loire River; there are human dwellings, too. Along the river there is a stretch of carved-out homes whose front doors are hinged to the rock and whose windows are cut out of it. They are not prehistoric sites left by troglodytes, they are still inhabited.

When you descend into one of the cavernous wine cellars and taste a gay, flowery Vouvray, you understand that this is a perfect environment in which to raise fine wine. Nowadays when I see a winery storing its wine outdoors, even if the stainless-steel tanks are temperature-controlled, I drive on past. As in rearing a child, the details of the home environment form a wine's character. Underground there is a confluence of factors beneficial to a healthy evolution: the cold temperature, the humidity, the mineral walls. Vouvray's wine is born underground where the vine roots suckle the cold, humid, chalky earth. The roots are wood. And there you have the constituents of a good cellar: low temperature, humidity, earth and wood smells. The air, the light and the warmth of the sun, so essential to the health of grapes, are enemies of wine. What ripens the grape cooks the wine.

Wine is happy resting in the caves of Vouvray. Look for a similar environment for your personal wine cellar, because, even in bottle, wine prefers to develop in the same conditions under which the vine roots were nourished. It is as if it never left the womb, and a bottle of wine which has the luck to remain in such conditions is really born only when the cork is pulled.

While it would be an improbable event these days, should you find a restaurant around Tours serving a *fresh* fish from the Loire, poached and sauced, summon up a bit of courage and order a Vouvray *demi-sec* to accompany it. The marriage is a good one, and serves to illuminate what seem to be three contrasting but harmonious layers to the *demi-sec,* the velvety outer texture, a ripe, saplike intensity, and a snappy, algid core.

Vouvray's chalky hillsides are not the only site that invests the Pineau de la Loire with a certain magnificence. Some tasters prefer the flintier dry white from Savennières, whose vineyards lie farther west toward the Atlantic, just past the city of Angers. The little highway between Tours and Angers runs along the banks of the

Loire, which makes it difficult to concentrate on driving because rivers have personalities. While the Rhône is powerful and swift, the Loire glides along with a stately air and makes you feel as if you are in too much of a hurry. Above, the sky fights for your attention whether it is in its luminous, majestic, deep-blue phase or filled with mountain-sized, salmon-pink clouds. Had Cecil B. De Mille filmed the Second Coming, he would have selected the sky above the Loire as its setting.

The area around Angers is called the Anjou. On the south side of the river, the wines are sweet. Coteaux du Layon, Quarts de Chaume, Bonnezeaux, these and other even lesser-known *appellations* are perhaps too dependent on their climate to develop a faithful clientele. In cold years, it is difficult to find a saving grace. In hot years like 1947, when the grapes are blessed by an attack of noble rot, then you have something memorable, great bottles to rival the Sauternes. Wines from even the finest *domaines* of the region have not had much impact in the States.

Across the river, however, at Savennières, there is a small quantity of dry Pineau produced, and if it is vinified in the traditional manner, the results can be fantastically good. Having tasted a good one, one can develop a weakness for Savennières, and for the wine buyer who gives a damn about price, it presents one of those happy situations, a great wine, a noble wine, but little-known and consequently undervalued.

If Vouvray has the chalk, Savennières provides the blackboard, and the two wines are strikingly different. The change in the soil is first evidenced as one approaches Angers. In the blink of an eye, heavy black-rock-shingled roofs begin to predominate. The stony soil here contains schist, which splits into layers quite conveniently for home builders. It also accounts for the nerve and firmness at the heart of Savennières wine, for its finesse and the attractive tinge of bitterness in its aftertaste. The aroma can be grandiosely expressive; there can be a vibrant steely freshness to it, and suggestions of honey, flowers, and unexpected fruit aromas like quince, pear, and red currant.

If Savennières does not sound like the Chenin Blanc of California, neither does it taste anything like it. With other grape varieties such as Gewürztraminer, Cabernet Sauvignon, and Chardonnay, the kinship between the California and French versions is easy to spot. With Chenin Blanc and Pineau de la Loire, the results seem totally unrelated. One can love Savennières and Vouvray yet remain aloof to Chenin Blanc. The difference is the soil, of course, and the climate. The Pineau is a late-ripening variety. Harvests usually do not commence until October, when the sun heads south and the daylight hours in the north grow noticeably shorter and shorter. This all means a long, gentle ripening season. The best vineyard sites have a southwestern exposure in order to catch the last gasp of sunshine. Other differences are due to the style of pruning the vines, the centuries of adaptation by the plant to Savennières soil and climate, the vinification, and myriad other details such as (who knows?) the brittle air of an Anjou winter.

There are only about a dozen wine *domaines* at Savennières. The most celebrated is the Coulée de Serrant. Its wine was drunk by D'Artagnan and his musketeer pals, thanks to the good taste of Alexandre Dumas. Was it Brillat-Savarin or Curnonsky who placed Coulée de Serrant alongside Yquem, Montrachet, and Château Grillet as the four most treasured French whites? Or was it Fernand Point, the great chef at La Pyramide, who began each day with a magnum of champagne and who tutored the likes of Bocuse and the brothers Troisgros? Whoever it was, Coulée de Serrant has long enjoyed an enormous if discreet reputation, and I had tasted old vintages which were quite impressive, so I was interested in importing it. However, accidents can happen to anyone, and the vintage for sale when I stopped by to taste suffered from excessive sulfur dioxide. In quantity, SO_2 is a suffocating gas because it repels oxygen. For that very same reason, SO_2 is a handy tool employed by nearly all winemakers. But if its malodor is detectable, a wine's natural aroma will be smothered. Sulfur dioxide smells like a matchstick the moment it has been struck, and some tasters have mistaken sulfur dioxide's matchstick nose for gunflint, an aroma, a desirable aroma moreover, produced by certain soils, including Savennières's! After all, it is not difficult to tell the two apart. Sulfur dioxide sears the nasal passage; gunflint is subtle and fine. When I returned to Coulée de Serrant the following year to lay my hands on a good batch, it had already been snapped up by another importer.

Instead, I began working with the Château d'Epiré, property of the Bizard family, who still followed the old tradition of fermentation and aging in wood.

A Château d'Epiré is two things. It is a wine, and it is a sixteenth-century château in the village of Epiré. The winery itself is lodged in the château's twelfth-century chapel.

I began importing Château d'Epiré with the 1971 vintage. Along with my order, Monsieur Bizard included a few samples of older vintages, the 1961 and 1947. Yes, Savennières is a white that ages well. And it is a wine particularly successful in what the wine journalists like to call "off-vintages." The 1977 was lovely stuff and attracted a good bit of interest in the American wine press.

Everything went smoothly until 1985, when I arrived a few months after the death of Monsieur Bizard. The family was crushed. I was emotional. Tears flowed. And there were problems, they said, because Monsieur Bizard's regular customers stopped buying once he was gone. Meanwhile, I noticed three new stainless-steel tanks standing on skinny, angular legs in a part of the winery where some of the old oak casks had once resided. Bizard's charming daughter explained that he had enjoyed a good income from his rather large business in Paris which produced *charcuterie* for supermarkets. Epiré was his country estate, more pride and joy than profit maker. He could afford to ignore the bottom line, which was usually printed in red. They would love to continue crafting the wine practically by hand, but economic necessity would no longer permit it. To keep the price competitive with their neighbors' wines, like their neighbors they would have to bring the vinification into the twentieth century. Making it in the old style was too labor-intensive. All those barrels to keep an eye on! And to avoid unhappy clients they had to make

Robert Daguin, winemaker.

Château d'Epiré

absolutely certain that the wine would never again throw a sediment.

Their dilemma gave us the opportunity to taste the same wine in two versions, the traditional and the modern-style vinification, side by side, because they had not yet converted all the cellar to tanks.

The modern style was already in bottle because modern methods allow one to coerce a wine to do quickly what takes months if the wine is left to its natural inclinations. It tasted bland and innocuous. It smelled of cardboard because it had been filtered through sheets of cardboard. Wine is incredibly impressionable. It is influenced by the most subtle details, from the soil in which the vines grow to a neighbor's black-currant patch. Squeezed through the sterile pads, the poor wine expressed sterility and cardboard.

Then we began tasting, from barrel to barrel, *cuvées* from the same vintage that had been vinified following a tradition developed over many centuries. There was one big oval cask, called a *demi-muid,* that was ravishing. Here it is, I thought. This is why I drink wine, this why I put up with jet lag and cold hotel rooms. There was every reason to express my enthusiasm for the wine. They agreed sadly. Of course it tasted better. Yes, they would bottle it for me by hand this year, unfiltered, if I would accept responsibility should it throw any deposit. But this year's might be the last like that because at the price there was no return, no profit. To survive, they had to change. It was depressing, and they were as dispirited as I was.

In fact, I would not buy the sterile batch no matter how low the price. What sort of person imports a wine he himself would not drink?

So I bribed them. I would pay a higher price, I offered, if they would continue to vinify grapes from their best parcels of vineyard in barrel, and bottle it unfiltered with a minimum dose of SO_2. They agreed, and this special bottling, which is labeled Cuvée Speciale, is an example of Pineau de la Loire at its best, as it might have tasted a century ago.

So far, none of the vintages has thrown any deposit, but it could happen. It *will* happen, and when it does, some clients will return their bottles as defective. Deposit in a white is a thousand times less acceptable than in a red wine. I have noticed, however, that wine lovers have a great thirst for knowledge, so when someone returns a bottle to me because of a deposit, I return their money without quibbling. Only then will I explain why the wine has a deposit. It is quite possibly the sign of a natural wine, and if they want an unnatural wine there are plenty available and they would be better served elsewhere. When the customer leaves, it is more often than not with the very same wine in hand, and when he or she uncorks it, the pleasure will be greater because their understanding will be greater.

Three or four times I have seen an unfiltered wine go bad, a minuscule proportion of the unfiltered wines I have imported over the years. It may be unrealistic, but I believe that customers who have such a wine go bad in their cellar should accept the loss and shut up about it. Complaining scares your wine merchant, who in turn scares the winemaker, who then for reasons of security begins to sterilize his wines. And who gains from all that? If one loves natural wines, one accepts an occasional calamity. We would not castrate all men because some of them go haywire and commit rape. At least I wouldn't.

There is a tribute due to the generations of anonymous *vignerons* who struggled to tame, nurture, and refine the Pineau de la Loire. Other grape varieties would have been easier. Summers are sunny in the Loire Valley and certain grape varieties would produce fruit ripe enough for harvesting in early September. But no, at Vouvray and Savennières, where the average harvest does not even begin until late October, the relevance and the inevitability of the Pineau de la Loire are now written into the laws of the *appellation*. Vouvray must be Pineau; Savennières must be Pineau. So the ancients took the hard road, and many winemakers still do despite the fact that the mass market, even the fine-wine market, shuns these masterpieces, despite the fact that the public would probably pay more for an Alaskan hothouse Chardonnay than for an exquisite Savennières. Perhaps the Pineau de la Loire with its delicacy, its purity and finesse, is too baroque a wine to be well understood today. Or perhaps its day will come again. In wine as in the art world, tastes change. Our generation throws bundles of money after Van Gogh paintings as if to make up for the absolute neglect by his contemporaries.

In the story of wine there is nothing more intriguing than trying to imagine the mentality of the ancient French *vigneron*. What a colossal oeuvre was created! It was a different mentality, certainly, guided by experience, taste, and instinct. The taste of the grape told them when to harvest. The taste of the wine told them when to bottle, what sort of oak to employ, the appropriate barrel size, how to prune the different grape varieties, and on and on and on. The traditions varied from village to village depending on differences of grape variety, soil, and microclimate. The traditions that were in place at the beginning of the twentieth century were the result of centuries of trial and error. If the taste of the wine indicated that a steep, stony piece of land produced better wine, then that was the land they worked, regardless of the labor involved. If the public taste changed, they did not rip out their Pineau vines in order to plant Chardonnay. Do not think for a moment that they were ignorant people who did not know better. They seem to have been instinctively directed toward quality. Only in this century have we seen the hard-earned knowledge of the ancients discarded, almost overnight, in the name of progress. Witness the almost unanimous change in the Loire and in Bordeaux's Graves district from fermentation in wood to fermentation in stainless steel. And now it has struck Puligny and Meursault, too. Witness the horrifying shift at Saint-Joseph, in the Rhône Valley, away from the steep, terraced hillside vineyards to the mediocre soil on the flat, easier-to-cultivate banks of the river.

Today's mentality is different. The motivating instinct is different. Progress is no longer measured by quality; it is measured by security and facility.

Today, in order to prepare the soil for new plantings at Savennières, dynamite is often employed to pulverize the rock. No
one can complain about that, but you might raise your glass
to the fourth-century monks who did such chores by hand, inspired by a grueling obsession to produce a finer barrel of Pineau
de la Loire.

BORDEAUX : "They are neither generous nor
vigorous, but the bouquet is not bad, and they have an
indescribably sinister, somber bite
that is not at all disagreeable."

—*Alexandre Dumas,*
quoting Cardinal Richelieu

Bordeaux lies due south of Sa-
vennières. In terms of driving time it is not that far, only a few
hours, but in terms of temperament it is a wonder the two are
in the same galaxy.

For most wine importers, Bordeaux is the foundation of their
business, but I arrived there several years after I had been working
in the Loire, Burgundy, and the Rhône. I recall my initial reaction
to the vineyard landscape when I arrived in the Médoc: "It is so
flat, how can they make fine wine here?" That was the first

symptom of a sort of personality clash with Bordeaux and the Bordelais.

One could probably accuse me of a tendency to rebel against façades. Bordeaux is a land of façades. In the city itself, there is the monumental façade of the Grand Théâtre with its twelve missile-sized Corinthian pillars, the smaller-scale façades of the numerous banking houses, the stolid façades of the *négociant* warehouses along the docks . . . Henry James wrote that "the whole town has an air of almost depressing opulence." As for good claret, James wrote, "I certainly didn't find it at Bordeaux, where I drank a most vulgar fluid." He did find "pyramids of bottles, mountains of bottles, to say nothing of cases and cabinets of bottles," but James concludes: "Good wine is not an optical pleasure, it is an inward emotion."

And there are the baronial façades and turrets of the châteaux . . . oh, the châteaux, the number of them boggles the mind. The landscape is bestrewn and plumed with them. All this presents to the observer an impression of class, stability, reliability, elegance, permanence, tradition, and unimpeachable status. But even the name château is a façade, because many châteaux are nothing but dilapidated sheds in which wine is produced. At Bordeaux you need not be a château to be a château!

As a Bordeaux proprietor, you do not even need a good wine-maker, although having one might mean a few extra centimes per bottle when the day's price quotes appear. You need only have been included in the classification of 1855, 130-some years ago. Your vineyard might now be ten times larger than it was in 1855, your production per acre five times larger, your grape varieties blended in different proportions, your vinification new-fangled (but concealed behind a façade of varnished oak vats) . . . No matter. If your château's name was included in the classification of 1855, you are on good terms with your banker. You may even be a banker.

No, the image cast by Bordeaux is not one of pious monks breaking up rocks in quest of unappreciated perfection. Here the world's currencies shower down like confetti.

An importer can buy Chambertin from its producer, Hermitage from its producer, Château Grillet from Château Grillet, but he cannot buy Château Lafite from Château Lafite or Château Margaux from Château Margaux. I arrived accustomed to buying wine nose-to-glass in the growers' cellars, and I attempted to conduct my affairs in the same manner at Bordeaux. It was like trying to enter a room without opening the door. At Bordeaux a château sells its wine to a *négociant* who then sells it to the importer. Bordeaux's *négociant* structure has a long history and an intransigent grip on its commerce. My nose got bent and my ego bruised more than once.

The *négociant* system works. The wines sell. Do not tamper with success.

And, after all, why should one resist? When I tried to circumvent the *négociants* and buy directly from the châteaux, some at Bordeaux assumed it was in order to circumvent the *négociant*'s commission and thereby obtain a lower price. Rarely was I given a hearing to explain that such was not the case.

I like to taste and discuss with the fellow who grows the grapes and vinifies the wine. There is so much more to divining a wine's quality than a quick sniff and taste, but at Bordeaux the attitude is usually: "The vintage charts rate the vintage eighteen out of twenty and it is a second growth. Here is its price. What more do you need?"

Most tastings occur in the *négociant* offices. I detest having to judge wine based on their little airline-sized sampler bottles. Oh, if you are a good boy, you will be fixed up with a visit to a château. Here is the occasion to gauge your importance. If you are a small fry, you receive the tourist bus tour. If you are a good client, there might be a meal at a fifth-growth château. If you are really a mover and shaker, you will dine at one of the first growths with a parade of older vintages.

I like to taste through a cellar, several barrels, several vintages, appraise the character of the winemaker, listen to his appreciation of his own wine, look at his terrain, try to get a feel of what is

going on there. Why does he do it the way he does it? I want
to discuss the treatment of the wine at the all-important moment
of the bottling. Will it be filtered? By what method? How
severely? Is it filtered because he wants to, or because he feels
he has to? By the same token, it is important that winemakers
hear from those of us who are not afraid of a natural wine. That
sort of give-and-take is valuable to both sides. However, most
of the Bordeaux wine trade is quite happy keeping everybody's
eyes on labels instead of wine.

And finally, I like to buy direct because it is the only way
that I can control the physical condition of the wine from the
moment it leaves the château cellars until my client walks out
of the shop with it.

In most instances, the public buys Bordeaux by vintage, label,
and price. The wine is not necessarily tasted before it is purchased,
but let us say you have attended a tasting of various 1983 Bordeaux and you decide you must have a case of Château Margaux.
Next you might shop around because several importers bring in
Château Margaux and several merchants stock the 1983 and
consequently prices vary enormously. You buy the cheapest of
course, because 1983 Château Margaux is just that, 1983 Château
Margaux. Or is it? Even if all the bottles were the same wine
when they left the Château cellars, there is no reason to believe
they will taste the same by the time you carry one home from a
wineshop.

A friend in San Francisco invited me to a tasting of several
vintages of Châteaux Margaux: 1983, 1982, 1981, 1980, 1979,
1978, 1961, and 1945. To reach San Francisco, the bottles had
to go from Château Margaux to the *négociant*'s warehouse by truck,
then to the docks to be loaded aboard ship. They are landed
either on the East Coast, in which case they are trucked or trained
overland to the West Coast, or they go directly to the West
Coast by boat via the Panama Canal. After they are unloaded,
they pass sooner or later through customs, then they are stored
by the importer or retail merchant. One can count several op-

portunities for spoilage by overheating en route, and every Margaux in the tasting had suffered to some degree (Fahrenheit or centigrade!) or another.

The 1945 was closer to black than brown in color, and it was undrinkably over the hill. Five hundred dollars had been paid for the bottle. The 1961 had only one foot in the grave. With those two older vintages, the problem was probably a combination of bad shipping and many years of bad storage. The same vintages tasted at Château Margaux are glorious. But the younger vintages, too, had all been cooked. Some were well done, some medium, but none tasted rare. Mistreatment had robbed them of nuance, rendering them practically uniform in aroma and flavor. After years tasting wines in the growers' cellars, one learns to recognize the taste of a vibrant, healthy wine. None we tasted were in mint condition, none tasted as they do at Château Margaux, all had lost some luster, which is not Château Margaux's fault unless one wants to reproach them for not taking the responsibility to insist that their pricey product travel at a proper temperature.

I prefer to buy wine direct because then I know that when it leaves the cold, dark château cellar to begin its voyage, it will be loaded directly into an equally cold, dark container.

For a retail client there is more to buying Bordeaux than nosing out the lowest price. Inform yourself of the history of the wine's shipping and storage conditions, or better, taste a bottle from the batch you intend to buy. Make certain the wine you are putting down is sound. Years later, when you decide your claret is mature for drinking, you do not want an unpleasant surprise.

Year after year I returned to Bordeaux, looking to unearth good winemakers who would work directly with me. There were some successes, some failures, some happy encounters, some strange.

The quality at Château l'Arrosée near Saint-Emilion impressed me, but on the matter of a direct purchase, I made no headway with the proprietor. After some persuasion, because he does not believe anyone is qualified to taste his wine until it is in bottle, he allowed me into his *chais* to taste out of barrel. The tasting was accompanied by his discourse on his château; he has the best wine at Saint-Emilion, the best soil, best exposition, barrels, and vinification. It was fascinating enough (although some might have found his self-congratulation a bit suffocating) because his is indeed a hillside vineyard, which is rare in Bordeaux. True, there are plenty of gentle slopes, but rarely anything steep enough to be called a hillside. As proud as he was about his wine, it did not interest him to take steps to ensure that it arrived in the States in pristine condition. When I returned to taste his next vintage, and the one after that, he delivered the same speech I had heard the first time, practically word for word, and when I tried to interject an opinion he continued with his script as if he had not heard me. If he did pause I would leap in, trying to cram a question in edgewise, but he would simply interrupt me and continue his spiel. It was as disconcerting as a gnat in the ear. The fellow had no off switch.

Here one sees an extreme example of the tendency among the Bordelais to erect a façade of vainglory. Perhaps they have nothing to hide, but when one cannot get past the façade, when one bumps up against it again and again, it arouses suspicions.

But then there are people like Jacques Marly at Château Marlartic-Lagravière, who is proud of his wine, loves to discuss it in passionate detail, enjoys differences of opinion, and has a most exquisite sensibility. Or Claude Ricard, who until 1984 was proprietor of the Domaine de Chevalier. In his youth Ricard trained to be a concert pianist, and dinner at his *domaine* might be preceded by a piano concert in the living room. At table he structures the wine service with the same attention a pianist gives to organizing a concert program. Ricard warmed my heart at one of those memorable dinners. After a taste of Beethoven, Chopin, and the Chevalier 1963 *blanc,* he served two of his old reds side by side. It was up to the guests to divine the vintages. One bottle had aged as one would wish oneself to age. It still had spirit and vigor. All its faculties were intact. The other wine belonged in a rest home, if not the morgue. Everyone came up with their guesses, and quite logically attributed to the healthy old bottle a great birth year like 1928 or 1929. Everyone guessed a different "off" year for the senile wine. Ricard then astonished his guests by revealing that both bottles were vintage 1928. The hale Chevalier had come out of the *domaine*'s cellar, the tired Chevalier he had purchased recently from the cellar of a Bordeaux *négociant*. His dramatic comparative tasting gave me the perfect opening to hammer away at my direct-buying policy. From time to time Ricard and I visited and discussed the possibility of a direct purchase, then just as I thought I was making progress he sold his beloved Domaine de Chevalier to an Armagnac company.

Jean Goutreau is a *négociant* who purchased a château in order to make his own wine. Strange that he of all people is one of those who are willing to sell to me directly, bypassing even his own *négociant* firm, but that is only one of the many things that set him apart from the norm at Bordeaux. He says things that one does not hear elsewhere. Speaking with his *négociant* hat on, he says, "If I offer a *petit château* at fifteen francs per bottle, everyone demands a sample. They must taste it before buying. But if it is a *château* at a hundred and fifty francs they will buy it without sampling. It is the label that counts."

When I arrived in early 1986 to taste Goutreau's own wine, Château Sociando Mallet, the stampede to buy the 1985s had already begun. The wine journalists had provoked a buying frenzy. "Year of the century! Year of the comet!" I asked Goutreau whether the vintage honestly deserved the hoopla.

"Look," he said, rolling a little cigarillo from one side of his mouth to the other, "in 1982 the Bordelais produced more wine than they ever had. A record harvest. A bonanza. In 1983, more or less as much. In 1985, *thirty percent more!* What do you expect? Sure, there are good wines, but don't be surprised if many are a bit liquid, a bit diluted."

Such candor facing a potential buyer is typical of Jean Goutreau. When we were tasting his 1982, he remarked, "1982 is a very special vintage, the first time we have not chaptalized since 1961." I began to worry for his safety. No one at Bordeaux speaks about chaptalization. Everyone's fingers are pointed at the naughty Burgundians, who openly admit to it. In the public's perception there is a taint on Burgundy's reputation because of chaptalization, while the word never arises when one is speaking about Bordeaux wine, but according to Goutreau the Bordelais chaptalize almost every year and some even chaptalized in 1982. "Either that," he said, "or the winemakers' wives made an awful lot of jam, because at harvesttime you could see the sacks of sugar piled up at the wineries."

The proprietor of the Château de l'Hospital in the Graves district near Bordeaux has thick graying hair that likes to fall into her lively eyes. Her attire is fine and careless, an earthy-brown-flecked sweater, a charcoal-colored wool skirt, and worn leather loafers. She has class, she has character, she *is* a character. Closer to seventy than to sixty, she is what the French affectionately call *la vieille France,* the old France. Some people probably think she is a chatterbox, but I love her chatter.

One of her favorite subjects is fraudulent or badly vinified wine.

"Near here," she begins confidentially, pulling her hair away from her eyes, "there is a little winery, and what a traffic there is through it. *C'est incroyable!* There are wines from Corbières, Italy, Algeria, wines from all over, both reds and whites. Sometimes after an evening out I come home by that route, and my God, you should see the trucks lined up. Those wines leave that cellar with a Graves label—*ça, c'est grave*—or with other Bordeaux labels. One of these days there will be a scandal there, I'm sure."

Her shattered expression, her eyes wide open and incredulous, conveys the seriousness of such a dreadful deed, a sin perpetrated against earth, man, and the laws of the *appellation contrôlée. "Incroyable,"* she sings, falsetto.

She has the same pained attitude toward the large, commercially oriented *châteaux,* including some rather famous names. "It's a factory," she will declare, or, "He's a good cook," meaning the winemaker concocts his wine from a dubious recipe with who knows what in it.

§ 63 §

Then she shivers with horror as she recounts the winemaking practices of her neighbors. "Right now there are only three proprietors here in Portets, including myself, who analyze the sugar content of their grapes before they harvest. No one does it! They pick the grapes, and then en route. If it is raining, they pick anyway. If it rains the night away, they pick the next day, and no one worries about it. The great *châteaux* as well as the *petits*. Last September I weighed my must, which was at 13 degrees alcohol. To make a good wine, you don't need more than 11 degrees. And someone said, 'I hope you've added some water to it.' What a horror. Add water to my wine? I don't want to see frogs crawling out of my vats."

I believe that wine can reflect the personality of the man or in this case the woman who makes it. Madame de Lacaussade has a flamboyant personality and her wine is far from bland. Then I realize that as true as my theory might be it is absurd-sounding. Can fermented grape juice express the personality of a man or woman?

Female winemakers are rare in France. It remains a male-dominated profession. Madame de Lacaussade took charge of the vinification when tragedy struck the first day of the 1964 harvest. The weather was perfect, and she had gone off to collect the grape pickers. When she returned, everyone was in a tizzy. "Monsieur is in the fermentation vat," someone cried.

Her husband had descended into a vat to make sure it had been properly cleaned. The ladder slipped on the moist wood and he fell over backward, breaking three vertebrae.

The doctor arrived and climbed down into the large oak fermenter to examine the injury.

"I said to myself, now there are two in the tank," Madame recalls. "My husband was suffering horribly. They tied him to the ladder to raise him out of the vat. The ambulance came and carried him to the hospital. I found myself faced with a fait accompli because the grapes were ready to be picked. It was beautiful weather, the pickers were there, so I had to proceed.

"I must say, I had a neighbor who was very kind, who came

over to give me advice. He told me, 'When the thermometer in the fermentation vat reaches 35 degrees [centigrade], you must rack the wine, transfer it to another vat, in order to cool it down.' After dinner I toured the cellar. I checked the thermometer. I couldn't believe it. I hurried back to the kitchen and told the pickers, 'We absolutely *must* rack the wine.' So we had some tea and worked through the night. We worked until five in the morning, and at eight we started again as if nothing had happened. It was a rough day, but in a way I was lucky because 1964 was an excellent vintage, relatively easy to make."

I have tasted her 1964 and it is as perfect a wine—aromatic, flavorful, and complete—as wine can be. It is not all that unusual for a first effort at vinification to provide results which might never be surpassed. My theory, another vague conjecture that cannot be proven, goes like this: The winemaker is nervous and lacks self-confidence. "There are the grapes—what do I do now?" So they stick to the book. They use the simplest, surest, most primitive techniques. They fuss over their wine as if it were their firstborn child. And then, *voilà!* something exceptional is bottled. So they decide that they are talented, gifted, and the next vintage they begin to intervene instead of allowing nature a chance to make the wine. I remember the words of California winemaker Joseph Swan, who told me that once you have good grape juice, the role of a winemaker is "not to screw it up."

Château de l'Hospital's vineyard is so small that Madame de Lacaussade is able to sell all her wine directly. She need not pass through the agent and *négociant* system that dominates the Bordeaux trade, a system which, she is quick to point out, is entirely male-dominated. They have no admiration for a woman in the cellar, she says, only distrust, and women who have larger *domaines* (there are a few) have a rough time of it because they must deal with those Bordeaux agents.

After her husband's death, Madame de Lacaussade's problem was with the private clientele that had previously bought from him. Sales dropped 80 percent. Not only did the clientele desert her, but the staff thought they could do whatever they pleased.

Those were difficult days, she says, and her two sons, Parisian businessmen, who in fact inherited the *domaine,* did not give her much help.

"After the death of their father, they told me, 'Mama, we'll buy you a little apartment in Bordeaux or in Paris, whichever you prefer. Or wouldn't you like a trip around the world, wouldn't that amuse you?'

"I told them I'd get bored all alone in a little apartment. I'm used to large rooms; I have my dogs, my cats . . . What would I do with them? No, that wouldn't please me. Not at all! In the country there's always something to do. I'm not claustrophobic, but I would have become claustrophobic."

Instead, she enrolled at the University of Bordeaux in the enology department in order to learn the craft of wine.

Her two sons saw the clients buying three bottles at a time instead of twelve and told her it would have been better if she'd listened to them.

"That was not very encouraging," she says with some bitterness. "At my age, it is painful to hear that.

"They say I'm impossible. But they're completely in the world of business. Business, business, business! They're bachelors, both looking for an extraordinary woman. Me, I always tell them: no one is extraordinary, and even if you have a mistress who is, the day you marry her she won't be extraordinary. They have many married friends and they see them arguing, you know, and they see the child with the measles, the mumps, and who knows what else. So, to their beautiful freedom, *adieu!* And that scares them.

"Here, I assure you, they had a very simple life. The family picked strawberries, dug up potatoes, and so on. The day they left the university and went to Paris, they began to drop their family. They made friends in the upper class—the easy life, you know, extravagant, superficial . . . I think that I . . . There's a saying here in the country . . . I won't be cold in the grave before they sell this château to buy a villa at Saint-Tropez.

"The other day one of my sons was here. He spent eight days here, and a bunch of his friends came, which made a lot of work

Madame de Lacaussade

for me. He had little pity for me; his friends came first. He telephoned a girlfriend in Paris . . . I don't know, a mistress . . . and I heard them. The girlfriend must have asked, 'How's it going, are you happy on your vacation?' Then I heard him say, 'What do you think, it's like always. There's nothing to do here but bang your head against the walls . . .' "

Despite the attitude of her sons, Madame de Lacaussade persisted, carrying on the tradition at the Château de l'Hospital. Happily, the clients have returned. She now faces another problem, if you can call it that—never enough wine to satisfy the demand. I'm fortunate if she supplies me with fifty cases of twelve bottles per year. More often than not, she'll promise fifty and later cut my reservation because she was not able to say no to people who ring at her gate to buy a few bottles.

While reducing my quantities, she's fearless when it comes to raising her price one healthy chunk after another. Upon receiving a hefty increase, I wrote her a note, trying to finagle a better price. Her reply is so perfectly true to her personality, and a classic example of how the small French growers conduct business negotiations:

Cher Monsieur,

Thank you for your letter. Agreed for shipment in early October.

I am absolutely devastated to know that you are upset by the price of the wine. I gave you a "friendly" price for the 1979, not thinking that it would become a habit to continue like that!

If I have the pleasure to see you again, I will show you the bills for the materials and the workmen who repaired my cellars! I don't count my own labor. And don't ignore the fact that these shipments to the U.S.A. take longer, too!

My European clients have given me no difficulty regarding the price increase.

The '79 was actually at 30 francs and there remains no more than 24 bottles and a few magnums that I'd like to keep for myself. It seems altogether normal to raise my selling price 3 francs.

Perhaps the 1980 is mediocre at other *domaines,* but not here.

Don't forget that my vineyard, though modest, though small, is an exceptional growth attached to the Graves of Léognan. In this area it is impossible to offer a price as low as other growths that practice the politics of quantity, of overproduction. Besides, their quality is not the same as mine.

As I don't want to ruin a man so nice and passionate about wine as you are, I would like to agree one more time to a "friendly" price of 30 francs instead of 33 for the 1980 vintage, in exchange for more rapid payment.

SIGNED : *Madame de Lacaussade*

Her eighteenth-century château is near the banks of the Garonne River, the waterway which flows past the vineyards of Sauternes and Graves, through the town of Bordeaux, past the vineyards of the Médoc and into the Atlantic. Madame says that when the château was constructed, one traveled by boat because of the constant danger of scuffles between Protestants and Catholics on the local roadways. The river was safer and faster, so the château was conveniently situated. The vines were already there when the château was built.

One approaches the iron grill gate of the château by a tree-lined dirt road. The first time I visited, I passed it by four or five times because there is no sign.

There are flowers, shrubs, trees, vines, and abundant vegetation all around the U-shaped château, with a pretty little garden in the central courtyard. During one tasting, Madame de Lacaussade went to the steps outside the main entrance to empty her glass into a flowerpot. She says plants *like* wine, especially red wine! "Wine is so very rich in nourishment. What I don't use for cooking I feed to my plants." Her plants appear to be abnormally healthy.

As châteaux go, there are grander by far, but the amazing

feature of the Château de l'Hospital is the interior, the furnishings and decorations, which remain exactly as they were a century ago. Nothing has changed. It is a glorious artifact which is still a home, full of old paintings, family portraits, grand vases, dishware, an enormous porcelain heater, and magnificent statuary cast from models at Versailles. "The king gave his authorization to reproduce them," says Madame de Lacaussade. It is a step into another era, a refuge from the modern world, and far, very far, from a little apartment in Bordeaux.

I remember rising from my chair during one luncheon, with a hand on the table to steady myself after several vintages of Château de l'Hospital, and I inquired where I might find the bathroom. Madame was busy talking to someone else, so she gestured vaguely toward the entrance hall. I crossed three large rooms, though room is a word inadequate to describe these *pièces,* as they are called in French, three vast rooms filled with period furniture and, here and there, vases of splendid cut flowers. Subsequently, I had to try many doors (most led into darkness, because few of the light switches were functioning), and I had to feel my way along until I found the quaint bathroom with its wooden toilet cabinet. It is flushed with a pitcher of water which one then refills for the next visitor. Going to the loo in the Château de l'Hospital is more of an event than we in the twentieth century are accustomed to.

My first visit to Madame de Lacaussade's was one cold November day, and we confined ourselves to a tiny, triangle-shaped room, surely at one time the servants' antechamber, trying to keep warm by a fire of old barrel staves while we tasted back through some older vintages. I'll never forget the view out the window, a wintry scene of leaves swirling down upon an icy, rippling pond with two stoic white swans cruising like props on a stage set.

Her neighbors tell her to cut down the little forest around the pond, to use the land for vines to produce more wine, creating more income, of course—perhaps enough to make the property financially viable. But she resists, she says, because it is a different soil there, a poor soil for wine grapes, and the character of her wine would change. Most would sacrifice quality in the name of economic necessity. She frets about it. Finances are a constant source of worry for her, but her passion for quality is stronger. She was angry that one of her sons had sold a few bottles to an industrialist friend just after the bottling, while the wine was still, as we say, bottle-sick.

"What if this Monsieur opens a bottle too soon? He might find the wine not at all good. And if it is a disappointment for him, he'll say, 'Madame de Lacaussade fobbed off a stinky wine on me,' which is not at all the case. Let's hope he waits a bit . . .'"

When I meet a winemaker who is so obviously seeking quality at any cost, I always try to get him or her to divulge other addresses. Madame de Lacaussade generously supplied me with a list of eight to ten producers in the Saint-Emilion/Pomerol area. The next day, armed with her addresses, I set out to reap the harvest. By midday I noted with a certain amusement that each proprietor I met was female. Was it solidarity? The Sisterhood of the Vine?

Madame has a horror of certain modern vinification techniques like chemical fertilizers and asbestos filter plaques, and a studied acceptance of others.

"Upon laboratory analysis, everything comes out," she says. "If the vines are treated with copper sulfate, you find traces of copper in the wine. Wines that have been in stainless-steel tanks have traces of steel, a metallic taste. So of course I don't allow weed killers in my vineyard, because I don't want it in my wine."

The vinification and style of her red Graves has not changed since the death of her husband. The vinification cellar is antique—most of the equipment is from the turn of the century. She continues to use it, she says, because it has proven itself.

Her red Graves is of Cabernet Franc, Cabernet Sauvignon, and a little Malbec. Malbec is a fragile varietal, difficult to grow, and Madame says that many of her neighbors have yanked out their Malbec vines. Instead of the rich juice of the Malbec, high in sugar content, they simply add plain sugar to their must. Of course, something is lost.

Fermentation and aging of the red is in wood. She thinks the taste of oak marries well with the earthy, berry, dead-leaf flavors she finds in her red.

For the white, however, she no longer uses oak. "For white wine," she says, "I think oak is harmful because one has a good white wine when there is the taste of the fruit, and if you put it into wood the flavor of the grape is masked."

I brought up the great white Graves from the Domaine de Chevalier because I knew that it sees some new oak aging.

"Oh yes," she said, "but Chevalier has a high percentage of old vines, sixty years old, which is very important. Then it can be done in oak. The wine has more nerve, more body, more strength, because the roots go deeper into the earth. Here they pulled out all the white vines and replanted. I was furious, but at that time I didn't have any say in the matter. The vines for my white are only ten years old. That is really young. So it is unthinkable to put it into new oak. My husband ran into problems because he had too many old barrels. They had to be replaced. Given the expense of new barrels, I really preferred to buy glass-lined tanks."

La vieille France. How relentlessly it disappears. During fifteen years I have traveled there, and the changes have been dramatic. And in the new France, corporate France, where the board of directors is the government, where agriculture is geared for production at any cost, is there a future for a twelve-acre *domaine* like Château de l'Hospital where weeding is accomplished by a flock of sheep and where organic compost is the only fertilizer? Or will it be only the giant cooperatives and corporate-owned *négociants* who supply us with their bland, impersonal plonk?

From Bordeaux with its celebrated châteaux and stock-exchange mentality, I head southeast through Toulouse to the Languedoc.

Research in vain through the winebooks for information about the Languedoc, that broad curved swatch of southern France west of the Rhône which stretches almost to the Spanish border and includes Carcassone, Narbonne, Nîmes, and Montpellier—in terms of liquid volume, the largest wine-producing province of France. Under Languedoc, in the 1970 edition of Alexis Lichine's *Encyclopedia of Wines and Spirits,* there is the following entry:

A vast plain in southern France embracing the department of the Hérault where quantities of wine are made, mostly mediocre. One of the better ones is Clairette du Languedoc.

Hardly a thirst-inspiring expenditure of verbiage for a province which in an average year produces 660 million gallons of wine—over 3 billion bottles! Thankfully, recent editions of Lichine's *Encyclopedia* have been more generous.

The Languedoc is a rewarding place to tourist, unless it is August, when Europeans who cannot afford the Riviera crowd to ravage its beaches. There is a wild, savage beauty to the landscape, stark and colorful at once, and the province abounds in medieval fortresses and cathedrals, impossible geological formations, sandy Mediterranean beaches, and unpretentious cuisine.

It is almost, but not quite, Provence. No, it is more austere, more Protestant, less passionate, less gay than Provence.

Let us begin at Carcassone, not for its wine but for its splendid (when seen from afar) medieval city, where you cannot find a decent morsel to eat, much less a respectable *cassoulet* or a glass of drinkable local wine. Corpulent air-conditioned buses evacuate streams of camera-laden tourists, who shove through the massive fortress walls into the city. It is a grand, depressing place that shouldn't be missed. Just don't eat there. Wander the ramparts, the windy streets, and imagine what once was.

Driving east toward Narbonne and the Mediterranean, you enter the Corbières, one of France's most handsome wine regions. Particularly in the fall, after the grape harvest, you gaze upon it and say to yourself, "Someone should paint this," but it would require a colorist like Van Gogh or Vlaminck to do it justice. The severe landscape (the impression is not altogether unlike one's impression of America's own Southwest) is transfigured by the change of season. Everywhere you look, there are vines. These are not neat little slopes as in Burgundy; here, as far as you can see, there is a rugged patchwork of vines, and as they give their last gasp in November, a rush of jubilant color bursts into the dying leaves. Whereas in Burgundy the plants are Pinot, here there are countless different grape varieties and each patch glows its own brilliant hue. The Alicante, I discovered, is responsible for those blasts of vivid purple, and there are orange, yellow, gold, red-red, even leaves of a luminous milky white, and so on. What a spell is cast by this radiant display even as the dead of winter approaches.

There you have the only reason I can think of for visiting the Languedoc in November.

As for hotels, I've not been the victim of all that much experimentation. I continue to return to the Relais du Val d'Orbieu outside Ornaisons, fifteen kilometers west of Narbonne and well-situated for all sorts of day trips. I return to the Relais even though the guidebooks keep adding stars, toques, and birdies to it, which has had an inflatious effect on the price of a decent night's lodging. But there is a swimming pool, which is useful in the Languedoc. And there is rosemary, thyme, and lavender everywhere you look, and comfortable rooms, and a welcome silence, except when the wind howls. The Relais sits by itself out on a deserted highway, battened down so you won't be blown away by that terrible and faithless wind, the *tramontane,* the Languedoc's version of Provence's mistral.

The restaurant receives kudos, but I am tempted to say that the best southern French restaurant is in Berkeley at Chez Panisse, where the menu changes nightly. At the Relais the limited menu varies not at all from night to night. What a bore. A bore not for me; I can move on, but what about the poor chef? How does he guard his sanity, stuck out there cooking the same thing night after night?

One evening I had the *loup,* a favorite Mediterranean fish grilled in the typical fashion, with a stalk of fennel shoved down its gullet. It was overcooked, so I asked for some olive oil with which to moisten its flesh. The waiter returned. "I'm sorry, sir, there is no olive oil," he whispered.

Incredulous, I enunciated, *"L'huile d'olive."*

"No, excuse me, but there is none."

I told him I didn't need a special presentation, just go into the kitchen and borrow a bottle of olive oil from the chef.

He returned once more, shaking his head. "There is no olive oil in the kitchen."

Dreadful! Unbelievable!

Another night I cleaned my plate of one of their specialties, a thing I would entitle Thyme and Catsup Chicken. I cannot really recommend it, but I sat there licking my fingers, slightly ashamed, which shows how difficult it is to ruin thyme and tomato.

Their local wines are intelligently selected, but the Languedoc has few proper cellars, so beware of the condition of older vintages. I learned my lesson when I had to send back a dead bottle of 1955 Yquem.

From their list I did discover one rare treat, a delicious white Corbières produced by Jean Berail almost next door, in Ornaisons. Because I argue so often against wines that have been too processed, people think that I am against technology, which is not the case. I pay for the equipment to ship my wines in refrigerated containers in order to assure these living creatures a safe voyage. That is utilizing a technology that was not previously available to importers. Jean Berail was first in the Corbières to employ cold fermentation and succeed in making a dry white there that was fresh and lively, instead of cooked and flat.

Side trips: Enjoy a *pastis* outdoors in *centre ville* Narbonne while you people-watch or devour an English-language newspaper found up the street. Avoid Narbonne's flat, windy beaches, which are overrun with tourists in campers and trailers.

Go south along the coast, almost to Spain, to Collioure and Banyuls-sur-Mer, two of the prettiest harbors on the French Mediterranean. If it is summer, jump in the ocean.

You can go ten kilometers south of Lézignan to Boutenac and buy a few bottles of Corbières *rouge* and *gris de gris* from Yves Laboucarie. This fellow is likable, dedicated, and has a heart so big . . . He may also be a bit bored there in podunk Boutenac, so don't be shy about stopping.

Vineyard in the Languedoc

Taking his wines in proper order of service, his *gris de gris* is a crisp dry beauty that leaves you smacking your lips—the wine drinker's applause. You hear a lot about the Rosé de Provence, but except for Domaine Tempier's Bandol rosé, I've yet to encounter a better rosé than Yves's in the South of France.

According to locals, Laboucarie's Domaine de Fontsainte Cuvée des Demoiselles is the finest red Corbières being produced in the 1980s. The twelve-acre Demoiselles vineyard rolls down like a carpet from a hilltop crowned with forest much like Le Corton. It is 80 percent Carignan, 10 percent Grenache *noir*, 10 percent a mélange of ancient varieties, including Mourvèdre. The entire vineyard consists of seventy- to eighty-year old vines! The Cuvée des Demoiselles is vinified in oak, fined with egg whites, and bottled unfiltered. It has rich, racy, mellow flavors marked by a spicy cinnamon aspect.

One can continue south from Boutenac on the little roads toward the Pyrénées. The land is burnt sienna and vast, but by no means barren; if you photograph, you'll find a lot to click about.

And there are vines everywhere. Brillat-Savarin noted two features which distinguish man from beast:

1. Fear of the future.
2. Desire for fermented liquors.

In this landscape you will delight in the revelation of mankind's tenacious pursuit of number 2, because you will see vines planted upon the most impossible-looking terrains. The trouble is, almost all of it is swill. Most of it looks, smells, and tastes bad.

Justifiably infamous for the volume of plonk it produces, the Languedoc is planted in grape varieties selected for the quantity they can produce. To almost all the winegrowers of the Languedoc, wine is a crop. They might as well be growing beans or potatoes. Yield is everything, and the price of their crop is normally based not upon its quality but upon its alcohol content. Consequently, one calculates the value of a plot of land by the volume of grape juice that can be tapped from it. Were one to use such standards to gauge value in California, acreage in the San Joaquin Valley would be more valuable than Napa's Martha's Vineyard or Stony Hill's priceless little plot of Chardonnay!

Of course, the liquid volume produced by fertile flatland soil is greater than that produced by stony hillside sites, but if you are searching for wines with character and flavor interest, you must head for the hills. Fortunately, the Creator littered the rugged terrain of the Languedoc with stony hillsides.

Alain Roux of the Domaine de Saint-Jean de Bebian says, "Often the best vineyards are the cheapest because no one else wants them. I buy them and my neighbors think I'm crazy."

Alain is a passionate young wine fanatic, an important pioneer in the development of fine wine in the Languedoc. One sees in Alain's 1980 and 1981—the first vintages he sold in bottle— that the Languedoc is a land of enormous possibility. These are wines that grab you by the nose and force you to pay attention.

Saint-Jean de Bebian's wine has changed since Alain took over. His grandfather made wine, but sold it off in bulk like almost everyone else. After his grandfather's death in 1954, Alain's parents did nothing to improve the *domaine*. Alain himself was uninterested until he went away to the university and developed a friendship with a young winemaker from Châteauneuf-du-Pape, who accompanied him home to Saint-Jean de Bebian on weekends.

His friend was struck by the similarity between some of the vineyards at Saint-Jean de Bebian and those at Châteauneuf-du-Pape. He toured the vineyards by foot, examining handfuls of soil, trying to determine the mineral composition. He studied the geological charts of the region. As time passed, he inspired Alain to look at what lay underfoot and finally convinced him that in terms of soil and climate he possessed something special. Alain became convinced that there was something that could be developed at Saint-Jean de Bebian, something that *had* to be developed—as Alain says, "a great growth which was sleeping, which was being ignored."

§ 79 §

In those days, according to Alain, the wine produced at the *domaine* had one important quality. It was *désaltérant*—a charming, thirst-quenching wine, easy to drink and enjoy. However, it lacked depth. It lacked length on the palate. It had no aging potential. And it lacked the intellectual appeal of a wine that results from a perfect marriage of *cépage* and *terroir*, grape variety and soil. It was what the French call a little wine.

Like the other vineyards of the Languedoc, Saint-Jean de Bebian was planted with high-yielding grape varieties. Convinced that he possessed a soil and climate capable of producing a wine of distinction, Alain decided to take the leap and rip out the old vineyards. Then, of course, the next question: Which grape varieties should be planted? With perfect logic, he looked to Châteauneuf-du-Pape for the grape varieties of which his wine would one day be composed.

If only it were that simple. Great wine is never simple. Great wine is the result of major factors such as Alain's decision to replant, but it also depends upon a complexity of seemingly insignificant details that add up to what you smell and taste in the glass. Alain discovered that there are thirteen different grape varieties growing at Châteauneuf-du-Pape. Pinot Noir makes red Burgundy. Gamay makes Beaujolais. However, there is no one grape that makes Châteauneuf-du-Pape.

I recall sitting around the dinner table at Domaine Tempier a few years ago at Bandol, discussing the wines of Châteauneuf-du-Pape with Lucien Peyraud and his two sons. We were praising this and that *domaine*, and one of the sons ventured the opinion that Domaine X made the finest wine of Châteauneuf-du-Pape. Lucien frowned, shook his head no, and put up his hand to cut off the discussion. "Domaine X is one hundred percent Grenache," he said. "It does not have the thirteen *cépages*." He popped out of his chair, disappeared out the door, and returned a few moments later, cradling a dusty old bottle in his arms. "This is the Baron Le Roy's Châteauneuf," he announced, "my last bottle of his 1961."

It was the most marvelous Châteauneuf-du-Pape of my life.

So much Châteauneuf is merely rich and heavy. This one had nuance, perfume, breed.

"Voilà!" said Lucien, "that's it, the true Châteauneuf-du-Pape, the Châteauneuf-du-Pape of the thirteen *cépages*."

Once upon a time, so the story goes, the vineyards of Châteauneuf-du-Pape were planted with thirteen different grape varieties. A blend of the juice of those thirteen grapes made the wine of the village. One gave color; another contributed a certain perfume; another, finesse, warmth, spice, and so on. However, by the beginning of the twentieth century, Châteauneuf-du-Pape had degenerated into little more than a blending wine for the big shipper companies up north in Beaune and Nuits-Saint-Georges. Except in rare, hot years, Burgundy was considered deficient in color, weight, and alcohol, so they imported these qualities from sunny Châteauneuf-du-Pape. Adapting to the demands of this hungry, cash-rich market for their wines, the growers of Châteauneuf-du-Pape pulled out the grape varieties that produce finesse and bouquet and replanted the varietals that give dark color and high alcohol. Even today, you can buy shipper-bottled Burgundies that yield an aroma suspiciously reminiscent of Châteauneuf-du-Pape.

Alain, without a grand *appellation,* located in the Languedoc, where wine sells for practically nothing, decided to rip out his producing vines and replant the thirteen grape varieties of Châteauneuf-du-Pape. What a gamble, when you think about it, the investment of time, labor, and money, all necessarily begun years before the results could be tasted and judged. He risked everything in order to create something fine.

For Alain Roux, there are three factors involved in the effort to make fine wine. It is not as easy as some would have us believe. You don't simply pick ripe grapes and use new French barrels.

The vinification is one factor, of course, and Alain's experiments with vinification will probably never be concluded. It is not his style to stand still. The last time I saw him, we tasted a *cuvée* of his 1981, which had been aged in new oak barrels, a very expensive, unprofitable experiment for such an inexpensive wine as Saint-Jean de Bebian. He was not satisfied with the *cuvée* because he felt the oak dominated, obscuring the natural fruit aroma. He thinks aging in giant oak casks may be the answer because the large casks will give his wine an opportunity to breathe, making it rounder, with more depth on the palate, but leaving it without a strong taste of wood.

Factor number two is the proper marriage of soil, climate, and grape variety. Marriage is perhaps imprecise; it is a *ménage à trois*. Alain is satisfied that he has created a successful *ménage à trois* now that he has the thirteen grapes of Châteauneuf-du-Pape growing in his soil and climate. Would that more vintners in California were aware of Alain's factor number two. The attitude in California often seems to be: "In our climate, everything ripens, so we can plant whichever grape variety we like. I think Château Latour makes the best wine in the world, so I'll plant Cabernet Sauvignon." Another likes the wines of Burgundy, so Pinot Noir is planted, right alongside his neighbor's Cabernet or Riesling or Chenin Blanc or whatever. The curious thing is that, in terms of climate, Napa Valley most resembles southern France, yet efforts to grow Grenache, Mourvèdre, Cinsault, or other varietals from the warm climate zones of France are rare.

Factor number three is the precise mineral composition of the soil in which the vines find nourishment, and Alain has revolutionary ideas. With his best friend, enologue François Serre of Béziers, there is an ongoing analysis of the mineral composition of the soils at Saint-Jean de Bebian and of the soils of the finest sites in France.

As an example of his findings, François Serre uses the white Burgundy vineyards of Meursault and Puligny-Montrachet. You look at the adjoining vineyards of the two famous villages, and to the eye there is no difference. They are on the same level of the hillside, they are both planted in Chardonnay, and the climate is identical. Yet wine connoisseurs know, even if they cannot define it precisely in words, that there is a difference between the wine of Meursault and that of Puligny-Montrachet. François Serre analyzed soil samples from each site and discovered that there is one major difference. Meursault soil contains a mineral that is not found next door at Puligny. He is convinced that Meursault's distinctive character and flavor are due to the presence of that mineral in Meursault's soil. Everyone speaks of *goût de terroir;* François Serre says he has isolated one. He seems convinced that, by tilling this mineral into the earth at Puligny, a wine could be made there which would resemble Meursault.

Alain and François are convinced that great wine cannot be produced from soil that is deficient in certain mineral elements. You can have a noble grape variety, they claim, and the right climate, but if your soil lacks certain mineral elements, you will be left with a little wine, a superficial wine, no matter what method of vinification you employ. The laboratory analysis of soil samples from France's *grand cru* vineyards is telling them what those mineral elements are and in what percentage they must be present. Alain firmly believes that any deficiencies in the soil at Saint-Jean de Bebian can be corrected by fortifying or adjusting the mineral composition.

When I asked Alain what his hopes are for the future at Saint-Jean de Bebian, he answered, "A wine better than Chave's Hermitage. The day that I do as well as Chave, well, that will be something! Chave achieves such depth and length because of his soil. By adding phosphates, one can do better."

Phosphates? I have heard all manner of theories about the secret of making great wine. Here was a new one, and I shuddered at the thought of Alain stirring chemicals into his wine vats. But no, he laughed, phosphates are tilled into the soil in order to enrich the quality of his wine.

"At Hermitage," I said, "you have that one steep slope with its perfect southern exposure. Here you have all the little plots that are so varied as to soil and exposure."

"At Hermitage," Alain answered, "they have only two soil types, granite and limestone. That's all. Here we have a myriad of types, so we can do better. Yes, there are problems, but once the questions are posed correctly, I'm convinced that we will be able to solve them."

§ 83 §

I am the first to admit that there are better wines than Alain's Domaine de Saint-Jean de Bebian. If he had vines at Chambertin or Hermitage, one would take his success for granted because the quality of those sites has been proven over the centuries and from them we expect extraordinary wines. But Alain's *domaine* is in the Languedoc. That is what gives his struggle a touch of the heroic.

And one can see from the 1984 Saint-Jean de Bebian that his gamble of yanking out his vineyards has paid off, that the *terroir* of the Languedoc possesses an unsuspected nobility, which was passing unnoticed amid the sheer volume of plonk that the region produces. The brilliant splash of purple in the glass is the first sign that you have something extraordinary. The aroma suggests thyme, fennel, black cherry, and black pepper. With an expressive personality that captures and sustains one's interest after repeated tastings, it has the warmth and generosity of a wine from the sunny south, but it is not too heavy, too alcoholic, nor is it mean with tannin.

Recently I opened one of my remaining bottles of 1981 Saint-Jean de Bebian. The aroma was wild, ripe, charged with herbs, exotic spices, and black truffle. It tasted like a top Châteauneuf-du-Pape with its stony *goût de terroir,* and the once chewy tannin had rounded out nicely. Violets and berry linger on the palate with a length normally reserved to the grand *appellations.*

Alain aims high. Many knowledgeable tasters consider Chave's Hermitage the finest wine of southern France. Few winemakers would dare to mention their wine in the same breath with Chaves's. Alain dares, and although his 1981 is not on a level with Chave's great Hermitage, it has already shaken up the wine world in France and blasted away preconceptions and prejudices about the wine of the Languedoc. It is *not* a little wine.

The roadways leading farther inland are lined with plane trees. Plots of vineyard are often bordered by rows of cypress. Rugged-looking mountains loom to the north. Faugères is a lazy little village whose robust red wine was recently elevated to its own separate *appellation contrôlée*. It consists of a few stone, tile-roofed houses shaded by the ever-present plane trees, which diminish the swelter of the Mediterranean sun. The streets seem always deserted. I have not seen a café, a bar, or even the inevitable *tabac*. The activity takes place in the cellars and vineyards. The winegrowers here are ignored, unspoiled, which means you will be received hospitably.

Then search your map for the Abbey de Valmagne near Ville-veyrac, an awesome, part-Romanesque, part-Gothic cathedral in a wildly beautiful setting in the middle of nowhere, whose gigantic naves are currently filled with the largest wine casks I have even seen. Under the guidance of Alain Roux's friend François Serre, the abbey has begun replanting with nobler grape varieties like Syrah and Mourvèdre, and I intend to return in order to follow their progress. Recent vintages look promising. For the moment it is a fantastic place to combine one's wine interest with the pleasures of sightseeing.

Also to be found in this part of the Languedoc, called the Hérault, is one of the most remarkable new wineries in the world, the Mas de Daumas Gassac, where the dynamic Aimé Guibert has created from what was *garrigue,* brush, and forestland a vineyard whose wine has captured the imagination of the wine press on both sides of the Atlantic.

Guibert's very first vintage, his 1978 from new vines, burst upon the wine scene leaving behind a shower of sparkling accolades which have been surpassed only by the notes accorded to subsequent vintages.

If I am not mistaken, the French magazine *Gault Millau* made the first public sighting, calling Mas de Daumas Gassac "the Lafite of the Languedoc."

As if such a paean could be improved upon, *The Times* of London reported that the wines are "actually more like Latour than Lafite . . . with their enormous colour and immense, hefty, tannic character." Enormous color? Can color have size, bulging perhaps beyond the boundaries imposed by its vessel, in this case evidently a wineglass? I shouldn't quibble because that sensational quote, "more like Latour than Lafite," served me well when I introduced Daumas Gassac to the California market.

Robert Parker, in *The Wine Advocate,* says: "In flavor it reminds me of a 30–70 blend of a great Bordeaux from Graves, say La Mission-Haut-Brion, and a great Châteauneuf-du-Pape, say Vieux Télégraphe. Don't miss it."

The Underground Wineletter, noting that Mas de Daumas Gassac is largely Cabernet Sauvignon, said "it may well be the very best buy for a wine of this type to be found anywhere in the U.S. . . . *nothing* from California comes close to this quality/price relationship."

Such to-do is somewhat reminiscent of the debut of California Cabernets and Chardonnays on the world wine stage following the well-publicized results of a blind tasting of California and French wines hosted by Stephen Spurrier in Paris. All of a sudden, Cabernets from the Golden West were selling for twelve dollars, then twenty dollars, thirty dollars, even forty dollars per bottle. I recall one limited production California Chardonnay released to the public at fifty dollars per bottle! And why not? On one given night, didn't one given California Chardonnay bolt from the pack and finish a nose ahead of a given white Burgundy, and wasn't this horse race witnessed by *Newsweek?*

And then it seemed as if every week a new superstar appeared from nowhere to beat Château Latour or some other great name in a blind tasting. How anyone can take a few swirls and sniffs and sips of two or more wines and pronounce a winner and a loser, can look at the wine and recognize its true breed . . . Oh well, I haven't noticed Château Latour pleading for mercy. The truth will out over many years as corks are pulled on magnificent bottles of Latour and on an array of flat, dead, blind-tasting champions.

With handsome gray hair and astonishing aquamarine-blue eyes—lively, piercing eyes that say "Let's go, let's not tarry"— Aimé Guibert is the proprietor of Mas de Daumas Gassac. Father of five sons, Guibert has spent most of his working life running a large leatherworks company, supplying haute-couture shops around the world. He is not a native of the Languedoc, nor does he have a Languedocienne personality. He is brimming with capitalist energy and he brings that spirit to his business. However, his wife was born in the region. She is an ethnologist who is passionate about Celtic culture, so I feel right at home; in fact, a Lynch can claim roots here, thanks to the remains of a sixth century B.C. Celt settlement unearthed near Béziers.

Several years ago they acquired their beautiful property, their country home, between Gignac and Aniane. There were no vines around the old *mas* (farmhouse), but even grown wild, it was indeed a little piece of paradise covered with trees and herbs, spectacular vistas wherever you look, a running stream, and air redolent with that wild complex of aromas that can only be found in the Midi.

As if that were not enough, shortly after they acquired the property, a friend visited and remarked upon the site's suitability for the propagation of the vine. This friend's opinion was not taken lightly, for the words were uttered by none other than geologist/geographer/enophile Henri Enjalbert, author of at least fifteen respected books, including the remarkable chapter, "L'Origine de la Qualité," in which one may read the following paragraph:

To define in a word the specific traits of a privileged viticultural terrain does not suffice to resolve the difficult problem of the genesis of the great wines. An in-depth analysis of these terrains—sites, soils, and subsoils—and a detailed history of the combined work of proprietors, managers, viticultural directors and cellar masters must be undertaken in a systematic way if we wish to understand each step in the elaboration of the great growths. But it must be pointed out that no one knew in advance which virtues a certain viticultural site (whose reputation is confirmed today) might be capable of producing. To empirically pursue, during dozens of years, the creation of a quality vineyard was a genuine adventure. It was necessary to grasp during the production the particular aptitudes of the soil and, at the same time, struggle on a double front to master the cultivation and the vinification: choice of grape varieties, system of pruning and farming practices on the one hand, how and when to pick the grapes, the production of the wine, and the techniques of conservation and aging on the other.

At the time of Enjalbert's death in the early 1980s, he had begun a monograph on the subject of the soil at Mas de Daumas Gassac. It remained unfinished; nevertheless, Monsieur Guibert has published it in order to have a tangible scientific foundation for his claim that the wine of Daumas Gassac deserves the designation *grand cru*.

Daumas Gassac apparently has a geological formation unique in the Languedoc: chalky, friable, poor in humus, the bits of earth ranging in size from mere grains of sand to little stones, a soil similar in aspect, similar in constitution, to that of the Côte d'Or and the Italian Friuli.

Blessed with a microclimate that retards maturation a full fortnight after that of the vines on the broiling plain below, this piece of earth possesses qualities that have led Guibert to dedicate himself to the production of a *grand cru* in a land where heretofore none have existed.

An undertaking of such dimension would be greeted with a ho-hum in California, where Hollywood moguls in their spare time create wines to rival the *grands crus* of France, but in France itself it is unheard of—France, where *domaines* normally pass from father to son and tradition determines matters such as grape variety, cultivation, and vinification. What Guibert has set out to do simply is not done, creating something out of nothing, and creating something not at all *typique de la région* at that! And he has met with resentment, resistance, and jealousy from his neighbors. Remember, Guibert is an outsider to begin with. However, I have not seen any crinkles of worry on his face. If he has noticed, he doesn't give a damn. But I have heard gossip in the cellars—Guibert may be unpopular, but not as a topic of conversation. For one thing, the locals ridicule his prices. I am

not totally convinced that his neighbors would refuse were the
same high prices offered for their wines.

The single most important decision was Guibert's choice of
grape variety. Going traditional in the Hérault would have meant
planting varieties like Carignan, Grenache, and Cinsault. I asked
him why he planted Cabernet Sauvignon in his "Burgundian"
soil in the Languedoc.

"God's inspiration," he replied. (These *vignerons* in the Languedoc are not the most humble race I've encountered. At nine
in the morning they speak with the pomp of an Irish poet after
he's had a few.)

"No," he continued, "it was actually a matter of personal taste.
I am not a partisan of the Pinot."

Then, following the advice of enologue Emile Peynaud of
Bordeaux, Guibert informed himself of the vinification practices
in the *chais* of the *grand cru classé* of the Médoc. His fermentation
proceeds at a controlled temperature lasting eighteen to twenty
days in order to produce a *vin de garde*. The wine then ages fifteen
to twenty months in barrel, some in new, some in used barrels
purchased from Château Margaux and Palmer. It is fined with
egg whites and bottled without filtration. In both his vinification
and his cultivation, Guibert follows the strictest organic prin-
ciples in order to produce a natural-tasting, healthy wine.

I must admit that I was not immediately swept away by
Guibert's creation. First, I have never been a partisan of the
Cabernet Sauvignon. It has always seemed too easy, almost monotonous. The difference between a Vosne and a Chambolle has
always intrigued me more than the difference between a Pauillac
and a Saint-Estèphe, or between a Heitz and a Mondavi Cabernet.

Cabernet is a vine that seems to make a decent wine everywhere
it ripens, from Spain to South Africa, from Chile to Australia.
And the distinctions between big oak-aged Cabernet Sauvignons,
be they Italian, French, Californian, or whatever, have never
struck me as that fine. "All right, yet another one," would be
my response, and that is how I responded when I first tasted Mas
de Daumas Gassac. I knew it was a top example, and indeed you

can match it against Cabernets from Opus One to Château Margaux, if that's your pleasure, and the Daumas Gassac will be anything but humiliated. I knew I'd found something that would create a stir, but my attitude remained more commercial than passionate.

Cabernet Sauvignon is a variety whose flavor tends to dominate environmental factors, unlike the Pinot Noir, Syrah, or Mourvèdre, for example, which express environmental factors. I buy an Italian white wine from a vineyard in which the vines share space with locust trees, and one can smell the opulent perfume of their cascading white blossoms in the wine. It fills the air, it fills the wine. Tasters in the northern Rhône always find *aubépine* (hawthorn blossom) in a good young Hermitage; it is a plant that grows wild thereabouts. And the various aromatic qualities expressed by well-made red Burgundies is well documented. Burgundy, there we have something to get excited about. Look at the wines from the vineyards around Gevrey-Chambertin. Those vines grown in soil that contains a proportion of marl, such as Mazis-Chambertin, have a definite licorice aspect. Another Gevrey-Chambertin, "Les Cherbaudes," communicates very little in the way of berries or fruit, but instead is very animal, almost like the smell of raw game. And right next door, at Clos de la Roche, there is a characteristic wild-cherry aroma that is not to be found in the wines of Gevrey.

However, except in rare circumstances (not nearly often enough if you ask me), Cabernet expresses only itself. Of course soil plays a part in the taste of Cabernet, but isn't it normally in terms of the structure and weight of the wine? When one compares Lafite, Latour, and Margaux, doesn't one notice primarily the difference in size, in tannin, in finesse?

The most impressive development at Daumas Gassac is the adaptation of the Cabernet Sauvignon to its environment. As the vines mature, that dominating Cabernet taste, so presumptuous in the 1978 and 1980, has gone from *forte* to *piano,* and one finds instead all those wild aromas with which the air there is charged. They are present in the 1983, a sensual, aromatic delight that shocks the senses by virtue of its originality and seems to penetrate right into one's bloodstream.

Normally I tend toward tradition, and that tendency may have blinded me at first to the adventure ("the miracle," says Guibert) taking place at Daumas Gassac. With the arrival of each new vintage, as the vines adapt, as their roots dig deeper into the earth, I find myself more and more amazed by the results.

There are many possible futures here. Will this be the first *grand cru* of the Languedoc, as Monsieur Guibert hopes? He is certainly expending a good proportion of his herculean energy to that end. Will he, with his capitalist temperament, wind up seduced by the economic potential the journalists have created? Will it lead him to overproduce? Right now, he permits a low yield per acre entirely in line with the Médoc's *grand cru classé.* Or will it lead him to plant vines on those less desirable sites surrounding his *domaine,* and to blend their wine in with the cream? The adventure continues at the Mas de Daumas Gassac.

I am always in a rush. As pleasurable as my business is, there is too much territory to cover. Hotel life makes me particularly anxious to get back home, so it is always onward to the next cellar. But if I were you I would stay and search these rustic meridional villages for that perfect inn, and I would spend a week or two exploring and hanging out.

When you do leave, you might enjoy a stop in Nîmes to see its Roman ruins, some of which are in remarkably good condition. It was at Nîmes that Henry James noted "a certain contagion of antiquity in the air." However, times have changed since his visit. There is a depressing difference between the reality today, those ancient Roman structures standing amid the contagion of garbage contributed by our own century, and the view of those same structures as seen in old etchings, where they stand nobly within their environment.

I wandered into Nîmes's Temple of Diana and happened upon two Norwegian-looking punks, tourists, one of whom chomped his chewing gum cudlike while he relieved himself upon a graffiti-covered Gallo-Roman pillar. I found it difficult to lose myself in pondering Henry James's criticism of Roman architectural efforts. He wrote: "The means are always exaggerated; the end is so much more than attained." It takes a Henry James to dare criticize such masterpieces in the first place. Most of us standing before them react with simple awe, despite the *croque-monsieur* concessions alongside.

Hoping you will not apply James's critique to my effort to introduce you to the wines of the Languedoc, I will not, because of my bad experience, suggest that you skip Nîmes, although you are not far from Avignon and Gigondas, Vaison-la-Romaine, Aix, and Cassis. But there will be some who decide it might have been better to sit back home enjoying a glass of *gris de gris*, scolding themselves for missing those ruins at Nîmes while their imagination, excited by the fruit of the vine, conjures up pristine images of magnificent Roman theaters, temples, and colosseums.

As one enters Provence from the north, there is a place that never fails to have a magical effect on my spirits. After Montélimar, the road passes through a gorge that pinches right up to the shoulder of the *autoroute,* then opens out upon a vast, vine-covered plain. The effect is emotionally exhilarating, like the untying of a mental knot, a release and a shock of open space within that mirrors the widening landscape without.

Shortly afterward, a large road sign announces: VOUS ÊTES EN PROVENCE.

Provence is good for the psyche. By the time I approach Cassis and that first breathtaking view of the glistening Mediterranean, I am singing, I am happy, I am *chez moi*.

Cassis produces the one wine I buy whose vines actually look upon the Mediterranean. This fishing village just east of Marseilles, long a weekend retreat for the wealthy Marseillaises, has nothing whatsoever to do with Cassis the black-currant liqueur. This Cassis is one of the least spoiled, most picturesque seaside villages in Provence.

The bay, the village, and its little harbor are visible from the *autoroute* far above. As you wind down to the sea, you see some of the geological formations that make Cassis so special; aeons of wear and tear have uncovered a series of huge, crown-shaped prominences the color of bleached bone that rise from the grayish-green, scrub-covered mountains. It is as if the timeless stony core of the mountains stands revealed. This rugged landscape has protected Cassis from undergoing what I call Rivierazation, the transformation of something deliciously inviting into something to be avoided. Developers run into problems erecting their high-rise condominiums at Cassis.

The roadway down from the *autoroute* cuts through one of the finest Cassis vineyards, those of the Domaine de Paternal, whose proprietor is Monsieur Cathinaud, a sly old gentleman who has seen ninety years come and go. In his youth he nearly learned English by studying Shakespeare in the original, and he uses my presence each year as an excuse to dust off his heavily accented Shakespearean vocabulary and grammar. He takes pleasure in concocting plays on words, so I laugh along as merrily as I can, although I rarely understand a thing he says. I am not about to let him know his English gabbling is incomprehensible, for fear of wounding his obvious pride.

Centre ville Cassis, the old section, is a lively colorful place with a beach, a mast-filled harbor, and a row of outdoor cafés where everyone is very animated, sipping *pastis,* soaking up the sun and sea air.

The subject of one of Frédéric Mistral's poems, Cassis also

attracted painters such as Vlaminck, Dufy, and Matisse. Today it is not uncommon to see a movie crew at work, using the alluring site as a backdrop.

The main beach is too crowded and pebbly to be interesting. Continue east half a kilometer and you will find an inlet with a small beach where the water is irresistibly inviting. Here is where most of the seminaked, young-starlet types seem to congregate. If you proceed farther, following the signs to La Presqu'île, you will pay eight to ten francs to enter a little parking area, a price that seems to discourage the multitudes, because once you have parked amid the pine trees, you are relatively isolated, by Riviera standards.

There is no sandy beach, however. You sunbathe on the rock shelf above the sea, but there are places to dip your toes into the water, or dramatic heights from which to plunge if you prefer a good wakening shock. The water at Cassis is said to be the coldest on the Mediterranean, because springs of fresh water from the Alps flow out from beneath the rocks. One advantage, however, is that Cassis is said to have the cleanest water on the French coast, and this, I assure you, counts for a great deal once you have gazed into the murk at certain Riviera spots where the city's waste is piped to spill out a mere few hundred feet offshore. I take a mat and towel and find a flat spot on the hot rocks and settle in. Every once in a while I try to concentrate on a mystery novel, I get baked enough to dive into the sea, I doze, I snack on a picnic lunch, I watch the fishing boats laying their nets and the tourist boats that plow by with binoculars and cameras aimed at the mostly-naked bodies scattered about basking. And I watch a fabulous light show; across the water the celebrated Cap Canaille, the highest cliff in France, rises ocher-colored out of the blue sea. As the sun travels across the huge sky, as clouds sail by changing the light, the massive face of the cliff changes color. Ocher to orange to rust to purple. And likewise the sea changes from blues to greens to grays, an infinite breathtaking variety. A painter would spend the whole day mixing and remixing colors.

There is even a decent restaurant nearby, La Presqu'île, where one can enjoy a bouillabaisse outdoors while the sea crashes on the rocks below and the Cap Canaille performs across the bay. The wine list offers the finest growths of Provence, including the Cassis of the Clos Sainte-Magdeleine, whose vines grow on a narrow fifteen-acre cape that juts right out into the Mediterranean. The fish can almost nibble the grapes. This must be one of the most valuable vineyards in France. However, it is not as a vineyard that it would attract a great sum, but as land to develop into a resort. This is an earthly paradise, the Clos Sainte-Magdeleine, and I wonder what Hilton or the Club Med would pay for it. I shouldn't even mention it.

Cassis produces red and rosé wine, but it is the white that merits attention. Quoting from *Les Grands Vins de France,* 1931, by Paul Ramain: *"Ils ont une saveur particulière due à l'exposition unique des terres qui les produisent"* ("They have a special flavor due to the unique exposure of the soils that produce them"). It is a quote typical of French wine books, but what does it say to give an idea of what Cassis *blanc* tastes like? It seems to say that Cassis *blanc* tastes like Cassis *blanc.* I suppose it is true that there are plenty of wines that have no personality whatsoever, that taste exactly like the wine from the next village, while the white from Cassis, thanks to the exposition of the vines and the limestone soil in which they grow, does have a character that cannot be duplicated. As to that character, most intriguing is its combination of nervosity and unctuousness. Nervosity can be found in a good Muscadet, unctuousness hopefully in a Montrachet, but the two poised together in a dry white have a special attraction. Cassis has a brilliant sun-drenched color and it marries perfectly with the local cuisine. This is garlic-and-olive-oil land, and in the local restaurants it would be crazy to drink a Muscadet or Montrachet with the catch of the day. The menus feature *oursins* (sea urchins), sea snails with *aïoli, soupe de poisson,* fresh *rougets* or *loup* grilled over coals, and, of course, the endlessly bastardized bouillabaise.

Cassis is one of the wines that people claim will not travel well. When I read the declaration of this or that gourmet or wine

Clos Ste.-Magdeleine.

Cassis

guru that such and such a wine (Cassis, Beaujolais, Chablis, Dolcetto, etc.) *must* be drunk on site, I know that they were having a high time and the local wine tasted better than ever. Wine travels well if it is properly shipped, which means temperature control. Motion will not harm wine, but high temperatures will. A little heat will hurt it a little; a lot of heat—say, three or four days through the Panama Canal or the month of July in an un-air-conditioned New York warehouse—and the wine is roasted. Shipped at around 55 degrees, followed by air-conditioned storage, your wine will not have changed between Cassis and the United States.

But then of course Cassis tastes better at Cassis! Debussy *sounds* better after a walk through the foggy, puddled streets of late-night Paris. You are in the midst of the atmosphere that created it. The wine is not different, the music is not different. You are.

The Cassis *blanc* of the Clos Sainte-Magdeleine has enjoyed a success at Chez Panisse restaurant in Berkeley, which is fitting not only because of the Mediterranean slant to the food there but also because the name Panisse was taken from the works of the great French dramatist Marcel Pagnol, who was born near Cassis. In fact, his mother was visiting Cassis when her labor began, and she traveled over those rocky mountains in a horse-drawn cart in order to deliver her son at home in Aubagne. Marcel Pagnol was almost a Cassisian.

Farther along the Mediterranean coastline, some fifteen miles from Cassis, lies the village of Bandol. Famous above all for the wine that carries its name, Bandol itself has no vineyards, but they decorate the landscape just over the hills from the sea.

Bandol has a bay ringed with sandy beaches, and a crowded, active harbor, which is home to a small fishing fleet. The catch is sold while it is still wriggling, directly from the boats along the quai. Bandol is a quaint, busy little vacation spot which seems to attract those French tourists who like to parade about with their poodles, pretending to be chic and well-to-do. Newspapers are available in English and German, but Bandol is far from being a Riviera hotspot.

There should be an entire book about the Domaine Tempier near Bandol. There would be an abundance of wine in it; oh, it would flow as if from a fountain, but it should not be a wine book, not one of those scholarly studies that appear on the grand châteaux like Latour or Lafite, because telling the whole story of the Domaine Tempier would require more than that. Today, Château Latour is controlled by English corporate interests. It has changed hands several times over the centuries, yet it still continues to produce wines of first-growth quality. Were an English corporation to acquire Domaine Tempier, I am afraid that would be the end of it. The rapturous exclamations of appreciation would peter out. The pilgrimage of celebrated chefs, wine merchants, wine writers, and winemakers would cease. I would treasure an ever-dwindling horde of older bottles, and each one uncorked would provoke tears and mirth, and so many memories.

Domaine Tempier is a place in Provence, a home with its winery and vineyards, its olive trees and cypresses. It is home to a large, joyful Provençal family. It is a wine. And while it must be inadvertent, one of those fortuitous miracles that embellish existence (there is no recipe for it dispensed at wine school), there is a certain vital spirit that one imbibes with each gorgeous swallow of Domaine Tempier's wine.

To write the book on Domaine Tempier, you would need Marcel Pagnol's understanding of character (Provençal character!) *and* a professional's understanding of enology. How to get *La Femme du Boulanger* and Emile Peynaud under the same cover? We need a big roiling novel with lots of room and several children growing up one after another that goes from the cellar right into the bedroom, a novel to which there is always a following chapter.

Domaine Tempier today makes the finest red wine of Provence, but it was not always that way. Up until 1941, the *appellation* Bandol did not even exist. In the story of the birth of the *appellation,* and of Lucien Peyraud's struggle to develop Domaine

Tempier into a fine wine, there is all the education one needs into the mysteries of what is involved in creating a fine wine.

During each visit to buy wine, then from friends and other winemakers, I gathered bits and pieces of the story. Over the years I constructed a history of the Domaine Tempier and its proprietors, the Peyrauds, but thanks to my slow-and-perhaps-never-to-evolve mastery of French, and partly because the story came in fragments both first- and secondhand, and certainly because the story lends itself to invention, I had actually constructed quite a mythical rendition of the facts.

Now that I have researched it more painstakingly, I am still reluctant to give up my mythical version. I like the way I (unintentionally) transformed it, and I invite you to share it with me before moving on to nothing but facts.

There is a village in the Ardèche between Hermitage and Côte Rôtie named Peyraud, and Lucien Peyraud's ancestors dwelt there with terraced Syrah vineyards as a backdrop, but Lucien himself grew up surrounded by snow-capped Alps in Grenoble.

In his teens he set out one spring, when the sap began to rise, to take his first job. He headed south, following the road from valley to valley until the mountains dwarfed him less and less and the snow disappeared. As he descended, a procession of plane trees appeared alongside to shade the roadway. Lavender and thyme baked in the sun beyond.

Lucien arrived in Aix-en-Provence to do a *stage* in a winery there, and the magic of this sacred land cast its spell. The air was hot and scented; traces of the great Roman civilization were there and of the Greeks before them; stone fountains poured out magical waters; the marketplace was alive with clamor and color; the vines eked purplish blood from the spare, stony soil.

This bold, golden-haired youth never returned to the mountains. How could he regret it? Lucien belonged in Provence.

At age twenty-one, Lucien proposed to Lucie (or Lulu) Tempier, eighteen, a fine Marseillaise beauty with vibrant dark eyes and black hair. Their marriage resulted in a procession of young Peyrauds, seven in all, one after another so quickly that at times it seemed there was less than the minimum period of nine months separating them.

On the day of the wedding, Lulu's father, Alphonse Tempier, had given a crusty old bottle to Lucien, saying, "This may be more of historical interest than a good glass to enjoy with lunch. It is from the old days, I don't know the exact age, before the phylloxera came and attacked the vines and we had to destroy them."

His other wedding present was the family's small wine *domaine* near Bandol, the Domaine Tempier.

One winter night with an icy mistral threatening to lift the old house off its foundation, Lucien carefully decanted his bottle by candlelight. The aged leathery aroma filled the room, but what caught Lucien's eye immediately was the wine's color, because normally Provençal reds turned brown after aging four or five years. This wine still showed some purple in the center. He sniffed it and found in the aroma a memory of all the wild perfume he had breathed in during his descent from Grenoble. He sipped it and wondered, because he tasted a great wine, a wine unlike any other.

The wine was a revelation, and his curiosity was passionate. He scoured the libraries, the old texts, the village documents, looking for more information on the wine that had been produced at Bandol in the nineteenth century, because in fact all the vineyards had been replanted in Provence as in the rest of France, thanks to the grimmest reaper the vine has ever known, the phylloxera.

Lucien discovered that the wine of Bandol had enjoyed a great reputation, that it had been sold at prices that rivaled all but the very grand at Bordeaux. Bandol's sturdy wine was considered to travel exceptionally well, and from the nearby port it had indeed been shipped all over the world, even as far away as California.

In one text, *Géographie de la Provence, du Comtat Venaissin, de la Principauté d'Orange et du Comte de Nice,* published in 1787, Lucien read about the wine of Bandol:

> These wines have the solidity, the bouquet and the finesse which are valued by connoisseurs who seek true quality instead of a label. Very simply, they sum up the true virtues of the Provençal soil and its products: *LOYAUTÉ, FINESSE et ARDEUR!*

And in the old texts he learned that, prior to phylloxera, the vineyards had been composed largely of Mourvèdre vines, a grape variety that had not been replanted, primarily because of its low yield. It had been all but forgotten. Lucien read that the Mourvèdre had originally come to Provence from Spain, that the old sources considered it a noble grape variety, the finest of the Mediterranean basin, where it went by many aliases such as Mataro, Buona Vise, Flouron, Balzac, and Benada, and that one of the Mourvèdre's traits was its stalwart resistance to oxidation. It was this latter quality, Lucien recognized, that accounted for the youthful appearance of the wine his father-in-law had presented him.

Excepting the gaggle of children appearing with notable regularity, all Lucien's energy was devoted to his research. It was as if he'd found the map to a buried treasure. His imagination was ablaze with the thought of what might be. Of what might be . . . again.

He saw the current reds, oh, they were decent *vins de table,* no more, although Bandol was producing an excellent rosé—one had to go to Tavel to find one as good. But what might be! That's what drove him.

The great name in wine during the late thirties was the Baron Le Roy of Châteauneuf-du-Pape, who through the force of his intelligence, vision, and personality was changing the history of

French wine, trying to preserve by law what made each region's wine original and worthwhile.

Lucien went to the baron armed with more pre-phylloxera bottles and with copies of the old texts.

The baron and his committee received Lucien's presentation. Here were men from the great *appellations* of Burgundy, Bordeaux, and the Loire, Champagne and the Rhône. They were staggered. There for all to see and taste was a forgotten treasure, a true *vin de terroir*. They agreed, "Here is certainly a very great *appellation*," and the committee did not hesitate to take the necessary measures to resurrect it. After a precise study of the geography, the geology, and the expositions of the ancient vineyard areas around Bandol, La Cadière, Saint-Cyr, Le Castellet, Le Plan-du-Castellet, Le Beausset, Evenos, Ollioules, and Sanary, they defined an area of *appellation* Bandol *contrôlée*.

It was not simple, because the terrain varied so much. In the end you might find one plot of land that had the right to call itself Bandol; its neighbor beside it was entitled to the name Côtes de Provence; and right next to that might be a less blessed plot whose grapes would figure in nothing fancier than a *vin de table*.

And it did not stop at that. There was the Mourvèdre to consider.

Contrary to popular belief, the creation of controlled appellations was not merely an attempt to define the best vineyard sites. It was also an attempt to preserve the traditional character of each site's wine. A vineyard within the Bandol *appellation* planted in Pinot Noir might produce a decent wine, but it would be a wine that lacked the traditional Bandol characteristics. Pre-phylloxera Bandol had been largely Mourvèdre. Thus, it was decided that, without a certain proportion of Mourvèdre, a wine could not call itself Bandol. However, there was no Mourvèdre left at Bandol, so a timetable was created in the bylaws of the *appellation*. The committee began in 1941 with a requirement of 10 percent Mourvèdre, and by 1946 it had to be 20 percent, forcing the *vignerons* to uproot the ordinary grape varieties and replant with Mourvèdre if they wanted to profit from the higher prices one could obtain by selling a wine with an *appellation contrôlée*.

Lucien was at the forefront, working tirelessly to replant the Domaine Tempier vineyards. Then in 1951 he acquired a new vineyard, a perfect terraced slope below Le Castellet called La Tourtine. Its previous owner had replanted a sizable proportion of the vineyard over to Mourvèdre in 1941 at the birth of the *appellation* Bandol, so now Lucien had some ten-year-old hillside vines with which to work.

The following year he added La Migoua to the *domaine*'s holdings. La Migoua is the wildest imaginable environment for a vineyard. High up in the hills, patches of vineyard struggle to survive in the midst of the rugged Provençal landscape. What a beautiful, primitive setting, and included were some old vines to add depth to Lucien's blend.

He experimented with *cuvées* containing higher and higher percentages of Mourvèdre, and when he saw the results he consecrated his life to the renovation of his vineyards, and to the *appellation* Bandol itself.

Lulu was not spending all her time in the delivery room. She had grown into a handsome woman and a great cook, and she received hordes of visitors at the *domaine*. The door was always open, it was easy to set another place at table, and there was a cool glass of rosé poured upon one's arrival.

Her lunches and dinners are legend in France. It was not rare to sit down at table with fifteen or twenty other guests, with of course a contingent of various Peyrauds. Even the president of the Republic attended one of Lulu's great Provençal feasts. And the wine was poured constantly around the table, which did nothing to harm the growing reputation of its quality. These were lively affairs, joyous affairs (Bacchus must have been delighted), and one tended to reminisce extravagantly about them.

By 1980, thanks to Lucien Peyraud, the proportion of Mourvèdre necessary for a wine to call itself Bandol had reached 50 percent, and at the Domaine Tempier, special *cuvées* were released containing 80 percent.

By this time, Bandol was being shipped regularly to California again, and Lucien, officially at any rate, had retired, leaving the cultivation of the vineyard to his son François, and the wine-making to his firstborn, Jean-Marie.

Thus was born an *appellation,* Bandol, and a family, Peyraud.

At least, such was my tidy little fantasy.

And the fantasy does have a lot of the right information, but the story did not unfold quite like that and it certainly was not that tidy.

Lucien was not from Grenoble. How did I manage that error? It seems he spent the war years in the service there.

It is my experience that when anybody makes the acquaintance of the Peyrauds and Domaine Tempier, he or she tends to my-thologize them. Everything seems so down-to-earth and won-derful and perfect. Even the names: Lucie and Lucien. And the setting contributes, too; the rugged hillsides, the sea, and the enormous blue sky create a landscape of divine dimension. And one's glass is never empty; reverie is natural.

Then, when you get to know the Peyrauds better and you see how human they are, "mad and wonderful" according to their friend Richard Olney, you love them and their wine even more. Yes, theirs is a wine that you end up loving. In my personal cellar I own more bottles of Domaine Tempier's bold-tasting, soulful red than any other single wine. It may not be rational; it is a love affair.

One could probably portray Lucien as comic or heroic . . . that's why a Pagnol treatment seems so appropriate. It would take Pagnol's special kind of genius to show Lucien with both facets intact . . . this short, muscular, crew-cut moral watchman railing against the march of progress, trying to resist single-handedly the vulgarization of his adopted home.

He fought, unsuccessfully, the construction of the *autoroute* from Marseilles to Toulon. Completed in 1972, it cuts a noisy, noxious swath through what was, since mankind appeared, an enchanted valley.

And he fought the construction of apartment buildings in the village nearest the *domaine*. I remember them going up, with Lucien snarling beside me, "Rabbit hutches! These aren't meant for men, they're for rabbits."

In shaping the *appellation* Bandol, however, Lucien knew success, and this kind man has brought so much pleasure to so many people . . . Raise your glass to Lucien Peyraud. He deserves a legend.

But there was nothing funny about his fear of the *autoroute* and the new housing developments. The *autoroute* did more than bring noise and pollution. Bandol is now a thirty-minute drive from Marseilles. One can now commute from the Bandol area to earn a living in the metropolis. The land becomes more valuable for living space than for what it can produce, and we in the United States know what that can mean. You work in a downtown office and drive through heavy traffic to sleep in your housing tract, where the rural quality has been destroyed. The French taste displayed in these modern housing developments is immoderately tacky.

One day, driving from Sanary, a charming little port between Bandol and Toulon where the weekly market is particularly colorful, Lucien pointed out a brand-new housing development, the boxy houses all alike and crushed up against one another.

"That was the Château Milhière," he said, "one of the greatest Bandol *domaines*."

I couldn't believe my ears, or my eyes! The housing development should have been prohibited on aesthetic grounds alone. I would describe it as carnage, even though everything visible was erect and intact. It was so new the tenants had not yet moved in.

"It was the property of Dr. André Roethlisberger, a man who understood very well the quality of the soil here. He made wines of a very great quality, red, rosé, but above all great white wines, due perhaps to the fact that he was of Swiss origin.

"It was he who prepared all the historical material for the presentation to the Baron Le Roy, he who went to the old *vignerons* to take down their testimony as to what had existed at Bandol.

"The Château Milhière had a *caractère magnifique.* Above all, it was the hospitality that was so charming. Madame Roethlisberger received so many people. I believe that the *appellation* Bandol was born of this hospitality, from the discussions that were carried on, not only on the theoretical side, but above all by way of the tastings that were presented there. The number of receptions they presented! I understood as well, thanks to Roethlisberger, that we wouldn't be able to make it, survive—we had created an *appellation* after all—if we didn't show every day in one circumstance or another the value of our *terroir* through the medium of what it produced: the wine of Bandol. That was indispensable."

As we drove on then in his *deux chevaux,* leaving the carnage behind, winding along the narrow road between the mountains and the sea, Lucien explained with emotion the gratitude he feels toward André Roethlisberger. Working with him was an education, *"une formation,"* says Lucien. "But the history of his *domaine,* the Château Milhière, is very sad, because there is no continuation."

Lucien stopped the car at the side of the road and turned toward me. "André Roethlisberger died in 1969. He left his widow alone, because their three children were not interested in the *domaine.* She tried to continue it but it was too difficult, and finally the *domaine* was divided between the children. This was serious because of the terrible appetite of the *urbanistes* who wanted to chop up the property for construction. And in fact that is what came to pass."

Lucien turned the key in the ignition and the little car shuddered and rattled back onto the roadway. "How can you ask people to remain *vignerons* when they are offered exorbitant prices for their earth? This is now the great drama of the *appellation,*" he concluded.

Imagine yourself in the place of a property owner at Bandol.

It is questionable whether one can imagine it until truly faced with the dilemma, but let us say you were forced to sell your twenty acres of vineyard on a hillside overlooking the Mediterranean ("forced," because no one in his right mind would move willingly). The projected income from wine production permits an interested winemaker to offer you a quarter of a million dollars. A developer of tacky vacation villas arrives, salivating over your sea view, and offers you a million. One might decide no, for the welfare of the rest of us, for the quality of life, that land would be better left a beautiful vineyard producing one of God's greatest gifts, wine. But how many would sacrifice three-quarters of a million dollars? Someone has to decide these questions. If it is left to each individual, there will remain damned few vineyards around Bandol. If it is left to the lawmakers, money talks, and payoffs could determine the fate of the Bandol *appellation*.

Now to the good news. Even Pagnol could not have designed better Peyrauds to continue Lucien's work than his two sons. One needn't worry about François or Jean-Marie selling out to an investment realty group and leaving Domaine Tempier to suffer the fate of Château Milhière. Those two would man the barricades before they would allow the developers to bulldoze their vines.

François tends the vines. Short, stocky, tanned, hairy like Esau, François works the hardest in terms of physical labor and he has the muscles to prove it. When I stayed in his home up on the crest of the hillside below Le Castellet, above the La Tourtine terraces, I was awakened every morning before sunrise as he maneuvered his spluttering tractor out of the garage. In California the tractors sail calmly across the fields, the driver charged with little more than setting a straight course. François rides his like a broncobuster, fighting to keep it upright. He wrestles with the steering wheel, careful not to lurch into a row of vines and wound one. His is equipped with a roll bar because farmers have been maimed or killed when their tractors toppled over on these hillsides. At noon he would return home and often as not collapse onto his bed without lunch. A siesta, some nourishment, and off he would go, bouncing along on his tractor until dark.

Tasting with François is a pleasure because what he smells in the wine he interprets in terms of the wild aromas he encounters out in the open air. I tend to taste structurally, looking above all for balance, for a wine that is complete, so to speak. If I am thinking "fruity," François goes to the specific—"apricot blossom, cherry pit, pomegranate," for example. I take another sniff and there it is right in front of my nose. It is a manner of tasting that deepens one's appreciation of wine. It inspires one to marvel at the talent for expression possessed by the vine.

He is a knowledgeable man and all of his learning seems directed to the upkeep of his vines. He knows biology, botany, horticulture, chemistry, geology, and natural history, and in conversation he is likely to leave me behind because he assumes that anyone in the wine profession knows, for example, what an *excoriose* is. (It is a fungus that develops when the shoots appear, which can inhibit the crucial budding of the vine.)

There cannot be good wines without good grapes, and François's job is to see that his brother Jean-Marie has the raw material (good juice) necessary to vinify a good wine.

If one imagines a vine's activity, commencing after the harvest, speeded up in the manner of a time-lapse botany film, and the twelve-month cycle were reduced to one minute of film, the director would say, "Lights, camera, action!" and nothing would happen, because from late October until early April a vine is dormant. It would stand as sculpted by the early-winter pruning. Generally speaking, you would see the gnarled trunk with four arms or branches neatly amputated to leave two eyes or buds remaining on each one.

In the film we would wait ten, twenty, almost thirty seconds before witnessing the tender green shoots bursting from the eyes, then a frenzy of motion and growth as the leaves appear, then the green bunches of flower buds, the blossoming, the grape set, and the maturation, until they are picked (hopefully, purple and ripe) and the vine is pruned back once more to its winter stance.

François may deserve one, but he does not take a vacation after the harvest. It is time to begin cleaning up, and to inspect each vine. Dead vines are removed, even their roots, to prevent them from rotting in the soil. He tills a furrow between the rows that will receive a compost, *la merde,* which is what remains of the grapes, the skins and the seeds after the vinification and the distillation of *marc,* a grape brandy. François does not fertilize, other than this *merde.*

In early November the earth is plowed; the soil is pushed up around the trunk (or foot) of the vine, to provide some protection against the cold.

The leaves have fallen and indeed it is turning cold, but it is time to begin the *taille,* or pruning.

The severity of this pruning goes a long way in determining the quality of next year's harvest. If too many eyes are left, there will be a lack of concentration in the grapes because there will be too many bunches on each vine, bunches that will not have attained maximum maturity. The pruning is reserved for dry days during the declining moon because the branches are harder then and the cut cleaner.

If it has not been too wet, December sees a finish to the pruning, and François is occupied with clean-up chores like gathering and burning the vine cuttings. Apart from the hustle and bustle of the harvest, this is one of the most picturesque sights one sees in the vineyards. All the foliage is gone, the sky is frigid gray. François stands bundled up against the December air, throwing vine cuttings onto a smoking fire. All over the hillsides, wisps of smoke rise into the sky as workers burn the branches from which the grapes of the vintage had hung. The fire comes in handy when his hands begin to hurt from the cold.

Another task is preparing the soil for the new plantings, which will commence in January.

In February and March, treatments against two fungi continue whenever there is a calm moment. Without these treatments— that is, if the fungi were permitted to thrive—François says he

Domaine Tempier's

La Tourtine

would lose 10 percent of his vines per year. Also at this time the soil around the foot of the plant is removed. Weeds are tended to by plowing and hoeing. He will not employ herbicides.

In early April the plant awakens, the buds swell, and out burst the shoots. One can visibly measure the growth from day to day. Leaves unfold. By hand, the plants are continually cleared of unwanted growth.

As necessary, the vines are sprayed with sulfur. The sulfur is in a pure form; it comes from the soil near La Laque, close to Bordeaux. François says there is a race now in the laboratories of the big chemical companies to develop something more efficient, but he doesn't seem to trust them to come up with something as healthy.

If the weather is wet, it is necessary to treat the vines with copper sulfate to prevent mildew.

As the shoots lengthen, badly formed vines are restaked.

At the end of May, there is a light pruning. The tops or ends of the branches are chopped off, so they don't fall over to one side or another and impede the passage of the tractor between the rows, and to ensure that the precious sap is concentrated in the bottom third of the branches, where the grapes are forming.

A vine lacks self-criticism. Moreover, it does not realize that its job is to produce wine grapes. François says, "The vine is a plant which needs to be bullied from the point of view of circulation of the sap. If the branches aren't pruned back now, the sap will always go to the extremities, the trunk is going to die while the shoots continue to push outward."

By early June, François has seen and smelled the flowering. The aroma fills the air. Then follows the appearance of the tiny green grape bunches. I walked down the rows with him one day as he pinched off a good 50 percent of these new bunches. He would not allow me to help him because "This is a delicate job. It is disagreeable to cast away half of your harvest, but it has to be done. I've studied the problem, and if it isn't done, the grapes stay pink. What we need is a grape with ripe juice, so we throw away one out of two grapes." The discarded bunches lay shriveling on the ground in the hot June sun.

In July, François continues to work the earth to keep it friable. Weeding continues in order to protect for the vine itself whatever water supply is in the soil. Irrigation is not practiced, nor is it permitted.

He must keep an eye out for fungus growth on the leaves because it could upset the process of photosynthesis. "I sulfur against oidium, if necessary, at least once during this period of the grape's maturation. Oidium is a fungus that develops at the leaf's stem and which would penetrate into the leaf. The leaf would whiten at a given moment—that is a manifestation of the fungus, which multiplies and paralyzes the leaf; it shrivels up to the point of dryness, and next the branch becomes stunted.

"Our work now is to see that the vine is in good condition, in good health, and to watch out for fungus."

I asked him if he knew each vine individually.

"I would say yes," he replied, after considering the question a few moments. His response may seem absurd to those whose image is of a vineyard on the flatlands, upon a valley floor, for example, where all the vines look alike in their perfect rows. But on the hilly terrain of Bandol, with its terraces, with olive and fruit trees growing in the vineyard, and with several grape varieties planted in the scattered parcels, François's boast, given his labor and his commitment, seems legitimate.

"Me, I want an intelligent production from my vines," he says. "Thirty-five hectoliters to the hectare, that's sufficient. But there are others who always want the maximum production possible. Their policy is to brew up lots of wine and still charge the same price per bottle. I think it's better to make less quantity, to take a good price, and to enjoy the pleasure of having made a great wine.

"I have seen in the Côtes de Provence this year—one hundred hectoliters to the hectare. They're practically doubling their production! I don't know how it can be good. It can be wine, but it will lack richness and depth. It is going to make a drinkable wine perhaps, but nothing more!"

In August, the vines are left alone. Work is concentrated on the maintenance of the stone walls or terraces that hold the soil in place on the hillsides. François wages a constant battle against the weeds that grow out from between the stones and whose roots tear apart the walls. Here again he refuses to arm himself with herbicides, even though he would be spraying them onto the stone (almost everybody else does), and could realize an incredible saving of time and labor.

"The first rain would arrive," he says, "and all those poisons would wash right down into my soil."

Born two years apart, Jean-Marie and François are brothers who idolize their father. Thus the stage is set for rivalry.

I asked Lucien how the decision was reached to divide the labor between the two, because it might have resulted in a resentful situation.

"No decision was required," he explained. "François was always outdoors in the vines and Jean-Marie was always in the *cave*."

It works, but it is not all sweetness and smiles.

Jean-Marie receives the claps on the back from the world outside because he is the winemaker. But at a winery itself there is the attitude that the quality of a wine is determined by the health and maturity of the grapes, so if François provides perfect grapes it remains to Jean-Marie a caretaker's role, to vinify the good juice according to the tradition developed by Père Lucien.

In fact, they both feel a trifle underesteemed. Jean-Marie wants recognition at home, while François is proselytizing outsiders on the fundamental importance of the viticulture. This subtle rivalry is good for the wine. They are tirelessly pursuing perfection, and if they cannot forget their father's pioneering achievement, they don't mind improving on it, even if the shadow Lucien casts is a large one.

Jean-Marie is a fervent record-keeper. When we taste through

Harvest,
Domaine Tempier

the different casks of a new vintage, he is flipping through his notes. "This is seventy percent Mourvèdre, fifteen percent Grenache, eight percent Syrah, and seven percent old Carignan," he'll say. "It is sixty-five percent La Migoua, twenty percent Le Plan, and fifteen percent La Tourtine. Fermentation lasted twelve days," and so on, detailing each *cuvée* as it is tasted. Eyeing his notes, he will remind me which *cuvée* I preferred the previous visit. He has even kept a record of every set of tennis we've played over the years!

Dining at Jean-Marie's rustic stone farmhouse up in the wilderness at La Migoua, I never get to see the label of a wine until he has put me through the paces. One night in 1985 he poured a rosé and asked how old it was. It was old, but the aroma was pretty enough, suggesting various spices like a good Châteauneuf-du-Pape. With the vagueness that experience brings, I guessed that it was at least ten years old.

Jean-Marie practically danced around the dinner table, crowing, "It's a 1958! Ha-ha, Kermit, twenty-seven years old!" Next came a 1955 Domaine Tempier *rouge*. I guessed 1969. Oh well.

Over the years I've tasted every vintage of Domaine Tempier's red except their first, the 1951. None of them was tired. None of them! How many Bordeaux or Burgundies can boast a consistency and longevity like that?

Today they produce about two bottles of red for every bottle of rosé. What qualities does Jean-Marie aim for in his rosé? "I think rosé should be a wine that is not too serious, a wine that brings joy, which is fruity and easy to drink, not a rosé which is rough or heavy with too much tannin. In 1951 Lucien made only five percent red. In 1960 it was up to thirty percent. In 1973 we finally made more red than rosé. I'd like to make nothing but red, because I think it would be more normal in a soil such as Bandol's, a soil that is made for great red wines. Let's leave it to the Côtes de Provence to make rosé. They cannot make reds like ours. Still, there will always be a demand for the rosé of Bandol. It has its followers."

I had to argue the case for the rosé of Domaine Tempier (argue with its own winemaker!) if only for selfish reasons, because I adore it.

"But, Jean-Marie, listen, you've got to have something to drink before the red is served. What good is a red without a white to precede it? And since you don't make a white . . ."

"I'm obliged to make rosé to satisfy the demand. A rosé can never be a great wine, but once in a while you want something to quench your thirst."

"There is a place for a pretty wine like that," I said, "and, moreover, the rosé has something to do with the personality of the Domaine Tempier, the joie de vivre. When one arrives, one is greeted with a cool glass of rosé. That's valuable."

"Absolutely," he finally conceded, "and in fact it is in that spirit that I make it."

The decision to begin harvesting the grapes is made jointly by Lucien and his two sons, but the primary responsibility is François's. Because of the different varietals and microclimates, the ripening does not proceed with regularity, so in early September, François picks a small sample of grapes from each parcel. He presses them, then analyzes the must for sugar and acidity. He repeats the process weekly, observing the evolution from parcel to parcel.

When they are satisfied with the maturity, the grapes are harvested by hand, beginning with the most forward parcels. There is no harvesting machine.

Fanatical care is taken to preserve the grapes intact from the vineyard to the winery, thus avoiding oxidation.

The grapes are destemmed 100 percent, which comes as a shock to most tasters, because Tempier's red is robust and tannic enough to satisfy anyone. And it has always been 100 percent destemmed! The Mourvèdre grape has sufficient tannin in the skin and the seeds. Furthermore, because the Mourvèdre's stems remain green in the interior even when the grapes themselves have attained maximum maturity, they would contribute an undesirable flavor—that is to say, a green, or stemmy, flavor—to the wine. At the same time, the grapes are lightly crushed before they fall into the fermentation vat. The fermentation starts of its own volition. Rather than introduce foreign yeasts, Jean-Marie prefers the native yeasts, which abound in the air and on the grape skins at harvesttime. The primary fermentation in which the grapes' sugar is transformed into alcohol, in which grape juice turns into wine, proceeds in cement or stainless-steel vats. Jean-Marie has no preference, but he does not like to leave his wine in those containers for more than the first few days. The wine's second or malolactic fermentation always begins during the alcoholic fermentation and continues to work after the wine is racked off into large oak casks called *foudres*. Even if the alcoholic fermentation is not completed after six to ten days, the wine is racked off its lees nonetheless, to finish naturally in wood. I say "naturally," because each wine has a mind of its own. Unlike the vine, which the Peyrauds will chop and bully into submission, they respect each wine's persona, its native intelligence, its ability to determine its own evolution, and they are reluctant to tamper with it even when its behavior seems capricious.

Their 1971 was four years completing its fermentation. Most winemakers would have panicked and attempted by artificial means to speed everything along. They might have forced it to finish more quickly, but the wine would have been altered, perhaps even tired out by those manipulations.

"The 1971 had lots of alcohol," explained Jean-Marie. "Over fourteen degrees. And it took four years for it totally to lose its sugar. It fermented each year at springtime or in the summer. Whenever the weather warmed up, it came alive and continued to evolve. We waited to bottle it until it had finished completely. Others would have heated their cellar and added yeast to hasten it along, but Lucien said no, it would finish by itself, and it did."

Today that stubborn 1971 is one of the most treasured of the Peyraud offspring.

To earn the *appellation* Bandol, the law requires eighteen months in wood. As evidenced by that 1971, eighteen months in wood is the minimum at Domaine Tempier. Their 1983, a

Jean-Marie Peyraud

wine with lovely black-cherry-like fruit and a more delicate structure, was bottled immediately after the requisite eighteen months in *foudre* in order to preserve its freshness.

Two quirks in the cellar treatment at Domaine Tempier are the source of endless dispute among those who follow their wines. Neither at the harvest nor at the bottling will Jean-Marie use sulfur dioxide (SO_2). It is never allowed contact with the wine, although it is used to clean winery equipment such as hoses and empty casks. Sulfur dioxide is a gas employed for its antiseptic qualities by practically all wineries. It sterilizes, stabilizes, and disinfects. In its free state the gas protects the surface of a wine and thus acts as an antioxidant. Unfortunately, it can also anesthetize one's olfactory organs, and nobody seems to know exactly how beneficial it may or may not be to one's health when taken in daily doses. Lucien sniffs SO_2 when he feels a cold coming on, and he maintains fiercely that his wine can be drunk to excess without fear of a morning-after headache because of the absence of SO_2.

Domaine Tempier's red has a tendency to sparkle or *pétiller* a bit. This bit of sparkle is carbon dioxide (CO_2), which has nothing to do with sulfur dioxide. Carbon dioxide is a natural by-product of fermentation, while SO_2 is an additive. All wines have CO_2, but it is usually removed before a wine is bottled, or quelled by dosing the wine with SO_2.

Some people like that CO_2 sparkle. Richard Olney finds it charming, the sign of a natural wine, and so do I. Other tasters are shocked and consider it a flaw. Restaurants form an important part of Domaine Tempier's trade, and this *pétillance* that appears in their wine from time to time (for example, when the weather warms up or storage conditions are not cool enough, or at the season of the grapevine's flowering and at harvesttime) drives restaurateurs crazy. Monsieur Big strides in with a cute young thing on his arm. The sommelier pours a glass of Tempier. Mr. Big puts down his cigar, swirls the glass in a grand circle that practically covers the circumference of the table, sniffs it approvingly, takes a sip, then he grunts, wrinkles up his nose, and announces that the wine is fermenting in the bottle! "Take it back," he commands while his date rubs knees with him under the table.

It is a great night for him, but the restaurateur is looking at a ninety-franc bottle of wine that must go into the sauce. Instead, his solution is to recork it and send it and all the rest back to Domaine Tempier.

While certain connoisseurs are clapping Jean-Marie on the back for the success of that same wine, enjoying that natural, freshening little prickle on the palate, he is looking at the loss of a sale, the loss of a client, and a painful round-trip shipping bill.

Still, Jean-Marie persists against the dread SO_2. "Besides," he says, "that little bit of carbon dioxide permits our wine to conserve its youthfulness longer."

Despite this dedication all along the way to produce as natural a wine as possible, Jean-Marie filters before bottling. "Lucien always filtered his wines," Jean-Marie avows. "I have continued in this tradition in order to avoid an excessive deposit. We might get by without filtering, but we sell about sixty percent of our production to restaurants and there are many who do not know how to explain to their clients that a wine that has aged awhile in bottle throws a deposit. If I didn't filter, I would have quite a deposit."

Why, then, does he refuse to change his policy concerning SO_2? Why not dose the wines with SO_2 to quell any possible *pétillance,* in order to please those same restaurateurs?

"Oh, you know," he says, "all they have to do is aerate the wine by decanting and that little prickle would disappear."

Yes, and all they have to do is decant it and the sediment would disappear at the same time!

But I did not say it. I did not persist in elucidating what is a quirky contradiction. I was afraid that if it were posed too nakedly he might solve the dilemma by gassing his lovely, lively wine with SO_2.

Instead, I began to select my *cuvées* each year before the bottling. My wine goes directly from the *foudre* into the bottle, unfiltered, with a tendency to *pétiller,* and I am convinced that the bottle of Domaine Tempier that you order in the United States is therefore more complete a wine than the same vintage served in France, which will have been filtered. Mine may have a little sediment, a delicate sparkle, but it is a natural wine; it is alive; nothing has been added or taken out.

No wine *domaine* would be the same without the personality of the woman of the house. Winemakers' wives play a central if rarely public role. Some are never seen to venture into their husband's cellar, and it is not unusual to glimpse a spark of jealousy when another woman does.

It is a favorite saying in France that a wine reflects the character of the man who made it. But is it not an equally persuasive argument that in the wine you see the character of the wine-maker's loved one? After all, like an artist (one would hope) a winemaker attempts to create a wine that satisfies his ideal of what is good or beautiful. And, one would hope (presume?), he has chosen a wife or lover because she personifies his ideal of beauty, beauty not merely in terms of appearance but in terms of personality and character, the whole person.

In one village from which I once purchased the wine of two *domaines,* Madame A of Domaine A had a chic haircut, peroxided hair, wore the latest fashions, lots of makeup, drove a new Mercedes, and struck quite a figure. Men noticed her on the street. Her husband's wine was flashy, too; it leapt right out of the glass, and for a while it quite seduced me. Beneath its rather dazzling perfume, however, I began to notice a lack of depth over the years, a superficiality, and I lost interest.

Madame Z of Domaine Z did not disguise her age. She loved to cook at home for her family and friends. To her, nothing was more important than her family's well-being and she stood solidly behind them, no matter what. She had a warmth and generosity that are rare. She was happy in her own skin. Her husband's wine does not shout or wave a red flag and I continue to discover qualities in it that were not evident upon first tasting.

Is it going too far to see a parallel between the women and the wines? Certainly, the wine of Domaine Tempier would not be the same were it not for Lulu, whose personality is similar to that of the *domaine*'s wine, with her qualities of vigor, earthiness, and finesse. Nor has Lulu's sparkle been gassed with SO_2, although there may be a light filtration from time to time to clean up for public consumption what is surely a saucy, even wicked sense of humor.

Discussing grape varieties with a grower in the Rhône, I mentioned that I bought a wine largely produced from Mourvèdre at Domaine Tempier.

"Ahh, Lulu"—and the grower sighed, as his eyes brightened—"she is a legend, you know," he said with a fond smile.

I cannot really talk about it knowledgeably because I arrived after those heydays of the fifties and sixties when she entertained so often and apparently so memorably.

One hears stories, however. Her beauty was remarkable, that is certain, and men would stare at her from around the table, their heads full of several vintages of Domaine Tempier, concocting fantasies about this spirited Provençal beauty who kept placing delicious platters of food in front of their hungry faces, satisfying at least one of their appetites.

With a racy twinkle in her eye, Lulu confided a story of one of those admirers who was always trying to corner her off in a room alone. She speaks the way Colette writes, in a voice almost infantile, and with the same imaginative detail. "One day he succeeded in getting me alone in his car. He was a handsome man. Nothing ever happened between us, but I admired him because he was so direct. 'Lucie' (he called me Lucie), 'I don't love you, but you turn me on.' "

With that, she broke into an infectious laugh, relishing the memory. "Oh, his words were even more graphic than that, I assure you, but I like that straightforwardness."

We were in fact in my car because Lulu had offered to give me a tour of Marseilles, her birthplace.

She claims that Marseilles, despite its renown, is not touristic.

"I don't know what it is," she said, then lowered her voice to a whisper. "Maybe it is because, you know, Marseilles has a bad reputation. Maybe tourists are afraid of it."

Our first stop was at the eastern outskirts of Marseilles, in a fishing village named Aux Goudes, situated in a *calanque* (rocky inlet) full of old wooden fishing boats. There were no fancy yachts as one sees at Bandol, Cassis, or in Marseilles's own Vieux Port.

Aux Goudes is mentioned in no guidebook; it is rustic, simple, with cheap little restaurants, and Lulu said it is where the working class of Marseilles, the postmen, the dockworkers, might hang out on their days off.

It is surrounded on all sides except its sea side by craggy, bizarre limestone formations. The white rock against the Mediterranean blue is striking.

If one follows the single road through town, it dead-ends across from the huge rock island Meiure, which is colored as if it had received a gigantic pigeon dropping.

There is a dazzling view of Marseilles across the bay, and of the impregnable-looking Château d'If on its Alcatraz-like island, from which Alexandre Dumas's Count of Monte Cristo escaped by feigning death and chuting out into the sea in a body bag.

I remarked upon the number of seedy nightclubs in the village.

"Oh, of course," Lulu said, her voice full of intrigue, "Aux Goudes is *très* Mafia. They come at night to make their deals. They might keep a woman out here to visit. Lots of racketeers come here."

We drove into Marseilles itself on the Corniche President J. F. Kennedy, a boulevard that runs right along the ocean for about five kilometers.

Lulu directed me to turn off down a one-way street . . . but in the illegal direction! "Don't worry about it," she said, as if she owned the city. The street was just a touch wider than our car. Without meeting another car head-on, we arrived at another *calanque,* a little inlet with houses built upon the rocks, "for the privileged," Lulu said. "It's always sunny here and you will see people sunbathing even in the dead of winter." These are grand old Marseillaise houses with stunning views of the sea, houses built during the last century, sporting individual features and plenty of personality.

"A movie star owns that one now," Lulu said, "and the one over there is a *hôtel de rendez-vous.* Two of my friends stayed there and they were regarded with suspicion because they were married. You know, people go there with their girlfriends. They didn't know what to make of my friends who wanted to stay two nights."

For lunch we arrived at our third inlet of the day, this one named Vallon des Auffes, and it will be found on the map should you find yourself with an appetite in Marseilles. The Michelin green guide says of the Vallon: "An animated little fishing port, it represents one of the most characteristic sights of Marseilles."

We parked illegally ("Don't worry about it," Lulu insisted) and walked alongside fishing boats and fishermen who were mending their nets. The Corniche J. F. Kennedy passes over the harbor atop a massive stone bridge whose archways allow the boats to enter and dock in the calmer, scummier waters of the Vallon.

The restaurant was Chez Fon Fon, and the septuagenarian chef welcomed Lulu with a big hug. We were seated at a window table looking out over a rather wild sea which crashed madly against the base of a lighthouse a few hundred yards offshore.

A *pastis* was served, on the house, for openers, accompanied by a bowl of black olives marinated in oil and herbs.

In this setting, one is wont to order something fishy, and the chef proposed a *bourride,* a sort of fisherman's stew not entirely unrelated to bouillabaisse. There is a broth thickened with *aïoli,* croutons, four fish served on a separate platter (that day *loup, Saint-Pierre, congre,* and *capelan*), and two bowls of *rouille* and *aïoli.* To the broth, one adds various chunks of fish and the croutons, which one tops with either the *rouille* or the *aïoli* or both. It is not something you eat with dainty *politesse;* there is slurping, dripping chins, and murmurs of appreciation.

Lulu was keeping me up to date on the situation in Marseilles. She explained that there is a vicious war on between the Corsicans

Chez Fon Fon

and the Arabs to control prostitution, and that assassinations are commonplace.

"In the winter we call the whores *les femmes avec les cuisses violettes* [the women with purple thighs]," Lulu explained, "because they wear such short skirts. When the weather is freezing, their thighs turn purple."

When we returned to our car after lunch, we found a lone fisherman next to it baiting his hook with a big morsel of sardine.

"You think you are going to catch something bigger than your bait?" Lulu asked.

"You see," she said turning to me, "no one in Marseilles says anything serious. Everything is a joke."

As we were driving up the circuitous route to the Basilique de Notre Dame de la Garde, a cathedral where seamen appeal for safe passage and where tourists appreciate the dominating view above the city, another driver started out directly into our path from a side street. I had the right of way, but he was charging out regardless, so I began to hit the brakes. When I noticed a slight hesitation on his part, I challenged him and swerved around the nose of his car as he jerked to a stop.

Lulu liked that. "You see? That is very Marseillaise, what he did. That is how they drive, and that is how they act. He was supposed to stop at the sign but tried to bully his way and get away with something. You did the right thing. It's the men, and they're even worse if they see a woman driving. Then they try to intimidate you, they just pull right out as if you weren't there. When I drive in Marseilles, I have to have courage and stand up to them. I won't let them get away with it. Now you know the Marseilles personality."

Next, Lulu directed me to the Porte d'Aix, a Roman-style Arc de Triomphe that greets drivers arriving from Aix-en-Provence. It is really rather thick, solid, and squarish, standing out-of-place today in the middle of a busy crossroads.

In her childish voice Lulu explained, "People around here always say, 'She has an ass like the Porte d'Aix.' I wanted you to see it so you'll know what they mean."

We visited a couple of museums near the Vieux Port, one featuring Roman artifacts, the other Provençal antiques and fabrics. Then we headed back toward Bandol. The weather had turned frigid and we were exhausted.

"Next time you come," Lulu said as we edged our way into the traffic on the *autoroute*, "I'll give you a tour of Marseilles by night."

Now, that should be something! Unfiltered!

One evening I dined outdoors with a dozen Peyrauds. It was almost nine o'clock, but the sky was still radiant, with a touch of fiery amber. Around a table crowded with heaping platters of boiled red beets, carrots, cauliflower, artichokes, fennel bulbs, baked sweet potatoes, hard-boiled eggs, sole filets wrapped around dill blossoms, and a heady octopus stew, the pièce de résistance was passed without cease despite its nearly impossible weight: a huge marble mortar filled with an *aïoli* that François had worked up by hand with a wooden pestle. *Aïoli* is Provence's garlic mayonnaise. Some poor souls find it indigestible; others feel their blood stir with excitement as they wolf it down. This *aïoli* had an entire head of garlic in it, two egg yolks, a pinch of salt, and a liter of Domaine Tempier's own olive oil.

Catherine, Jean-Marie's wife, coughed and sucked in air to cool off her mouth.

"It's not too strong, is it?" asked Lucien, reaching again for the mortar. "You think there's too much garlic?"

"No, no, I have a little cold," Catherine replied.

"An *aïoli* is good for colds," Lucien said, and plopped another heaping spoonful onto her plate.

Jean-Marie poured more Bandol *rouge* into each wineglass, empty or not. "You've got to have a cool young wine with *aïoli*," he said. "An old wine would be lost. Papa, remember when Madame Blanc invited you to dinner with Gigi?" (Gigi has worked in the Peyrauds' cellar since the early fifties. He is a huge hunk of a man, with a gristly Provençal accent.) "Madame Blanc served an *aïoli*, and after one bite Papa glanced over at Gigi and shook his head because there wasn't enough garlic in it. 'Do you like *aïoli?*' Madame Blanc asked. 'Oh yes, madame,' Papa said, 'it's very typical of Provence.' The next year she invited Papa and Gigi and again she served them *aïoli.* 'Do you like *aïoli?*' she asked. 'We love *aïoli,*' Papa answered, 'but maybe it could use just a little more garlic.'

"These dinners became annual events," Jean-Marie continued, "and Madame Blanc always served the same thing, and Papa always complained that there still was not enough garlic."

"It's true," Lucien interjected. "She was a nice woman, God bless her soul, and a good cook, but she didn't understand *aïoli.*"

"So one time Papa and Gigi showed up and there sat the big bowl of *aïoli* on the table. Gigi took a bite and practically choked on it, but he was able to swallow it and of course he had to clean his plate to be polite. 'Do you think there is enough garlic in my *aïoli?*' old Madame Blanc asked sweetly."

Jean-Marie squeezed his hands around his throat and breathlessly mimicked Lucien: " '*Yes, madame, that is a true aïoli!*' Madame Blanc announced with pride that she had used one head of garlic *per person.* Gigi didn't eat garlic for ten years after that, and Papa was sick for days."

"Oh, Jean-Marie," scolded Lucien, "you always exaggerate."

Everyone around the table was laughing except Jean-Marie, who was clearly offended by Lucien's denial. "Okay, Papa, tell us what really happened."

"Oh, my son, why must you exaggerate everything? Gigi was back eating *aïoli* within a year or two."

"Aha, but you see, it's almost the same thing." And Jean-Marie turned his attention to another ladle of octopus stew and another scoop of the dwindling *aïoli.*

Rhône wine, we say, but it is badly said because a Rhône wine can be red, white, or pink, sweet or dry, still or sparkling. It can be from one grape variety or a blend of several. It can be among the handful of France's noblest wines, or it can be a simple wine whose proper place would be in a carafe alongside a quick steak and french fries.

Rhône tastings are conducted in which such diverse wines as Gigondas, Saint-Joseph, Hermitage, Châteauneuf-du-Pape, and Côtes du Rhône are tasted blind, as they say, then judged and ranked. Such a grouping has a single characteristic in common:

the grapes that produced them are grown near or somewhat near the Rhône River. There is as much difference between a Gigondas and a Saint-Joseph as there is between a Saint-Joseph and a Beaujolais, yet blind tasters would never square off a Saint-Joseph against a Beaujolais. The fact that Gigondas and Saint-Joseph are lumped together in Rhône tastings is a symptom of confusion, an unfortunate confusion, because each wine expresses itself in its own language, and in the Babel-like jumble of such a blind tasting one misses what each has to say. The winner is usually the most powerful wine, the one that speaks in the loudest voice, so one leaves having learned nothing.

Sorting out the Rhône is not difficult, and several wine books explain the different *appellations*. Dividing the Rhône into north and south is the first step. Such a division is altogether practical and natural. The two regions, north and south, are about an hour's drive apart. There are profound differences between the two in terms of landscape, soil, climate, and grape varieties employed (although they overlap a bit as we shall see), and finally in the taste of the wines themselves.

South of Lyons (the French spell it Lyon), a few hundred yards past the limits of the old Roman city of Vienne, the vineyards of the northern Rhône commence in grand fashion with the Côte Rôtie, or "roasted hill." For the great *appellations* of the north, it is best to keep in mind two dominating factors: *Syrah,* which is the only red grape permitted, and *steep,* because the vines are planted on dramatic terraced hillsides that rise from the narrow valley floor. One does not see these dazzling carved mountainsides in the southern Rhône. The dominant grape variety in the southern reds is the *Grenache,* which is usually blended with other varieties, and the terrain is comparatively *flat*.

The northern Rhône consists of a long, narrow, stingy stretch of vineyards along the river between Vienne and Valence, the source of such exalted growths as Côte Rôtie, Hermitage, Saint-Joseph, and Cornas. I hesitate to include Crozes-Hermitage because the committee that defines the limits of the controlled *appellations* has allowed commerce to be its guide, and most Crozes today comes from flat, sandy soil. An extraordinary Crozes is hard to find, and it is objectionable that the growers have the right to tack Hermitage onto their name.

By contrast, the southern Rhône is a vast, productive, almost circle-shaped area, and here one finds the vineyards of Châteauneuf-du-Pape, Gigondas, Tavel, Cairanne, Rasteau, and countless others. The most important city of the southern Rhône is Avignon, but the most important for the wine lover is Châteauneuf-du-Pape.

In terms of worldwide renown and prestige, Châteauneuf-du-Pape is the greatest *appellation* in southern France, which is not to say that it is always the source of the finest wine. A perfect Côtes du Rhône will inspire more pleasure than a badly made Châteauneuf-du-Pape. It is well to remember that the system of *appellation d'origine contrôlée* (AOC) is not a rating, not a judgment of the wine in bottle, but a definition of the terrain, the soil, the grape varieties . . . the raw materials!

Over the years, wine writers have yielded to the temptation to classify the top *domaines* of Châteauneuf-du-Pape much as the Bordeaux châteaux were classified in 1855. However easier such a ranking might appear to make the life of the wine consumer by helping him decide what to buy, such a classification is dangerous work. In 1832 a French writer, A. Jullien, placed La Nerthe at the top of the Châteauneuf-du-Papes. More recently an American author, Robert Parker, Jr., left La Nerthe out of the top category and rated Vieux Télégraphe, Beaucastel, and Fortia *grand cru classé*. Vieux Télégraphe's vines are planted on a very privileged site. Thanks to this site, their vinification, and their consistency, it is one of the two or three finest *domaines* producing Châteauneuf-du-Pape today. But what is to prevent Vieux Télégraphe from buying another block of vines in a less privileged part of the *appellation* in order to pump out more wine and take advantage of the commercial possibilities created by their new *grand cru* status?

Classifying a *domaine* or a château rather than the soil or terrain misses the point. Rating the specific vineyards of Châteauneuf-du-Pape is a good idea, overdue, in fact, because the area of the *appellation* is so enormous (over seven thousand acres) and includes nobler and less noble sites. If *domaines* had plots of vines in several parts of the *appellation,* which is often the case, they would have to vinify their *grand cru* separately if they wanted to name it on their label. A perfect example of such a system can be found in Burgundy. La Romanée-Conti (the vineyard) is a *grand cru,* but the Domaine de la Romanée-Conti (the winery) is not. If it were, the proprietors could bottle a simple Bourgogne *rouge* and call it *grand cru.*

Henri Brunier of Vieux Télégraphe agrees that the vineyard site is of supreme importance. The source of his wine's quality, he says, is his stony terrain, situated upon the slope of the highest ridge in the Châteauneuf-du-Pape *appellation.* Because of the superior elevation, it was on this ridge that a telegraph tower was constructed in the eighteenth century, one of the relay points for communications between Paris and Marseilles. The crumbling stone ruin of this tower gave Vieux Télégraphe its name, and there is a rendering of it on the *domaine*'s label. To the eye there is no soil here and one would think it is barren, but living vines poke out from the thick layer of smooth, oval stones. Walking the Côte Rôtie vineyards, one is impressed by the difficulty of climbing such steep hills. In Brunier's vineyard it is hard to walk because the stones slip and slide underfoot. An unreal landscape, it sticks in the mind like the volcanic Kona coast of Hawaii or the surface of the moon. It is totally unprotected from the elements. I have been there in the summer when the stones are too hot to touch. I have heard the sound of vine branches cracking in a fierce mistral. Nowhere does the mistral blow with such force. It can knock you over, and when it turns cold, the mistral cuts right through you. You cannot move your fingers, your teeth chatter, your nose and ears turn red. You are glad you are an importer who can head for the fireplace and a glass of Vieux Télégraphe and not the poor fellow out there pruning the vines.

One visitor from California revealed perhaps the difference between the American and French mentality when he asked,

"Why did they move all those stones into the vineyard?" The French cultivated this ridiculously stony site, this nearly impossible surface, because it gives a special character to the wine. Typically American would be to plant on the valley floor and use land-moving equipment to move in a layer of stones.

They look like Sierra riverbed stones and were formed by the same geological process. They are glacial deposits, shattered and shaped by the weight and crunch of the glacier's movement, then rounded and polished by the flow of water as the ice melted.

One tastes the influence of the stones in the wine. Experienced tasters in the area recognize a Vieux Télégraphe by its expression of *pierre à feu,* or gunflint. A great Châteauneuf-du-Pape tastes almost as if it had been filtered through the stones, and indeed rainwater is filtered by this thick stone layer before it reaches the underlying soil which nourishes the plants. In addition, the stones account for Vieux Télégraphe's characteristic power and generosity because they reflect and collect heat, and it is believed that during the ripening season this store of warmth works throughout the night contributing to the grapes' maturity. Brunier considers adding some sandier parcels to his holding because in hot years he wonders if his wine is not too alcoholic, lacking perhaps a certain finesse, which a proportion of less-ripe grapes would palliate. Americans who buy Vieux Télégraphe are not at all of this opinion. The hottest years producing the strongest wines, such as 1983, are the object of a real buyers' scramble. A more elegant vintage like 1984, by no means a light wine and which Brunier prefers to his massive 1983, is slower to disappear from the shelves.

One is immediately at ease with Henri Brunier. He typifies the Provençal qualities of warmth, friendliness, and candor. The rugged cut to his features and his ruddy, sunbaked cheeks attest to the years he has spent outdoors with his vines. He looks the way the winemaker of a robust wine like Vieux Télégraphe should look.

When he shows off his new vinification cellar, completed in 1979, he stands back with his hands on his hips gazing up at

Royaume des Craux

the towering stainless-steel *cuves* like a sculptor regarding a grand new work. *"Eh, voilà,"* he says, as if letting the installation speak for itself. He is still awed by his creation. The envy of many of his neighbors because it is so rational and functional, Brunier's new winery permits him unusual control over the elaboration of his wine no matter what the vagary of the vintage. Each harvest means different problems, yet most winemakers are predestined to a certain vinification by virtue of the equipment at hand. Their vinification will be essentially the same whether the grapes are shriveled, thick-skinned, and sugary, or plump with water from unseasonal showers. Brunier's cellar is built up against the hillside next to his house. The grapes arrive at the rear and enter on conveyer belts, a rather gentle reception. They can be partially or totally destemmed, or not at all. They can be partially or totally crushed, or left intact. Henri is free to decide according to the constitution of each variety as it arrives. By an ingenious system of movable bins, the grapes then fall directly into whichever vat he chooses, without having suffered the stress of mechanical pumping. Once the must is in the fermentation tank, Henri can control its temperature, which is of exceeding importance in the South of France, where it is often brutally hot during the harvest. In 1985, for example, many growers saw their wines cooked right from the start because temperatures soared in the vats during an unusually ebullient fermentation. The result is a wine lacking freshness and fruit and marred by excessive volatile acidity. At Vieux Télégraphe, Brunier kept the fermenting mash down around 30 degrees centigrade, and his wine shows splendidly ripe fruit without a trace of volatility.

Dwarfed by this costly, gleaming, high-tech facility, one might imagine that Brunier had forsaken the chewy, old-style wine that made his reputation . . . until he explains that here the wine spends only the first twelve to fifteen days, the most tumultuous days, of its life. It could be compared to an obstetrics ward, because during this initial fermentation a wine is born and it can develop certain faults or virtues that will remain with it and mark its personality.

The second fermentation, the malolactic fermentation, takes place in glass-lined tanks under the most sanitary conditions possible. Brunier then has a clean, healthy wine which is racked into his huge oak casks, or *foudres*—the traditional aging vessel of the Rhône—to develop slowly for six to eighteen months.

When I arrive in the fall after the new vintage has finished the initial fermentation, we begin our business by tasting the new wine drawn directly from the glass-lined tanks. There are several *cuvées* to taste. The final *assemblage* will occur when the wine is racked into the oak *foudres*.

We usually begin with a *cuvée* of 100 percent Grenache. The aroma is reminiscent of pit fruits, like cherry, plum, and apricot. Certain years produce a sumptuousness that is blackberry-like. Typically, there is an extravagance of alcohol (sometimes between 15 and 16 degrees) and a lack of acidity. The wine fills the mouth, but there is no center.

The next sample is from a *cuvée* with a high proportion of Syrah. Disputes occur because I often arrive with the aftertaste still lingering from tastings of the noble Syrahs of the northern Rhône. The Syrah expresses itself in more vulgar terms in the southern soil and climate, where it seems more peppery and earthy, often leaden with rude tannins. The Bruniers see the violets and raspberry, the stuffing and length of it.

Mourvèdre dominates the next *cuvée* with its wilder (the French say *sauvage*), more vegetal aromas of *garrigue* and herb. The Bruniers value the Mourvèdre for its structure, nervosity, and, in contrast to the Grenache, its resistance to oxidation. However, there is also a sapid, delicious fruitiness recalling black cherries picked ripe off the tree, and an intriguing soulfulness, a darker, more mysterious nature than expressed by the pure Grenache. Mourvèdre has a leaner, intense feel to it, and in fact it normally ripens to only 12.5 degrees to 13 degrees alcohol.

Brunier still has some Cinsault in his vineyard, but little of it is destined for the final *assemblage* of what will be sold as Vieux Télégraphe. For the most part, it is blended with Syrah to make the Bruniers' everyday house wine. A pure Cinsault passes over the taste buds without sticking, almost like water.

In a normal year Vieux Télégraphe is 75 percent Grenache, 15 percent Syrah, and 10 percent Mourvèdre. Recently, they planted five more acres of Mourvèdre, which, when the vines are old enough, will significantly alter the proportion of Mourvèdre in the final *assemblage*.

Then we move into the old cellars to taste the previous vintage. The walls are humid and moldy, lined with *foudres*. From twelve to twenty *foudres* contain wine, depending on the size of the year's crop. Each *foudre* differs in size, but the average in Brunier's cellar holds about seven thousand bottles of wine.

Henri's son Daniel does the work of drawing the samples from the *foudres*. He has a robust, self-assured presence like his father. In his mid-twenties, he is curly-haired and well built, with a firm cut to his jaw. He has an irrepressible mischievous streak that grows more and more effective as he learns how to disguise it behind a serious expression. "Which one do you want to taste?" he asks, tossing a glance at the row of casks.

"Well, all of them," I reply.

He grimaces. "They're all the same."

"Let's taste them and see."

Theoretically, each *foudre* contains the same wine because the final blend was made when the *foudres* were filled. However, the *foudre* itself has an influence, subtle or profound, on the wine as it ages. Therefore, I like to taste each and select the ones to be bottled and shipped to me.

Daniel grabs the wooden ladder and slams it up against a *foudre*. He pounds down on it once or twice to make sure it is secure, and climbs up on top, crawling between the cask and the roof.

All of us taste, Henri, Daniel, his brother Frédéric, and I, but they don't contribute much in the way of opinion. I wish they would because they certainly know their wine better than I do. On the other hand, they appreciate *all* their offspring. How often do you hear a father say, "This child I don't like"? And perhaps they like to stand back and judge my judgments.

Each sample means Daniel must scramble up and down the ladder one-handed because he has to carry the glass "thief" with which he draws the wine from the top of the cask. After the fifth or sixth *cuvée* he starts acting like it is a real pain in the ass, but over the years it is always the same routine; it is a playful pose for the sake of his father and brother.

Henri says, *"C'est bon, ça,"* about one *cuvée*, "This has the aroma," about another. If I comment that one *foudre* seems to me the most complete, he says, "That cask always makes a good wine, but it really is strange because they were all exactly the same to begin with." Each year he seems to learn anew that the evolution within each *foudre* is different.

As usual, when we went through the 1984s I jotted down a quick note on each *foudre* to remind me later on of the differences among the twelve to twenty tasted:

1. Spicy, a bit hard.
2. Lacks nerve.
3. Closed. Excellent palate. Finishes dry.
4. Nose lacks charm.
5. Spice and black pepper. Ripe, stony, long.
6. Most complete so far. Spicy, vibrant, deep, long.
7. Closed. Quite round but finishes abruptly.
8. Still full of CO_2. Difficult to judge today.
9. Deep purple. Classic V.T. nose. Powerful, tannic, long.
#10. Short.
#11. Well balanced, a bit dumb.
#12. A bit tarry; lacks finesse.
#13. Lovely robe. Finesse. Typical flavors. Finishes a bit short.

And so it continues. Finally Daniel marks *foudres* 5, 6, and 9 with a *KL* in chalk. One cannot say that I necessarily receive the best. For one thing, returning three months later, I might replace one of my selections with #8, which was that day so difficult to judge. Or another might develop unexpected qualities, which often happens. Finally, it would be surprising to find two tasters who could agree on a ranking of so many similar wines. However, I do get my preference, which adds a certain personal involvement to my work.

When I reminded them to bottle my *foudres* without filtering, our annual to-filter-or-not-to-filter discussion begins. With the 1982 vintage they began bottling my selections unfiltered, but the rest of their production was filtered. We have been arguing filtration a long time. Daniel sums up their position when he says, "There are filtrations and then there are filtrations. And then there is the system we use. It doesn't change the wine at all."

"If it doesn't change the wine, why do it?" I ask.

"Just to take out the heaviest sediment."

"Oh, you have a filter that thinks, that looks through the constituents of your wine and decides what needs removing? That *is* quite an advanced system."

Then they surprise me by pulling out two bottles of 1983. "One is filtered, one unfiltered," says Frédéric, the quiet Brunier whose expression tells you more than his utterances.

For years I have been waiting for just such a face-to-face comparison. Bizarre as it seems, it is the first time I have been provided with two glasses of the same wine, one filtered, the other unfiltered. Up to this moment, my lecturing winemakers all over France has been theoretical. One would think all winemakers would bottle such samples as a matter of course in order to experience with their eyes, noses, and palates the results of their manipulations.

The entire family is assembled for our blind comparison. Maggie Brunier leaves her *pot-au-feu* on the stove to join us. There is silence as we taste, then a secret ballot.

"It is unanimous," Daniel announces, and pauses dramatically. "The unfiltered wins."

What a victory! It is not astonishing, after all, because the

A *foudre*
at Vieux Télégraphe

difference between the two bottles was striking. The filtered was a limpid, one-dimensional ruby color, boring to the eye. The unfiltered was deeper-colored, shimmering with glints of purple and black.

The filtered smelled as clean as it looked, but what little nose it had seemed superficial compared to the unfiltered, and it gave an impression of fatigue, which is not illogical because filtration involves pumping, or pushing, the wine through a long series of cardboardlike plaques. The less you work a wine, the more vitality it retains. The unfiltered had a deep, healthy aroma. One might say that its aroma had *texture;* it seemed dense and full of nuances of spice and fruit. It smelled as good as the wine fresh out of the *foudre.*

On the palate, too, the filtered bottle lacked texture. It had body, but it didn't coat the taste buds with flavor like the unfiltered, which was chewy and substantial.

The difference in the aftertaste was dramatic. The filtered wine clunked dryly to a halt. In the unfiltered, the typical Vieux Télégraphe perfumes kept returning.

The Bruniers are keeping a stock of each bottling in order to compare the evolution over the years.

The difference between the two was dramatized by the face-to-face comparison. The filtered is not a bad wine. The Bruniers are conscientious and skilled; they do not practice severe or sterile filtrations. However, side by side, the filtered seemed merely decent, the unfiltered grand. There was more wine in the wine!

"But look at this," Henri says, and he holds up to the light an unopened bottle of the unfiltered. "That's what I don't like, that *petite tache.*"

There was a *petite tache,* or smudge of deposit, that had settled on the underside of the bottle. Already. Even though the wine had very recently been bottled.

"What's wrong with that, Henri?"

"It's worrisome."

"It's nothing. I like it. It shows that you respect your wine too much to subject it to filtration."

"The clients don't like it."

"Wait, I'm a client and I like it. For someone who doesn't understand fine wine you are going to trade the color, the aroma, texture, and flavor for a spotless appearance?"

"What can one do? They return bottles like this. They think the wine is not clean." He shrugs helplessly.

"Don't sell to clients like that," I insist. I could see that even after my secret-ballot victory the battle was not yet won. "Almost all my reds arrive now with this *petite tache*. People who love wine prefer to have it intact, even if it means there is a little sediment, which falls harmlessly to the bottom anyway. You watch, Henri. Soon it will be fashionable, the sign of a serious winemaker, to bottle without filtering. Your customers will be demanding an unfiltered wine."

Daniel speaks up. "We'll have to uncork our bottles and add a little deposit to make them happy!"

It is a relief to terminate with laughter what is actually a dispute of passionate importance to both of us.

One must not have the impression that the problem of filtration is easy to resolve. It is not as simple as saying, "I shall, or shall not, filter." Foremost is the problem in the marketplace. If a vintner chooses not to filter, he limits himself to the minority of wine buyers, the true connoisseurs who care about quality and will accept some gunk at the bottom of the bottle. For superstar producers like Brunier, the problem is not as big as he makes it out to be, because there is never enough Vieux Télégraphe to supply the demand. He has certainly reached the point at which he can choose his clientele and bottle the finest, most natural wine possible.

But there is also the question of how to bottle a wine without filtering. One cannot proceed just like that, leaving out the filter. Above all, it is a matter of clarification by natural methods: fining, racking, and time, allowing the unwanted material to fall to the bottom of the cask and drawing off the clear wine. The ancients understood how to do it; they had to because they had no filters. However, today's is a hurry-up world, time is money, and fining and racking require more patience, care, and attention than mashing one's wine through a filter pad.

Also, winemakers in France pay a tax on their stock. Thus, today's scarcity of old bottles and the rush to bottle and sell as quickly as possible. Châteauneuf-du-Pape used to spend three to four years in *foudre*. Some growers today bottle before a year has passed. No one likes taxes, especially a Frenchman.

Vieux Télégraphe was not filtered until the 1979 vintage. One might claim that they earned their reputation with unfiltered wine, but in fact very little Vieux Télégraphe was bottled at the *domaine* until the 1978 vintage. For the most part, it had been sold in bulk to *négociants*.

The *domaine*'s origins go back to the turn of the century, according to Henri. "My grandfather, Hippolyte Brunier, was a peasant, meaning he lived off the land. He grew melons, lettuce, almonds, apricots, wheat, and he had two acres of vines in the heart of this plateau, which was known as the Royaume des Craux." (Royaume means realm or kingdom. Crau is an arid plateau dressed in stones which supports little in the way of vegetation.)

"My grandfather put a little of his wine in bottle. He saw that it pleased the clients, so he and my uncle purchased another forty acres. Forty acres of *garrigue*, scrubland, woods. After the first war, they began to transform it to vines. My grandfather worked the land, my uncle handled the business side of it, and my father built the original *chais* with his own hands."

Henri began working with them in 1940 at age seventeen. During World War II, they acquired additional acreage. "It was cheap. No one wanted it. There was no market for wine then. Some simply gave us their land. It was believed worthless because it was covered with scrub. To clear it by hand . . . Then you Americans arrived and introduced us to the bulldozer." He lets out a deep chuckle. "And then, after the war, people began to ask for the wine again.

"When I sold my wine to the *négociants,* I always received the highest price," he says proudly. "Our wine was called a *vin de médecin* because the *négociants* used it to remedy the ills of their less successful *cuvées*."

Henri Brunier is a proud man without a trace of haughtiness or self-importance. Such a man, who rightfully takes pleasure in his achievements, is rare and a joy to behold. With so many people who have attained success, one has the impression that their thirst for it will never be quenched because they never take the time to celebrate their blessings. Above all, the source of Henri's pride is his family; they are close yet notably individualistic and independent, and they love him. As he surveys the great plateau, the Royaume des Craux, one sees his pride now that it is planted and productive. He succeeded in introducing modern technology into his cellar without compromising the robust, old-fashioned character of his wine. He guided the commercialization away from bulk sales toward *domaine* bottling with his name on the label. And you see his pride when he says, "It is a wine that pleases."

Price and celebrity; adorned with these diadems, Châteauneuf-du-Pape reigns upon the throne of the wine aristocracy of the southern Rhône. As to quality . . . ? Yes, bow and scrape, but not to all pretenders to the throne. At Châteauneuf-du-Pape, one finds the drinkable and the undrinkable, the majestic and the tired, orange-colored, overalcoholic flop. Drinking a great one is an event.

There is both an official and an unofficial hierarchy of *appellations* in the southern Rhône. Officially, Châteauneuf-du-Pape is not ranked above Lirac, Tavel, or Gigondas. The four have the right to stand on their name alone.

Bulky as it is, the official hierarchy defining the areas of *appellation contrôlée* is not engraved in stone; it is ever-changing, overcomplicated, and confusing. In its present form it exists more to soothe the pride and commercial instincts of the thousands of local growers than to serve as a guide or guarantor of quality to the consumer.

After Châteauneuf-du-Pape, Lirac, Tavel, and Gigondas, there are the villages and communes (twenty-seven in 1985) that have the right to state their name on their label as long as it is tied to the designation Côtes du Rhône Villages: Rasteau, Côtes du Rhône Villages, for example.

Then there are the forty-seven communes (in 1985) that can also call their wine Côte du Rhône Villages, but which are not allowed to specify more precisely their origin.

There must be a better system than this!

By far, wine from the largest surface (producing 1.4 million hectoliters in 1983) is bottled under the vaguest label, Côtes du Rhône. Without question, the logic of the system *appears* to be: vagueness equals inferior quality. In fact, one can encounter unpotable Tavels and snappy Côtes du Rhônes. Actually a precise label means only that the official controls on production, grape varieties, and alcoholic content are more severe. Still, there is an *implication* of quality control, and the consumer responds to that implication.

Meanwhile, there is a humble *vin de pays,* or "country wine" (an upstart, an outcast, because its vines lie just outside the official Côtes du Rhône zone), whose wine can outluster a good many of its titled neighbors. The vineyard is the Domaine de la Gautière, near Buis-les-Baronnies. Paul and Georgette Tardieu are the proprietors of the Domaine de la Gautière. It is worth visiting and they look forward to visitors. Paul especially likes Americans. He gave me a discount because I am an American. He remembers the war. Their *domaine* is only about forty miles northeast toward the Alps from Châteauneuf-du-Pape, but give yourself plenty of time because the territory in between has an endless, ageless allure, and there are several villages en route in which you may wish to tarry.

For example, Orange, the city, has a chunky-looking Roman theater, a well-preserved (as they say when there is nothing better to be said) Arc de Triomphe, and, on a more transient level, a master cheese merchant, Monsieur Alan Parant, whose tidy, jam-packed shop is on the Place de la République, just a few steps from the tourist congestion around the theater. Parant has a fabulous assortment of the very finest cheeses available from all over France. Ask for a taste of what interests you, or take his advice. He knows more about cheese than any ten million Frenchmen, and he is eager to share his enthusiasm and his treasures. Orange was one of the important Roman cities; however, most traces have been destroyed or covered over by succeeding habitants. The last time I tried to park in Orange's block-large central parking lot, it was fenced off because of new excavations. From what I could make out, an elaborate public bath has been unearthed a stone's throw from the theater, about twenty feet below the asphalt surface of the parking lot, leading one to wonder what else lies underfoot. With each step you take in downtown Orange, you are only a few feet from another civilization.

Around here, each village has some wonderful distraction. Drive east to Sarrians, where Marius Dumas (great name, with its Pagnol and Monte Cristo connotations) still bakes bread in his wood-fired oven. It is worth a short detour to taste what French bread used to be, and you might require a loaf to go with your cheeses. As for mouth rinse, vines are everywhere!

The village of Beaumes-de-Venise was constructed in levels up a hillside on which you also see isolated groves of olive trees and vines, the former producing an olive oil touted by Elizabeth David, the latter producing a succulent sweet Muscat, one of France's loveliest dessert wines. A local restaurant once served an interesting little refresher between my fish and lamb courses, an ice made with the local Muscat in which rosemary branches had been macerated. It was not sweet, simply a breathtakingly aromatic ice that smelled like Provence in blossom and left the palate lively and alert for the garlic-studded leg of lamb that followed.

Just around the bend to the north is the village of Vacqueyras. Truly a wine village, every house, it seems, has a cellar underneath. There must be interesting wine at Vacqueyras, but often the search for good wine involves simple luck, a question of whether or not one's leads pan out. After several scouting trips to Vacqueyras, I still have not found one to import.

Village in
the southern Rhône

Artifacts reveal that the Romans, smart fellows, enjoyed a good quantity of wine at Gigondas. The name is supposedly from *Jocanditus,* which means "merry or joyous city." While the village as it stands is not *that* ancient, it is old enough. With tile roofs and cavernlike dwellings—the doorways appear to lead right into the hillside—it is an altogether idyllic, surprisingly lazy, secluded spot. What a wonderful place for a wine merchant to retire, surrounded by vines, olive and fruit trees, wild herbs, ruins of the medieval fortified city on the hillside, and a population of only 750 with whom to share it all.

There is not a white Gigondas, but a rosé is produced, better to cope, perhaps, with the summer's blazing heat. However, winter means cold weather ofttimes in concert with a howling mistral, and few of the homes are heated except by fireplace, which is where the cooking is done, too. In such a setting, the sturdy red wine of the village comes in handy. A glass or two for warmth while the pot simmers and we poke at the coals . . . a glass or two *in* the pot of course . . . Hand over that corkscrew, will you; we've drained the bottle and dinner's just ready.

I have imported several Gigondas over the years, but I stick with old man Faraud, whose home is right at the entrance to the village. It took several visits and some outside interference before Faraud agreed to sell to me. The first time I broached the subject, he began trembling and quaking as if I had suggested some wildly deviate act. Export? Send his wine several thousand miles away? The idea scared him to death. I kept returning, each time buying a case or two, putting them in the trunk of my car like a retail client. He warmed up a bit, but my attempts to purchase a serious quantity were answered with a nervous smile and shake of the head.

One year Aubert de Villaine, a grower in Burgundy, accompanied me to Gigondas. We tasted in several cellars, then stopped at Faraud's.

"This is the one I want," I told Aubert, "but he is afraid to export."

"He probably thinks he won't get paid," Aubert said.

We stood in the cramped entry hall that serves as Faraud's office, tasting the latest bottling out of water glasses with him and his wife. Madame Faraud has lean, birdlike, sharply etched features, no cosmetics, gray hair, and bright, vigilant eyes. Her clothes are faded and oft-repaired. There is a sort of rural, aged beauty to her. She spoke no more than a word or two and left from time to time to tend to lunch, which smelled like turnips and carrots. Once again, I made my pitch to Faraud, while Madame watched warily.

Faraud twisted at the cork on his corkscrew. "I don't export," he said.

"I ship my wine to Kermit," Aubert said. "It is not at all complicated."

In his creaky, fusty voice, Faraud said he didn't have enough wine.

"I'm not looking for large quantities," I said. "You tell me how much you want to sell."

He shook his head no.

As we drove off with a case of Faraud Gigondas in the trunk, Aubert gave me some advice which has proven useful again and again in dealing with small growers like Faraud. "I know what the problem is. It is not the quantity. You're talking to the wrong person. In the old French families—well, it is more or less true today, too—the wife handles the accounts. You didn't say more than *Bonjour* to Madame Faraud, and she is the key. Ask about her garden. Bring up the names of others that you buy from around here."

It worked. Nowadays, Faraud pesters me to buy larger quantities.

Faraud's Gigondas is ultratraditional. A visit to his cellar, seeing his winery equipment, is like a visit to the nineteenth century. Once I found him seated on a wooden stool bottling by hand, bottle by bottle, from a brass spigot in the ancient oak *foudre*. A *foudre* holds several thousand bottles. Once you have begun bottling, you must finish it or risk oxidation, and it is monotonous work. That is why almost all winemakers hook up a bottling machine and an electric pump and press the START button. However, as wine simply doesn't like to be shoved around, it is exhausted after passing through the bottling line. Faraud's method is an anachronism, but it is kinder to the wine.

His production averages thirty hectoliters to the hectare, which is about half the production of a Meursault vineyard in a normal year. Thus, the power, the sap, the concentration of flavor in his wine. Thus, his Spartan life-style. Small production is not the most profitable policy. Faraud drives a tractor, not a Mercedes.

Some are put off by the rusticity of his Gigondas. It can be a shock once one is habituated to the taste of the overproduced, overelaborated wines that dominate the marketplace. Others revel in its punch and genuineness. Some neighbors say his vinification is outdated, but his wine is like a remembrance of things past. Were Faraud the type to verbalize a philosophy he might say, "It has worked for centuries. Why change?"

The contrast between Faraud and André Roux at the nearby Château du Trignon could not be greater. If Roux were not constantly searching to improve, *"mieux faire,"* as he says, he would find a different line of work. Faraud has barely noticed the twentieth century's arrival; Roux will try anything in order to progress. His cellar is lined with cement vats, and there is not a *foudre* in sight. He drives a BMW, not a Mercedes.

Short, stocky, closing in on his sixtieth year, André Roux has a thick brush of hair in which the pepper is giving way to salt. Thick jowls, thick lips, a thick waist. Either there is something Saint Bernard-like about his appearance, or one is too influenced by the giant, furry dog blocking his doorway.

André is a thinker, and of the many pleasures he derives from wine, the intellectual aspect is what motivates him. He makes consistently intriguing wines.

He makes Gigondas, Rasteau, Sablet, Côtes du Rhône Villages, and both red and white Côtes du Rhône, all of which he vinifies by carbonic maceration, a method that evokes images of fresh, inconsequential quaffing wines like Beaujolais *nouveau*. Critics bad-mouth the method, in which the alcoholic fermentation occurs within the skin of each uncrushed grape in airtight vats under a preservative layer of carbon dioxide, calling carbonic maceration wines insipid, spineless, short-lived . . . In a word, carbonic maceration wines are not considered *macho*. However, when Roux's wine is poured, the glass is stained with deep, vivid color. The aroma is lively and complex. It fills the mouth with flavor and it is tannic enough. Destroying once and for all the notion that carbonic maceration wines do not age well, Roux will pull out a Côtes du Rhône Villages that he vinified in 1966. It is not a fluke. He can also uncork a 1967 or 1969 to prove his point. Tasted in 1983, even an unsung vintage like 1974 was at a rather glorious peak. Roux explains that for Beaujolais *nouveau* there is a very short period of maceration before the wine is drawn off the skins and seeds, while his maceration continues for almost a month, plenty of time for the maximum extraction of color, tannin, and flavor components.

Each visit finds André seized by a new idea. He is planting a large parcel of his Sablet vines over to Mourvèdre in search of structure and flavor interest. He is studying with the faculty at Montpellier the question of optimal maturity in order to harvest his different grape varieties at the moment they give their finest perfumes. Contrary to almost universal opinion, ripest is not always the finest. He has planted a vineyard of Viognier and one of Marsanne to see what these noble whites from the northern Rhône will give in his *terroir* and climate.

Like artists and cooks, most winemakers want to hear only compliments. André wants serious feedback. Simply saying you like one of his wines leaves him unsatisfied.

Tasting the 1983 Rasteau out of the glass-lined vat, I told him that I would like to see it spend a few months in *foudre* because it needed to breathe through the wood a bit. It seemed closed in upon itself. He led the way to another corner of the cellar which held three spanking new Burgundy barrels. Holding a glass thief in one hand, he tried to knock the barrel's wooden stopper loose with the other hand, then went off to find a hammer.

He banged tentatively at the stopper because he did not yet have the knack that comes with familiarity.

"We'll see," he said, easing the thief through the bung. "The same wine, but it breathes in a barrel."

"Yes, it breathes, but it is not the same as a big old *foudre*," I said.

We sniffed. It was a good wine, but it lacked what I call "typicity." The new oak had rendered it an anonymous red wine, masking its characteristic aromas.

André agreed. "The wood dominates. Too much vanilla. Well, it is an experiment. We have to top off the barrels almost daily because it is too dry here. The wine evaporates through the wood. It breathes too much!" he joked.

For centuries, the *foudre* was the traditional aging vessel for wine in the South of France. Before that, wine vats were carved out of the rock. The walls of the stone *cuves* that have been unearthed show hand-struck chisel markings. The result obtained by aging a wine in a glass-lined tank is probably little different from aging in rock. Andre's experiment with new barrels demonstrated that the ancients had a rationale. After all, they could have stored their wine in small oak barrels instead of large *foudres* just as easily as did the Burgundians or Bordelais. Small barrels were not employed, because the arid climate of the Midi sucks out too much wine, the loss in liquid volume would simply be insupportable on financial grounds, and the taste of wood obliterates rather than marries with the southern grape varieties. Grenache, Mourvèdre, Syrah: in a new oak barrel, they have a muted expression. At Vieux Télégraphe, when Brunier must replace a worn-out *foudre,* he puts his *vin ordinaire* into the new one for two or three vintages to leech out the wood flavors before he will use it for his Châteauneuf-du-Pape.

"Personally, I don't like the taste of oak," Roux said, echoing the sentiment of most winemakers in the Midi, "but I don't want to have a closed mind about anything that might improve my wine."

* * *

One night, owing André Roux and his wife Colette a favor, I invited them to dinner. It had to be somewhere special because during one of my trips they lent me a four-hundred-year-old town house in downtown Sablet, a rustic little village near Gigondas. It was paradise, a house instead of yet another hotel, a kitchen in which to dabble rather than the hit-or-miss risk of yet another restaurant. During the daylight hours I worked the wine villages of the southern Rhône, tasting in dark moldy cellars and bright stainless-steel-furnished installations, tasting hundreds of wines—mostly powerful, tannic wines—until my mouth felt like the inside of a barrel. Returning home evenings, I would search across the flat, vine-covered plain for Sablet's Romanesque bell tower in order to gauge the distance I still had to cover before I could kick off my shoes, pour myself a glass of André's refreshing white wine, and begin concocting some simple dinner based on olive oil, garlic, and usually one of the small-leafed basil plants that are available in the markets during the spring and summer months. I would read myself to sleep to the sound of the gurgling stone fountain outside my window.

I invited André and Colette to a nearby restaurant of some repute. The cuisine was fine enough; I ate it, then forgot it because of everything else that occurred. The wine list was dazzling. One page listed *domaine*-bottled reds and whites from nearby Châteauneuf-du-Pape. The right-hand page listed rare old Bordeaux and Burgundies. The great growths. The great vintages. At irresistible prices! I fell for the 1929 Château d'Yquem. I had never tasted the 1929; I knew I would never see it again at such a low price, and I thought it would make a rather memorable thank-you gift to André and Colette, whose eyes widened in disbelief when I ordered it.

Even though I had invited André, we had to fight over who would pick up the bill. It is an unceasing battle to "outgenerous" André. With one hand I held him back by the throat, with my other I tossed out my American Express card.

"We don't accept credit cards," the waiter announced. My

high good humor turned to shock and silence. I felt as defenseless as when I first noticed my thick head of hair turning thin. No credit card? The '29 Yquem was cheap, but not so cheap that I had enough cash on me. Of course André reached for his checkbook, but I stopped him firmly with a glance that let him know that I was not playing. He was my guest; he would *never* have ordered that '29 for himself.

There had to be a way out (apart from the back door). This is a serious restaurant, I told myself, and upon arrival I had introduced myself to the chef/proprietor and transmitted to him the best regards of some mutual friends. I would simply explain my dilemma to him and he would offer a solution.

I left my guests and asked at the cashier's desk for the owner. He came out of the kitchen in his white chef's suit, toqueless, unsmiling, and I explained that I had expected to pay with a credit card . . . The man exploded into a tirade against credit cards. He had never accepted them and never would! He made me feel like a credit-card salesman.

"I understand," I said carefully, even if I did not, "but I am in a delicate situation. Normally, I carry enough . . ."

"Your friend can pay," he said.

"He is my guest. Believe me, that is not the solution."

I was coldly informed that *none* of the great restaurants take credit cards.

What was his problem? I told him to check his *Guide Michelin* and show me a three-star restaurant that refuses credit cards. A three-star meal is so horridly expensive, only drug dealers would carry enough cash to pay cash. The French have checkbooks, of course, but the gastronomic palaces rely on foreigners for survival these days, so they accept cards as a matter of course.

I was imagining walking out without paying. Instead, I proposed that I go to a bank the next day and send him a cashier's check. He accepted this solution, this obvious solution, which any gracious restaurateur would have proposed at the outset.

The taste of that fabulous 1929 Yquem stayed with me. One of my favorite wine-drinking companions is Jean-Marie Peyraud, the winemaker at Domaine Tempier. We both love wine, we are longtime friends, and we never agree about anything we taste. If a wine seems tannic to me, Jean-Marie is just as likely to say it lacks tannin. If it is tart for me, it is flat for him. We discuss, dispute, define. One night I was rhapsodizing the qualities of the 1929 Yquem. We decided to return to the scene of the crime together to celebrate something and try another bottle of the '29.

When I arrived alone, the chef was at the door, but neither of us acted as if we had ever met. I gave the name Peyraud because the reservation was in Jean-Marie's name.

At table, Jean-Marie and I spent half an hour going over the wine list. There was an old La Tâche, Latours and Lafites from the thirties and forties . . . not exactly cheap, but, relative to the going price, irresistible. One red could not be ignored, the legendary 1947 Cheval Blanc. Some have called it the finest Bordeaux of the century. From our waiter, who seemed to be strangely breathless throughout the meal, we ordered a 1947 Cheval Blanc and a 1929 Yquem. The chef arrived a few moments later and apologized; there were no more '29s. "An American took the last bottle last spring," he said. "However, there are some older Sauternes in the cellar which do not figure on the wine list. Climens 1928, Yquem 1921 and 1947, Coutet 1947 . . ."

"Why don't you remove the '29 from your list if it is no longer available?" I asked.

Jean-Marie spoke up quickly. "Fine, we shall discuss it and let the waiter know our decision."

A platter of *amuse-gueule* was placed on the table, then the waiter arrived with our 1947 Cheval Blanc. It lay in one of those straw baskets for decanting. He carefully cut the lead foil, removed it, and then his mouth dropped open. I followed his eyes to the top of the bottle and my mouth fell open, too. There was no cork there.

"*Ça, c'est curieux,*" said Jean-Marie.

I thought to myself, now this is going to be interesting. The waiter could take the bottle away and start all over with another. However, it must be difficult to pour a rare hundred-dollar bottle into the stockpot just like that. He was torn for a moment, then he lifted the basket and poured a taste into my glass. The wine was brown. I sniffed it. It was oxidized. I shook my head no, that it would not do. He left with the bottle. Jean-Marie and I raised our eyebrows at each other, awaiting the next scene.

"How could it happen?" I asked. "Was there ever a cork? Did it fall into the wine, carrying it up from the cellar? Or has the capsule been the wine's only protection all these years?"

Our waiter reappeared with the news that the chef had tasted the wine in the kitchen and pronounced it drinkable.

"We did not order it to have something merely drinkable," I said, thinking to myself that it was about as drinkable as warm prune juice.

The chef sped from behind the curtain across the dining room to our table, causing other diners to perk up and pay attention. He moved rapidly, without much upper-body movement, as if he were riding a unicycle. He plopped the enormous wine list into my lap and asked, "Maybe you would prefer something else?"

That surprised me. I expected him either to refuse to take back the bad bottle or to offer us another. Was he going to resort to his "last bottle" routine? Given our history, it would have been more politic had I left it to Jean-Marie, but I said, "We ordered the '47 Cheval Blanc. It was a bad bottle. We would like to stay with 1947 Cheval Blanc."

His jaw turned to steel; he grabbed his wine list out of my hands, spun away, and pedaled off. I began to think that dining out is not all it is cracked up to be. Then the waiter appeared with the second bottle, pulled its cork, and poured a healthy splash of purplish/black liquid into my glass. I swirled and sniffed, thinking any wine that looked so good must smell good, and it did. There was an impressive aroma, thick and dusty like the door to Ali Baba's cave opened. Jean-Marie started laughing out loud when he sniffed his. It was that good. I looked up at the waiter, who was waiting for a sign of approval, and I nodded yes, good, this is it, all that we hoped for . . .

Throughout our meal, we argued about which Sauternes to take. The 1921 Yquem seemed a likely substitute for the '29, but once before I had fallen upon a '21 Yquem that had not aged gracefully. After the corkless Cheval Blanc, I was in no mood to take chances. As we nibbled our cheese, we agreed, "Let's stick to the year 1947 and follow our Cheval Blanc with Yquem." I signaled to our waiter and ordered the wine.

"Très bien, monsieur," he said and walked back to the curtain. After enough time to pronounce the words "1947 Yquem," the chef came bursting out and accelerated triple time to our table.

He glared at me and spoke through clenched teeth. *"C'est la deuxième fois que je ne suis pas content avec vous, Monsieur Lynch, c'est la deuxième fois que je ne suis pas content avec vous!"* Perhaps he repeated himself for emphasis, or did he think my French lacking? And now, all of a sudden, I was Monsieur Lynch! And what did he mean by *"la deuxième fois"*? Which had been the first time that I displeased him, the credit-card dispute or the corkless Cheval Blanc? I sat waiting. It was all rather delicious.

"For a great bottle like the 1947 Château d'Yquem," he proceeded, "one must order at the beginning of the meal so it can be properly prepared."

Prepared? What is there to do? You pull the cork and pour. "Is it in your cellar here?" I asked.

"Of course, but it must be at the proper temperature."

Proper temperature? What an odd thing to say.

"Why? Is your cellar too hot?" I asked.

At that he turned purple, and of course my question was insulting, but what else might the problem be? For an old Sauternes, especially Yquem, cellar temperature is likely to be the perfect serving temperature. Too cold and its qualities will be deadened; too warm and it is unpleasant. If cellar temperature is not quite right, you simply slip the bottle into an ice bucket for a few moments or minutes as necessary. I told him to serve it at cellar temperature, "and we shall see if it needs further chilling."

The bottle required five minutes in an ice bucket. It was an impressive wine but still young, a bit tight, a bit closed. We enjoyed the perfection it promised, fifteen or twenty more years down the road.

When the bill was presented, Jean-Marie reached for his checkbook, because we had agreed to split it. I stopped him, pulled out my wallet, and laid my American Express card on the dish. When our waiter arrived, I spotted the chef peeking out at us from behind the curtain. I thought the waiter was going to faint away when he saw the credit card. "We don't accept credit cards," he said warily. I winked at Jean-Marie, who knew the whole story, and we pulled out our checkbooks. Between the two meals, I had opened a French checking account.

Dining offers travelers the most important diversion of a day on the road. At the end of the meal, the pocketbook is pulled out to pay for the food, service, and ambience. One walks out of the restaurant altered by what transpired at table. Generally I try to avoid certain starred restaurants where empty pomp and circumstance reign, especially in the Rhône, where the best food is found raw in the village markets. Once Provençal cooking takes on airs, it is no longer Provençal. You would be better off with a simple roadside picnic. In the starred establishments today, good taste is usually ignored or insulted at a high tariff. At one three-star restaurant, the butter on my table sported a little flagpole advertising the dairy. In return, presumably, the restaurant received a discount? Meanwhile, the meal totaled over a hundred dollars per person. With commercial announcements! Do not be surprised if the cigarette girls of yesteryear make a comeback. Just as you are sniffing a cognac at the end of your meal, a young woman will appear with her tray of goodies suspended beneath her breasts. "Troisgros mustard, sir? Alain Chapel corkscrew? Bocuse wristwatch?"

One restaurant that I return to is l'Oustalet, the only restaurant in *centre ville* Gigondas. The cuisine is not spectacular but they do know how to make a vinaigrette, how to fry a potato, I do not think they have a freezer, and it is a comfortable setting even if the locals receive prompter service than the tourists. Here you can enjoy simple family cooking, Provençal-style. There is a careless selection of local wines and a sorry assortment of packaged cheeses. Still I go back—day after day when I am working nearby—and help myself to the generous cart of salads and *charcuterie.* There is grated carrot, cucumber, celery root, cold boiled potatoes with black olives and little morsels of anchovy, rice salad with peppers and mussels, sausages, and more. Then comes a main course such as grilled lamb cutlets or chicken in a spicy tomato sauce. How unlikely it must seem that such a place deserves mention, but it does because the food is hearty and genuine and will not devastate one's digestive system. In France in the 1980s, that makes it worth a detour, and even though it is well off the beaten path, it fills up with truck drivers and traveling salesmen . . . *if it is open.* There's the rub. How many times have I crossed the Rhône Valley to enjoy a decent lunch at l'Oustalet only to find the door locked. I swear there is no rhyme or reason to their business hours. As if France did not already have its fair share of holidays (three three-day weekends in May alone), but they are not of a sufficient number to satisfy the proprietors of l'Oustalet, who throw up the closed sign whenever the mood strikes. Their attitude is as Provençal as their cooking. Expect to be underwhelmed, but you will have had something authentic and you will walk out satisfied.

Of course, my point of view is different from that of a tourist who is in France for a once-in-a-lifetime vacation. Going to a gastronomic shrine is a shared experience for visitors to France; when they return home, they can talk to friends and compare notes about what happened at Taillevent or Bocuse. No one is going to ask how they found the cuisine at l'Oustalet. French tourists in the States have their own "don't miss" list of places to go: Las Vegas, Disneyland, and the Grand Canyon.

I am on the road in France four to five months of the year, and I crave home cooking.

* * *

Not far from Gigondas, medieval Seguret clings to a solid-rock, half-dome-shaped hill. On a clear day the village is a dazzling sight when the sun shines on its silvery limestone cliff and stone buildings. There is a ruined castle atop the hill, narrow winding streets that discourage motorists, and though you are only about twenty-five miles from Châteauneuf-du-Pape, with another twenty-five to go before reaching the Domaine de la Gautière, you might, after all the distractions, require a hotel for the night. The view from the rooms of the hotel La Table du Comtat is unforgettable. It overlooks a vast plain, La Plan de Dieu, with its colorful sea of vines, and looking back toward Gigondas, one has a view of the Dentelles de Montmirail, those skyward-pointing rocks that stick up like teeth from the broom-and-oak-covered hills. *Dents* means "teeth." I tell everyone that they were named the Dentelles because they are so clearly toothlike, but not one Frenchman has agreed with me or even listened patiently to my etymological fancies. *Dentelle* means "lace," and can't you see, the Dentelles are a lacelike fringe on top of the hills.

Vaison-la-Romaine is only a few miles farther along, and the guidebooks devote several pages to its diverse pleasures, most notably its Roman ruins.

Then one heads east on D-5 toward Buis-les-Baronnies, where 85 percent of France's herb harvest is traded. The air smells good. The scenery changes. More and more mountains thrust up boldly from the fertile valley floor. To the south is the Mont Ventoux, which at 6,200 feet has a dominating presence. To the east the summits heighten and crowd together; these are the foothills of the Alps, yet it is still Provence, which makes a wildly beautiful combination.

Shortly before Buis-les-Baronnies, there is a sign directing visitors up the hill to the Domaine de la Gautière. The dirt road winds up through olive trees to the old stone farmhouse, where you will be greeted with a smile, a handshake, and a cool glass of Paul and Georgette Tardieu's red wine. The warmth of the sun cooks up a wonderfully spicy fragrance from the vegetation.

Then a bowl of herb-flavored black olives appears, with a platter of sliced sausage. "The sausage is nitrate-free," Georgette says matter-of-factly.

Their dark, purplish wine does not have an *appellation contrôlée.* It has the right to call itself simply *vin de pays,* or "country wine." While it is a characterful, delicious wine, which can outluster a good many of its titled neighbors, nothing in your wine dictionary or encyclopedia or atlas of wine will guide you to it. And most American merchants do not want to fiddle with it, because their customers demand Napa, Bordeaux, Burgundy, the big guns, as if everything grand had already been discovered and categorized, as if price and label always deliver what they promise.

In 1982 Gautière's *vin de pays* sold in California, with difficulty, at $2.50 per bottle!

At that time I sent along a case of Gautière's wine as a gift to Madame Gruère, who ran my office in Beaune. She is Burgundian, related to the Louis Latour family, and she worked for years as private secretary to Robert Drouhin. She owns a vineyard at Savigny-les-Beaune. In other words, she is heart and soul Burgundian right down to the *terroir* on her shoes. No one can accuse her of prejudice.

She wrote back saying that she appreciated my little gift of twelve bottles. "We had a large group over last weekend, including a few people from the Burgundy wine trade, and several different wines were uncorked. There was a Chambertin on the table, but me, I drank the *vin de pays.*"

Is the Gautière *vin de pays* better than Chambertin? It depends on which Chambertin, does it not? The Gautière is delicious and it has soul, while many bottles labeled Chambertin have no deliciousness, no soul, and precious little Chambertin. But what a question: Is it better than Chambertin? "Better for what?" is the only proper reply.

Better when dining at Taillevent, the Parisian gastronomic palace? No, at Taillevent the noblest bottles are appropriate.

Is it better than Chambertin if you have Richard Nixon over

for dinner? No. There is the story that Nixon, aboard the Presidential yacht *Sequoia,* served his guests plonk, but his glass was filled with Château Margaux from a bottle masked by a white towel wrapping. Better to serve Nixon Chambertin, making sure to turn the bottle so he can see the label.

Is Gautière's *vin de pays* better than Chambertin served alongside black olives and sliced sausage? Yes.

With *ratatouille?* Yes.

Hot onion omelet with vinegar sauce? Yes.

Soupe au pistou? Yes.

At home, alone, for a quick lunch? Yes, then it is preferable even to a great Chambertin. One cannot do justice to a great bottle alone. Someone with whom to ooh and aah is indispensable, someone with whom to share the intellectual and aesthetic stimulation that a great bottle inspires.

The boundary that determines the limits of the *appellation* Côtes du Rhône stops two miles west of the Domaine de la Gautière. If wines from the slopes around Gautière could wear a Côte du Rhône label, there would be more vineyards planted because they would fetch a worthwhile price, higher than they can manage now with their vague *vin de pays* label, and Gautière's wine demonstrates that these slopes can outperform many areas that possess an official *appellation.* The French system of controlled appellations can sometimes legislate against quality wine, which is of course just the opposite of the intended result. Nothing new here: legislation has often sown the seeds of injustice, no matter how well-meaning our intentions. The *appellation contrôlée* system is an ingenious expression of the French mentality, a mentality that has deep roots in France's aristocratic past. Under the aristocracy, a person of value could fail to rise in society because of the lack of birthright. So it is that valuable vineyard land can go for naught for the lack of an *appellation.* The Tardieus keep a sense of humor about it all: *C'est la vie.*

Never mind, the quality of the wine is not the only thing that makes La Gautière interesting anyway. What is fascinating is the history of Paul and Georgette Tardieu, the proprietors. Georgette says she is tired of recounting their story. "People envy us because we gave up everything to move here to La Gautière. They would all like to change their lives as we did, but they don't dare because they're afraid that if they did they wouldn't have anything on their plate to eat. But they question us as if we could provide the key to solving their problems."

The Tardieus live a life many of us only dream about. They turned their backs on city life and created a self-sufficient country paradise. Above all, an aversion to the pollution and congestion of the big city inspired them to risk everything and head for the hills. Paul says he wanted to "grow old in good health," so he took measures to ensure that he would. "We isolated ourselves from the pollution, we consume fresh, natural products. Consequently, we know we'll make a healthy old couple. Often we receive visits from merchants who try to sell us chemical products. We give them a little glass of our organic wine and explain our philosophy before saying *Au revoir*. They're wasting their time with us."

"Organic" is a word that does not work in a wineshop. *Vin de pays,* strike one. Organic wine, strike two. The word seems to have a negative impact on most wine connoisseurs. And it is true that many organically produced wines are liable to fizz, gurgle, and stink to high heaven because no chemicals have been used to kill possible yeasts and bacteria.

However, there is another side to the question. Would that I were a health nut, but I am not. Still, I look very closely at organically produced wines when I hear of them because what you have is the unadulterated product of earth, vine, and man. Man's part of the equation, the vinification, can be well or poorly executed, but if we find a winemaker of talent who knows how to bottle a clean wine, then an organic wine has a good chance to be interesting. Once you start throwing chemical fertilizers into the soil to increase production, chemical treatments onto the vines to kill pests, and yet others into the wine itself to stabilize it, you change the quality and personality of what comes out through the vine into the grape and ultimately into your wineglass. That fundamental expression of soil and fruit is distorted. Chemicals increase production, they protect the wine from nature's quirks, but they also muck up the elemental statement that wine is capable of making.

Georgette is Provençale by birth. Paul is from the Massif Central, a province he describes as cold and harsh. Wisely enough, he headed south, where he met Georgette. "Once you know Provence, you don't ever want to leave it," he says. "No one ever heads back north. No one!"

He worked in Avignon selling fruit and vegetables. He developed a passion for wine and beekeeping, and at the same time grew to hate city life. "Avignon was already a big city," says Paul, who has never seen New York or Los Angeles. "We decided to move to the country, to recycle ourselves, to work in direct contact with nature."

Georgette says she got her passion for nature from her father. "He built a house five miles outside Avignon in a *garrigue*. Do you know what a *garrigue* is? In a *garrigue* there are cicadas, green oaks, poor soil, and wild herbs. We had no plumbing or electricity. I was raised barefoot, naked to the sun, swimming and boating in the Rhône, gas lamps—that's how I grew up. Then I was obliged to move to Avignon to earn a living. As the years went by, I watched the countryside, places where we used to go camping, eaten up by civilization. It used to be so different. There was nobody there. And now? Imagine how I feel when I see the Ardèche River, which was such a wilderness when I was young. It has turned into a thoroughfare. It's like the Champs-Elysées, the Ardèche, with thousands of canoes descending one after another.

"Paul came and I showed him my Provence. We watched it nibbled away by man, by civilization, and we said, 'All right, it's all over now. We'll have to go farther away to find any peace.' It just wasn't in our nature to buy a house in the city and hide behind a high fence. We discussed leaving for two or three years. We went for a walk through a field of lavender and Paul saw the bees gathering honey. And that day it was stronger than we were! We had to have someplace where we could work with the bees and make honey. One beautiful day I brought Paul here to the land of my ancestors. My cousin told me that this property, La Gautière, was for sale, and we closed the deal very quickly. And it was a good deal, too!"

Paul sold his little produce business. Georgette sold a piece of property that she had inherited from her father. Off they went.

They speak rapidly, and often one will complete a sentence begun by the other. "When we bought the property, bought a tractor, tools, cleared the land and planted, we ran out of money. A year and a half after starting! We survived with chickens, bought some goats, planted a garden, and Paul had his beehives so there was a little income from the honey they gave us. We lived on very little, but we were economically self-sufficient.

"I like to cook," Georgette says, "and I made very cheap meals with what we had. We had olive oil from our trees, wine, cheese, eggs, potatoes. I bought very little. We managed, barely. Then the crops started coming in. You, Kermit, you arrive now, ten years since we started, and you probably have the impression that it's an easy life. But this is the first year that we're beginning to breathe freely. We've had several years of difficult struggle. When we arrived, we found an overgrown, virgin soil. We started from zero. We've been exhausted, there have been serious accidents, a lot of worries . . . We had to horsewhip ourselves to keep at it. We worked like crazy, but with faith and enthusiasm. We knew what we wanted—our products produced under our conditions and sold by us. We knew that this was a touristic region with potential, and we figured correctly, because it took off quickly. One day we put up a little sign down on the highway, and that very day three or four people came. When we saw the first car coming up our dirt road, we cried, 'It works, it works! A customer!' We were crazy with joy. There was only a little lavender honey and a few bottles of olive oil to sell, but we were thrilled. We treated the customers like friends. We had them sit down with us, poured a little wine, *et voilà*! Each year new clients show up and they come back again and again."

Their vineyard is just behind their modest tile-covered house on an amphitheater-shaped hillside facing south. When his crop yields 40 hectoliters to the hectare (4,000 liters per hectare, or 2,200 bottles per acre), Paul says he is satisfied. For a cheap *vin de pays* it is a drastically minuscule production. In an abundant year such as 1979, the Meursault vineyards in Burgundy yield twice as much juice per acre and the wine sells for five to six times the price of La Gautière's.

But Paul says, "Forty hectoliters per hectare is enough for me. Our vines aren't pushed or forced to produce. They give just what they have to give and no more."

I asked how others manage to produce two to three times more from an equal area of vineyard.

"Oh, it's easy. When you prune, you leave longer shoots. You use fertilizer. That's all there is to it. It's what we call *fait pisser la vigne,* making the vine piss. Listen to this. I took a course at the wine school at Vaison-la-Romaine to learn more about bottling. Next to me there was a guy who makes wine down near Montpellier. Go ahead, guess, what do you think his production is per hectare?"

I guessed 120 hectoliters per hectare, three times Paul's production.

Although we were alone, Paul leaned over and whispered in my ear. "The guy swore he gets two hundred thirty! It's easy. Fertilize, irrigate. What a crop, eh? Two hundred thirty hectoliters! By making shit wine, he makes six times more money than I do. And those guys down there, then they block the roads and demonstrate to get the government to give them even more. It's not right."

Paul planted the typical Rhône grape varieties such as Grenache and Cinsault, but he also put in a higher than normal proportion of Syrah. Grown on his well-drained hillside soil, the noble Syrah gives its special perfume and helps explain why his red has a finer aroma than most Côtes du Rhône.

"For the vinification," he says, "it's quite simple. We arrive there at the cellar with the grapes. As they fall into the fermentation vat, that's how we leave them. They are not stemmed or pumped. We don't add anything. They ferment gently, because we control the temperature. We keep it low because if it gets too high you lose all the bouquet, the flavor, the perfume. That's what everyone remarks upon when they first taste our wine. There is so much perfume. But it doesn't surprise us because we're used to it. We drink our wine every day. When they ask how we do it, how we obtain such a perfume, I just tell them it comes from our grapes."

I pointed at the vegetation growing wild around the vineyard and asked Paul if he found traces of their various aromas in his wine.

"Yes, I think so. I don't know if you noticed, but the 1979 has a little black pepper, a little resin. That's typical here. I think it comes from this wild environment."

"How do you think it is transmitted?" I asked.

"By the atmosphere, the air, which is impregnated. The vines breathe through the leaves, you know. Everyone who visits says it smells good here. We're surrounded by wild hyssop, sage, lavender, pine, thyme, rosemary, broom in blossom . . . all that counts enormously. I think there is an osmosis of perfumes, of aromatic qualities.

"For me, wine is a passion. When I drink water, I'm sick. Even in my youth I loved wine. If you love wine and you plant vines, you take a great deal of care with it, you treat it with love and respect, you do everything you can to make it be good."

Winemakers tend to be single-minded. They make wine and live wine from dawn to dusk, and then there is likely to be a dinner with clients. It is fascinating that Paul and Georgette, with their commitment to organic culture, their apricot and cherry trees (they sell jam, too), their beehives and olive groves, still have succeeded in making something special, a wine that intrigues even such a jaded palate as my own, a wine that has been favorably reviewed now by *The New York Times*, the *International Herald Tribune,* and *The Wine Advocate.* And I am pleased that in today's world of so-called agricultural "progress," Paul and Georgette can tell the chemical peddlers to get lost and still manage to show a profit.

Nowadays, when heading north
from Provence, I hear Paul Tardieu's passionate exclamation,
"Once you know Provence, you don't ever want to leave it.
No one ever goes back north, no one!" If over the years I have
grown attached to Provence, in terms of wine itself my heart
belongs to the great reds of the northern Rhône. The best combine
a reminder of the sunny Mediterranean with the more self-
conscious, intellectual appeal of the great Burgundies farther
north, which is not a bad combination. And these prized wines
of the northern Rhône are France's rarest: Hermitage has 300

acres planted in vines compared to 7,900 at Châteauneuf-du-Pape. Gigondas has 2,600; Cornas, only 130. To bring it into perspective, Vieux Télégraphe, a single *domaine* at Châteauneuf-du-Pape, has the same surface in vines as all of Cornas. Vieux Télégraphe's vineyard can be cultivated by tractor despite the stones, whereas at Cornas a tractor would topple sideways down the hillside. Yet Châteauneuf-du-Pape and Cornas sell at about the same price, which explains why so many of the northern Rhône's best vineyards have been abandoned: they must be worked by hand, and the pay stinks.

By *autoroute,* Cornas is only one hour from Châteauneuf-du-Pape, but everything changes.

That vast luminous Provençal skyscape is gone, and with it the expansive feeling it engenders.

In the north, you see what spawned the name Côtes du Rhône in the first place, the "hillsides of the Rhône." Most vineyards have a view down to the river.

The talismanic olive and cypress trees disappear, and though one sees aromatic herbs like rosemary and thyme in the northern Rhône, they do not grow wild but must be cultivated.

Butter and cream replace olive oil in the cuisine of the northern Rhône. Garlic and tomato play a lesser role. This is the midlands, so the fish markets exude a less appetizing odor.

The northerners are supposedly harder workers, and more cerebral. They accuse their neighbors to the south of being lazy and superficial. But the southerners pity the uptight northerners, who are thrashed this way and that by their cold winter wind.

Those stonework walls that define the northern vineyard landscape are not to be found in the southern Côtes du Rhône, although farther south at Bandol the hills are once again adorned with them, so let no one slander the Provençaux for being lazy. The hand-made walls transform the landscape to an extent the artist Christo would envy. Painstakingly constructed over the centuries, the dry-stone terraces bear witness to the value the ancients accorded these viticultural sites.

After the dizzying number of *appellations* in the south, the northern Rhône is easy. There are but a handful, including some of France's noblest: Saint-Péray, Cornas, Saint-Joseph, Hermitage, Crozes-Hermitage, Condrieu, Château Grillet, and Côte Rôtie. And in contrast to the numerous grape varieties permitted down south, the northern Rhône reds are the result of a single variety, the Syrah. One would think that a blend of grapes could create a more complex range of aromas and flavors than a lone variety, yet the Syrah juice eked out from one of those steep hillsides can produce wines of dazzling complexity, wines whose exotic aromas seem to shimmer and change like the flashes of color gleaming from a jewel.

The first wine village encountered as one enters the northern Rhône produces white wine exclusively. Old wine books mention Saint-Péray's "taste of violet," boast that Pliny and Plutarch both regarded it highly enough to single it out in their writings, and that it was a favorite of composer Richard Wagner. What more could you ask?

No one can argue with past appreciations because we cannot taste the Saint-Péray they were obviously enjoying, but in our day and age something has gone haywire. Saint-Péray is full of subterranean cellars. Someone must be making good wine because the ingredients exist: hillside vineyards and the same grape varieties that make white Hermitage. But each time I go to Saint-Péray I am so indifferent to what I am offered that it takes two or three years to overcome the taste memory and convince myself to return and try again. It is useless to discuss whether Saint-Péray has a taste of this or a taste of that. The problem is finding any taste at all. The wines seem to have been concocted by freshmen students trying to pass an enology exam in sterilization. A+! No one is going to write a *Parsifal* with a glass of technological Saint-Péray for inspiration.

As you survey the terraced slopes from below, the boundary between Cornas and Saint-Péray is indiscernible. It is weird, because in terms of what you find in your glass the two are opposites. Unlike its neighbor, Cornas does not produce white wine, but calling Cornas red does not do it justice. Should your pen run dry, fill it with Cornas, but this is not the wine to uncork the evening of the day you paid to have your teeth cleaned. Actually, there are wines as dark and darker, but rarely as remarkably vivid.

Because the vinification has remained old-fashioned, there are several excellent producers at Cornas. For some reason, *Invasion of the Enologists* has yet to appear at the Cornas cinema. Underground in one of the several cellars it might as well be 1885 or 1785. And with a dense, vibrant Cornas in your glass, you are tasting a wine not unlike what was poured in 1885 or 1785. The curé of the parish wrote in 1763, "The Mountain of this village is nearly all planted in vines which produce a very good black wine which is sought after by the trade because it is so heady [*fort capiteux*]."

This is Syrah country. Cornas is the first village where the grape shows its true colors, so to speak, and it does not start off timidly. The taste of Cornas is as bold as its appearance. You chew it around in your mouth and it seems to stain the palate. There is nothing like it.

Why, then, is there so little of the stuff? Why are there only 130 acres planted when there are 1,300 acres of Cornas available for planting? Is there not enough demand worldwide to sop up 1,300 acres of Cornas?

Auguste Clape, the best-known grower in Cornas, regrets that there has never been a *négociant* of importance with vines at Cornas, someone who understands commerce better than the small local growers, someone who could help the *appellation* become better known, as Guigal has done for Côte Rôtie. It is a point well taken; after importing Cornas for years, as recently as 1982 I felt obliged to offer an "introductory price" in order to tempt my clients to try Cornas.

Then again I think I would just as soon Cornas stay lost lest the twentieth century take notice and decide to sophisticate this monumental relic. And yet, if it remains unknown, if its price does not soar, the Cornas slopes will not again be covered with vines.

Even if the price becomes more interesting to the growers, replanting the abandoned terraces is not certain. Once untended, oak and pine trees seem to multiply and sprout up like weeds. In order to replant vines, the trees would have to be uprooted, but most of those terraces are too narrow to permit the kind of earth-moving equipment necessary. Manually? Today? Forget it. A recent menace is the appearance of several new homes in the heart of the Cornas *appellation.* In the old days, the villagers worked the slopes and lived on the plain. Now they want to live on the slopes for the breeze and the view and cultivate the flatlands because it can be done by tractor. But, God help us, the results are not the same, and the difference between the two wines is not subtle. One is Cornas and one is not. Auguste Clape has Syrah growing on both terrains, and he says of his flatland wine, "It makes a decent table wine, but nothing more, and yet it is exactly the same Syrah clone that makes my Cornas. The only difference is the *terroir.*"

Qualms aside, let us consider how Cornas is drunk, once one has mastered the art of bending one's elbow and swallowing. In the wine literature, it is repeatedly advised that Cornas must be aged several years before it is worthwhile, but there is something about a brand-new Cornas that should not be missed. Muhammad Ali may have grown more savvy as he matured, but who can forget the young Ali, that dazzle and explosiveness? A bottle should be uncorked when it appears on the market, in order to experience its youthful extravagance of color and size. But then Cornas shuts down for three or four years, after which its aromas begin to develop. For some reason, a perfect Cornas is never as aromatic as a perfect Hermitage or Côte Rôtie. When asked how else Cornas differs from Hermitage, Auguste Clape answered with a trace of a smile that Cornas is more *rustre* (loutish or brutish), while his friend up the road, Gérard Chave, who makes Hermitage, used the polite word *rustique* (rustic).

Both agreed that Cornas is less elegant and more tannic than Hermitage.

Clape advised following Hermitage with Cornas at table. "I

have often been to meals where the order was Saint-Joseph, Côte Rôtie, Hermitage, then Cornas. When we tried the reverse, Cornas followed by Hermitage, the Hermitage did not stand up well. A rustic wine," he concluded, "will overwhelm a finer wine."

Yes, normally when several wines are served, the progression is from light to heavy, following the theory that a heavyweight will knock a lightweight out of the ring. By the same token, the progression should go from simple to complex, from rustic to aristocratic, from young to old, the guiding principle being: one's judgment is going to be influenced by whatever went before. The question is of some import because you do not want to diminish your appreciation of a perfectly good wine by serving it inappropriately. Hermitage is no lightweight, but we do not want it to *seem* so in the rough, tannic presence of a Cornas; a lighter wine following a heavier wine can actually seem thin. Likewise, a perfectly lovely country quaffer served after a noble growth might seem ignoble, or a young wine raw after a mellow old bottle. Cornas after Hermitage? To me, there is something jarring about the notion. Might not the Cornas seem *rustre* rather than *rustique?*

The dilemma helps bring into definition the difference between these two great Syrahs. A proper Hermitage will have a stronger, more eloquent bouquet. It is more distinguished, more the aristocrat. It sings like a chorus of several parts. Cornas sings great bass.

The solution is to give some attention to the vintages chosen, once it has been decided to serve Cornas and Hermitage at the same meal. I would refrain from serving the two at the same stage of maturity. Cornas 1980 could lead into Hermitage 1971, or Cornas 1976 into Hermitage 1966, and so on. A progression toward the older, more aristocratic bottle is a safe guideline to follow, but improvisations are not forbidden. An old Hermitage with roast bird could be followed by a purplish blast of young Cornas with cheese to wake up your party.

* * *

Saint-Joseph *rouge* possesses neither the dimensions of a great Hermitage nor the substantiveness (there is a lot of there there) of Cornas. Consequently, it is not respected to the same degree. But in reality Saint-Joseph is not a substitute that fails to measure up. Here Syrah can be enjoyed in another role. When in doubt about anything, it can be helpful to turn to Mozart, who in *Don Giovanni* provides an analogy: Zerlina (Saint-Joseph) may not match the emotional dimensions of Donna Elvira (Hermitage), nor is she as "heavy" as Donna Anna (Cornas), but Don Giovanni certainly finds Zerlina's "farmer's daughter" seductiveness distracting enough. Then Zerlina sings a playfully erotic song of comfort to her poor, bruised fiancé, Masetto. No self-respecting music critic would start throwing rotten eggs merely because her song lacks the emotional extremes of Donna Elvira's passionate outbursts, but I believe today's wine critics would. For them, big means good, light means less good; serious means good, playful is less good. What a humorless way to look at things. Which deity handed down the law that serious, heavy wines are better than gay, playful wines? It certainly was not Bacchus. Was it America's Puritan God, who refuses to accept that wine can be pure unadulterated *fun*? When ranking Syrahs, the critics want us to believe that you can apply the same standard to all of them, as if when you uncork a bottle of Syrah you are always looking for the same qualities. The truth is, if a perfect Hermitage deserves an A+, or 20 points, or 100, or five stars, so does a perfect Saint-Joseph. Perfection is perfection, even if the wines taste different. Thank God they taste different! One of the miracles of French wine, one reason it is so endlessly enchanting, is its diversity, even within the same region employing the same grape variety. Rather than belittling it, exalt Saint-Joseph for being different. Here one can breathe in that wonderful, wild, hillside Syrah aroma without waiting years for the wine to soften or open up. And Saint-Joseph *rouge* is the one Syrah that might even be placed in an ice bucket on a summer day and served cooled down a bit with lunch, outdoors.

The white wine from Saint-Joseph is not easy to obtain because

Cellar in
the northern Rhône

little is produced. It is a white that must be aged in wood in order to be worthwhile. In stainless-steel tanks, which have all but taken over in the cellars, the wine's wonderful pit-fruit flavors do not develop. It remains closed and unpleasantly aggressive on the palate. But if it is vinified in used oak and if it has not been emasculated by efforts to clean it up or stabilize it, Saint-Joseph *blanc* can be a gorgeous, expressive dry white that ages well. A 1972 tasted in 1985 had a quincelike aroma, a chalky edge on the palate, and a fleeting suggestion of apricot skin in the aftertaste.

Originally, Saint-Joseph referred to a single hillside between Mauves and Tournon which is now the property of the Chapoutier family. Then the name Saint-Joseph began to be applied to the wines from the series of terraced slopes between Châteaubourg and Vion, which included the exceptional vineyards of Mauves, Tournon, and Saint-Jean-de-Muzols, whose wines had once been marketed under their own names, such as *vin de Mauves* and *vin de Tournon*. In those days, prices varied from parcel to parcel even within the same village because the ancients knew the lay of the land and the quality of the juice it gave.

And what of Saint-Joseph today? How did it grow from 240 acres in 1970 to over 700 today? Why, when the quantity produced is increasing, is Saint-Joseph an *appellation* in decline? The answer is to be found on the abandoned hillsides, grown over with weeds and straggly remnants of vines.

The French wine bureaucrats of the INAO (Institut National des Appellations d'Origine) enlarged and redefined Saint-Joseph, lumping together practically everything on the west bank of the Rhône from Cornas to Ampuis, approximately forty miles, including flatland soil along the riverbanks that had never been planted with grapes. They allow bottles of this stuff to sashay out onto the marketplace decked out in a Saint-Joseph label. Never mind the consumer or truth-in-labeling. Never mind some possible twinge of responsibility to our predecessors who labored to carve those steep hillsides into a shape hospitable to the vine, who left behind thousands of miles of hand-built stone walls because the wine was finer from up there. Nothing is sacred to these officials of the INAO who continue to devalue these historic sites even though they were hired to protect them.

Think about it. *Côte* means "slope," or "hillside." *Rôtie* means "roasted." Today, wine from the flat plateau above the "roasted slope" can legally call itself Côte Rôtie.

In Celtic, Cornas meant "roasted slope." Now the INAO is considering allowing the plateau above Cornas to be planted in vines whose wine will be sold wearing a Cornas label. Welcome to our brave new world of French wine in which there may be no *côte* in your Côte Rôtie and no *cornas* in your Cornas.

When I praised the wine of Saint-Joseph, I did not mean the ordinary wine whose grapes were mechanically harvested on flat terrain thirty miles from the original Saint-Joseph hillside.

But let them plant the plateaus, the hollows and sinks, let them grow grapes in their belly button if they want to, laissez-faire, but do not call it Côte Rôtie, Saint-Joseph, or Cornas.

The French are capable of such *noblesse*. At its inception, the system of *appellation contrôlée* was elaborated with admirable rigor. Here was a noble idea. But when they set their minds to it the French can outwhore anybody. Imagine someone trying to convince you that red is green, or a square, round. The current bunch in control of the INAO would have us accept the notion that a slope is flat. This is more than preposterous, it is legalized fraud.

Crozes-HERMITAGE? Here we go again. Hermitage is that one majestic hillside tilted south like a solar receptor. If there is any single vineyard that the Creator obviously designed expressly for wine production, it is Hermitage.

I suppose someone might be inspired to try a Musigny after tasting a good Chambolle, or a Montrachet because of a good Puligny, but would sampling a bottle of Crozes-Hermitage motivate anyone to try an Hermitage? It is as likely as Muzak leading someone to Bach.

Crozes-Hermitage is by far the largest *appellation* in the northern Rhône. It includes terrain that does not even deserve to be called Côtes du Rhône. Where's the *côte?* Since the *appellation* was redrawn and expanded to include sandy flatland soils, that is where most of the growers have moved because they can attack with tractors and harvesting machines and because the yield per acre is so much higher. Profit! Facility! The best of all possible worlds!

In other words, by changing the legislation the INAO has, purposefully or not, encouraged the growers to abandon the sites that give the best wine.

The grape variety at Crozes, at least, remains the same as at Hermitage. However, Syrah without a hillside is like Saint George without a dragon: boring.

In reality, Crozes is a sleepy village just behind the Hermitage crest. There are vineyards near Crozes, above the Rhône at Gervans, for example, which provide an environment for the vine similar to that at Hermitage. In olden days the wines from certain of these sites even commanded the price of the lower parcels at Hermitage, and their wine can indeed be reminiscent of Hermitage, thus the reason for coupling Crozes to Hermitage in the first place.

The best parcels of Crozes, of Saint-Joseph, Cornas, and Côte Rôtie include some of the world's finest vineyards, yet many of them lie fallow. It is a twentieth-century failure. Two thousand years ago, a Roman chronicler observed that the slopes on both sides of the Rhône were covered with vines! One way to encourage replanting these historic sites would be to permit certain wines to have more specific information on their labels. As a wine buyer, you should have the right to know whether your Saint-Joseph comes from one of the great hillside sites or from a flat one. The INAO should permit growers to specify: Saint-Joseph, *vin de Tournon* or *vin de Mauves,* or Crozes-Hermitage, *vin de Gervans* or *vin de Mercurol,* for example. As time passes and the consumer begins to distinguish and judge the different qualities, the price of the wines produced from the best sites would rise (just as in Burgundy a Pommard "Rugiens" is pricier than a Pommard), perhaps making the tremendous task of replanting the hillsides a profitable venture.

Once upon a time I imported a *vin de Gervans* from a producer whose vines were well situated. His soil was granitic; his exposition was almost as south-facing as l'Hermitage; he had the old Syrah, not one of today's superproducer clones; and his vinification was traditional.

I purchased 1970, 1973, 1974, and 1976. His red lacked elegance and so did he, but it was always a big wine, stuffed full of Syrah flavor. And he was a big-boned Porthos-like figure with a red bulbous nose. An ordinary wineglass looked like a thimble in his hands.

The first danger sign that my Crozes source might be drying up appeared in 1977. There was a disturbing lack of consistency from cask to cask. One exploded with wild raspberry, the next approached vinegar, the next was beginning to oxidize. He downed his glass of each, nonetheless. Then he uncorked a 1970 and filled our glasses to the brim. Well, it is difficult to smell well when your glass is too full to swirl, but one whiff was all that was necessary to see that we had a corked bottle. It happens. There will be an occasional off bottle no matter how expensive the wine or how fancy the label. You pour it down the drain and fetch another. But he seemed not to notice, and he drained his glass in one go.

The next time I drove up the hill, his wife came out to meet me. Her nose had the same colorful glow as her husband's. When I asked how things were going, she moaned, "We don't have enough wine to satisfy the demand." Then she added brightly, "We're getting twenty-two francs per bottle now." That was not far from the price of Hermitage itself! Madame was re-creating a scene French wine families must be taught in school: tell your buyer he will be lucky to get any wine at all, and should he be so lucky he will pay dearly for the honor.

Her husband hulked through the doorway. He had a faraway look in his eye, which suggested that he had been a trifle too

attentive to his wine's evolution, and evidently he had had his
fill, because instead of taking me directly to the cellar for business
as usual, he led me to his garage, which he opened with one of
those electronic gadgets. Inside, there was a spanking new car.
He invited me to seat myself in front of its majestic dashboard.
For the next twenty minutes I sat there watching him demonstrate
accessories. Things glowed and twinkled. The windshield wipers
click-clacked. Water sprayed. The seat retreated, advanced, and
tilted with a purring vibration. The air conditioner exhaled. The
roof slid open. Finally he shifted into reverse, gunned it, and
backed out a few yards, then he nosed it back into the garage.
I glanced over at the odometer: 18 kilometers. I asked when he
had purchased it. "Six months ago," he answered, which meant
a drive up the hill from the dealer, and an in-and-out-of-the-
garage every day for six months.

I miss the great Crozes that he used to make. It is as if a
chapter were missing from my favorite book. I have never been
back. Years later I noticed his Crozes *blanc* on a restaurant list
and ordered it with hope and curiosity. It was not *blanc* at all,
however, but brown, oxidized, and undrinkable.

When asked what people should know about Hermitage itself,
winemaker Gérard Chave replied, "When people think of the
Côtes du Rhône, they always imagine huge *domaines*. They should
know that the surface area of the Hermitage vineyard totals only
three hundred acres. It is tiny, even smaller than Côte Rôtie or
Saint-Joseph. And it should also be known that the area planted
in vines has remained the same for centuries. An *appellation* that
has not been altered is an extremely rare thing, especially in the
Rhône."

Gérard Chave's Hermitage appears under his father's label,
Jean-Louis Chave. The label will once again be perfectly appropriate when Gérard's son Jean-Louis takes over, continuing a
succession of winegrowing Chaves which began in 1481! The
family still possesses the original document showing that a property was given to Charles Chave by the Seigneur d'Yserand in

return for an unstated service rendered. That property, however, was not at Hermitage itself. Vineyards at Hermitage were acquired much more recently, in 1890.

Some might think the métier would grow a little stale after five hundred years, but no, you could not design a better, more enthusiastic Chave than Gérard. During the centuries there must have been several flowerings of talent in this winegrowing family, but it would be difficult to surpass the impact Gérard has had. Guigal, the *négociant* at Ampuis, has also had a tremendous influence on the Rhône market. Chave's impact has been less flamboyant, less commercial than Guigal's, very much like the difference between their wines. There is a moral force behind Gérard Chave's respect for tradition and tireless search for quality. Here is a man who comprehends the heritage left behind in those mountainsides, one after another along the Rhône River, carved and sculpted and planted over the centuries in order to produce an annual flowering and fruition and finally a thing of liquid beauty. Chave is capable of communicating the responsibility that heritage imposes, and he does it not like a preacher handing down commandments but with a questioning mind, the smile of a man who loves a good joke, and a contagious joie de vivre. On top of all that, it is not easy to name a finer winemaker. Whatever qualities we might include in a listing of what makes a wine great, they all seem present at once in a glass of Chave Hermitage.

The Chave winery is a few miles from Hermitage in cellars under their home in Mauves, a thin strip of a town that supports itself growing fruit and making wine. Nowhere in Mauves is there evidence of the French flair for storefronts, or any outward flair at all for that matter.

Main Street is the Route Nationale 6, pinched in size by the buildings of the village, which, according to old postcard photos, were constructed with narrower horse-drawn vehicles in mind. This circumstance does not slow down the lead-footed French truck drivers who blast past, full throttle, an arm's length from where I must stand waiting for a Chave to answer the doorbell.

The diesel fumes are trapped between the buildings on each side of the highway, coloring Mauves not mauve but a charmless sooty gray.

All is instantly forgotten when Gérard Chave appears in the doorway with a bright smile. He is a good-looking man in his early fifties, a cross between Gene Kelly and Buster Keaton, with candid, friendly eyes and a nose designed for wine sniffing. Often he greets me with his glass thief in hand, and before I can even pay respects to his wife, Monique, we are descending into the cellar. Suddenly I stand with a glass of the current white Hermitage vintage in hand and I am gazing into one of wine's most magical colors. It is golden, with much nuance, from glints of green and straw yellow to just a suspicion of something like peach skin. Even if we start tasting at nine in the morning, it always looks good enough to drink, but that first taste is only the downbeat of a lengthy set of variations to follow, so spitting is mandatory if I want to make it back up the steep dirt path out of the cellar.

One taste of white is drawn from a glass-lined tank, another from a large chestnut oval, another from an oak barrel gray with age. One was fermented in new *limousin* oak, the next in *vosges* from Alsace. There is also an experimental batch to taste and compare, some new technique that Gérard had heard about and wanted to try in order to see the results for himself.

Here is a place to study the influence of wood on white Hermitage. I always voice my alarm at the success the *négociant* Guigal enjoyed with one batch of Hermitage *blanc* because I am terrified Chave might be tempted to follow the current new oak fad. Guigal's bottling inspired a French journalist to write, "It is the best white Rhône I have ever tasted, and a lesson in vinification for the other winemakers of the Rhône." Guigal wines do seem to drive wine writers to daffy extremes. The irony is, according to the story I heard in a cellar in Tain l'Hermitage, the white Hermitage in question was purchased, not vinified, by Guigal. The actual producer sold it off in barrel as a failed *cuvée* because it was so oaky. I had the chance to taste it. It showed no Her-

mitage character. It had one smell: new oak. It is a dull, monotonous odor, but it is amazing how many tasters fall for it. I
say if you are going to pay the price for an Hermitage it might
as well smell like Hermitage. Chave uses new oak as a seasoning
whose presence is one of the many facets in the aroma of his
bottled wine. He likes the analogy of a chef using salt in the
kitchen: a little can improve a dish, but too much covers up all
the other flavors.

On the other hand, there are Hermitage growers who have
begun bottling their white without any wood aging at all, and
some now prevent their white Hermitage from undergoing its
malolactic fermentation, which necessitates a supertight filtration
and a good dose of SO_2 lest the wine follow its natural inclination
and burst into a stinky, bubbly "malo" after it is bottled.

"Such wines," Chave says, "are not bad, but they are not in
the style of the classic Hermitage. Vinification in wood," he says,
"allows a better development of the aromas because there is a
phenomenon of osmosis in the wood that you don't have in glass
or metal. In stainless steel, the wine remains more anonymous.
It does not reflect the originality of the *appellation,* by which I
mean those characteristics that make Hermitage Hermitage. The
definition of Hermitage's character does not date from yesterday.
Winemaking methods that have been employed over the decades
also contribute to a wine's identity. Here is where the rules of
the INAO are altogether incomplete. The INAO regulates the
grape varieties, the number of buds to leave on each branch, the
form of the pruning, all sorts of things, but on the subject of
making the wine, they say nothing. You can do whatever you
like. If I decide tomorrow to make my red Hermitage by carbonic
maceration, no one can tell me I don't have the right. It would
still be considered Hermitage."

The multiple *cuvées* of his newest white Hermitage are followed
by a procession of bottled vintages reaching back over several
years. Today, from all the *appellations* of the northern Rhône that
produce white wine, there is only one sure thing year in and year
out, and that is the quality of the Chave Hermitage *blanc.* Be it

1986, 1985, 1984, 1983, 1982, 1981, or 1980 (picking the decade I know best), it is a white to be enjoyed young, old, and in between. And there is a pleasure to be obtained by laying down enough bottles of one single vintage to be able to observe its evolution over ten, twenty, or thirty years.

These descents into Chave's inner sanctum are the ultimate thrill for a wine taster. Deep underground you hear nothing from the outside world, and never are those professional tastings disturbed unless there is an emergency. His cellar is composed of several chambers. One in particular is unforgettable. It is filled with barrels and, in bins along the walls, the family treasury of old bottles, some of which are completely engulfed in mold. The wisps, webs, and curls of mold are colored from velvety black to silvery white and everything in between. Some have a green tinge, some blue. Some patches glisten with droplets of moisture. The stuff hangs from the ceiling, the walls are draped with it, and while it is not exactly teeming, it does appear to be taking over. Thus, the visual backdrop as you regard the robe of the wine in your glass. The cool, damp air is pleasantly thick with aroma. There is the rowdy, backward smell of new red wine in barrel, the mysterious hoary/fresh smell of the fungus, and the continual evaporation of all the wines that have been spit onto the dirt and gravel floor since who-knows-when. It is a setting in which you feel a lineage with the ancients who preceded you, who made the same clinking sounds with a glass thief as the glasses are filled, the same slurping, chewing, spitting sounds, the same lip-smacking, murmurs, and grunts of approval.

Chave has vines growing in several parcels scattered over the Hermitage *appellation,* and his bottled red is always a blend of them. In the wine literature we find the names of these separate parcels cited well before we come across any reference to Hermitage itself. A document from 1389 mentions Bessards, Méal, Rocoules, Baumes, and others, but the earliest appearance unearthed so far of Hermitage as Hermitage is from 1598.

In April 1983 I arrived to taste Chave's 1981 Hermitage *rouge.* He had not yet assembled and bottled his various *cuvées,* so we

Chave's cellar

wandered from one part of the cellar to another, taking tastes from various *foudres, demi-muids,* barrels and casks.

"We will start with Les Dionnières," he said, plunging his thief through the bunghole of one of his barrels, drawing out some purple wine and, aiming carefully, splashing a bit of it into my glass and his. "Les Dionnières is at the bottom of Hermitage, below Les Rocoules. It always gives a fine, elegant wine, never very tannic. You mustn't think that the higher slopes always give a wine better than those down below. In fact, when we have a dry year, the lower slopes will give the better wine because the vines are less stressed. In a normal year, yes, the higher, steeper slopes are better. But in terms of the different parcels, to have a good balance, a little of each is essential. In 1981 the higher slopes *are* better, but you can see that the lower parcels give an elegant, fruity wine. Still, it is certain that if it were bottled as is, separately, it would not be completely representative of the *appellation* Hermitage."

I asked if the lower parcels like Les Dionnières were flat.

"At Hermitage there is no flatland. It is not like Crozes-Hermitage. But the soil is lighter at the base of the hill, which favors the grape's maturity.

"Here, this is Les Baumes. It always has finesse as well as being tannic. Fine but strong. Les Dionnières has a perfume like little red fruits, raspberry and cherry, but Les Baumes is more like wildflowers. The aromas can change from year to year, however. It depends on the maturity of the grapes and above all if the year was dry or not. It would be too simple if every vintage were alike. Then I could put the same blend into bottles every year. Ten percent Baumes, twenty percent of this, fifteen percent of that . . . It would not hold the same interest for me."

I gave him my impression of Les Baumes, that it seemed fuller and richer but also shorter on the palate.

"That shortness is due to the astringence of the tannin. It dries out the mouth so it seems shorter. For aging, it has more strength than Les Dionnières. You could make a good *little* Hermitage by blending the two.

"Here we have Peléas. It has more depth. There is an aroma of violets.

"And this is Les Rocoules. There is not much red grown there. Les Rocoules is almost entirely white."

I asked how he decided whether to plant red or white grapes in the different parcels.

"Oh, there is not much of a decision to make," he answered. "That decision was made centuries ago. The nature of the soil decides for you. The sections of limestone and clay are destined to be white, but white in granite won't work, the result is not elegant enough. This was all determined a long time ago. But I've experimented and learned for myself that granitic soil is not suitable for white wine. On the other hand, Syrah grown in white-wine soil works better. See how it gives a fatter wine with more glycerine, more like a white.

"Now, Le Bessard. Can you smell the hawthorn blossom? I pointed it out to you up on the hill yesterday. It grows around here and we often find its aroma in our wine. Bessard has a more tannic structure than the others, without having higher alcohol. There are elements here that you do not find in the others. It is less floral, but longer on the palate. . . . For me, none of them can stand alone."

I asked if the differences between the wines was a question of exposition, or the level of the hill, or the soil.

"It is always the soil. At Hermitage the exposition is practically the same everywhere on the hillside. But Bessard is essentially granitic."

"Is it the same clone of Syrah as Peléas and the others?"

"They are all the same. I graft from our old vines when I replant."

He hesitated and glanced down a row of large oval casks. "We have another *cuvée* of Bessard to taste, but we'll get to it later because it is so tannic. First, let's taste Le Méal."

Le Méal seemed solidly structured, but less aromatic, less rich than the others. I asked what in particular it imparts to his final *assemblage,* or blend, in bottle.

"It is a combination of tannins. In the *assemblage* there is the tannic side to consider, and the floral or aromatic side. Some *cuvées* bring a certain finesse, a perfume or aroma to the blend, others a tannic support. And then some tannins are harsh; others finer, smoother."

When I asked him what he thought of Le Méal's aroma, he said it reminded him of cherry. "But that can change," he added. "One day you find black currant, and shortly afterward it is more like cherry or vanilla."

"You don't find cherries year after year in Le Méal?"

"Absolutely not. It is too simplistic, saying a wine is like this, this, or that. Only the journalists get away with that. They might taste it once or twice a year at most, but when you taste a wine several times a year, you perceive that it is not as easy and definitive as all that!

"Now, here is that other *cuvée* of Le Bessard I told you about. Notice that this one is in *foudre*. There is a huge difference between the *foudre* and the barrel. This is less mature. Less finished. What a difference! Leave the same wine in two different containers and two months later you have two different wines."

I asked if they had been precisely the same wine at the outset.

"Absolutely, so one can conclude that a wine 'makes itself' more rapidly in barrel than in *foudre*. That is why I like to have a little of each. I'm going to transfer this one into barrels and the other one will go into these *foudres* before I make my *assemblage*."

But why not leave it all in *foudre* in order to have a slower evolution once it is in bottle, a slower aging process?

"No, there is a different kind of oxidation in bottle. What is aging? It is an oxidation. But the sort achieved in wood you will never achieve in a glass bottle."

I told him about my experience in Raymond Trollat's cellar in nearby Saint-Jean-de-Muzols. "He has fifty-year-old *demi-muids*. Some are chestnut, some oak. After fifty years, of course there is absolutely no taste of wood imparted to the wine, yet the character of the wine from each kind of wood differs."

"And fifty years from now there will still be a difference," Chave said, "because the pores of the wood are different. Oak is tighter, more compacted, so the exchange with the air is slower, resulting in a firmer, more closed-in wine. The pores of chestnut are larger. It breathes more easily, resulting in a wine that is more supple, more advanced."

After we had tasted each *cuvée* of 1981 separately, we revisited each one and Chave carefully squirted out a bit of this, a bit more of that, a touch of Peléas, until he presented me with a glass of red Hermitage and declared, "Today, this is my conception of what the 1981 *assemblage* will be."

If Betty Grable was able to insure her legs, Chave should be able to insure his nose. He lowered it into his glass. "No, it needs something floral . . . here, a little more Les Baumes . . . there, see . . . the nose comes out better." Then he counted down a row of barrels and took out a few drops of another wine which he added to his composition. "Just a bit more Peléas to soften that tannin. I don't know. It is imprecise like this, without a measuring device. And it would be simpler if there were only three or four wines to blend, but it is fascinating because here there are so many possibilities. Imagine a composer who had only three or four tones to work with. But wait now, see if a touch more Bessard . . . from the *foudre* . . . no, it isn't any more satisfying, is it? Before I bottle the 1981 I will spend two weeks working to find the proper *assemblage*. Afterward, you won't be able to recognize any of these *cuvées* we tasted, but there will be a certain harmony on the palate. Today is like a first sketch."

Afterward the corks began popping. We tasted his 1980, 1979, 1978, and 1977.

The vintage chartists had made the 1977 difficult to market in the United States. I asked Chave if he had some sort of chart or system for rating his different vintages.

"For me, once a wine is in bottle, I have another conception of its quality which is not at all of wine as wine alone. Once you have a sound wine in the glass, your reasoning must be different, and each time you taste a wine you've got to imagine it with a dish. Otherwise, you are just saying you prefer this wine a little more than that wine, which is not very interesting. And this is where one can reproach most wine critics. You must be knowledgeable about cuisine in order to recommend a wine, in order to say this wine would go well with game, for example. The ultimate destination of a wine is on the table, with food. Serve the same wine with two different dishes and you will have two different opinions of it."

Chave then pulled the cork on his 1976 *rouge,* 1975, 1974, 1969, then the 1942. Blissful appreciation replaced the immense effort of concentration required to appraise the younger *cuvées.* Going back through the decades of Chave's Hermitage, you witness as wild, turbulent youth evolves into something sophisticated and profound.

"Here, let's change everything," Chave said, turning once more to what his English importer Robin Yapp has called "that sinister sea of fungus." He pulled out a bottle and scraped a thick puff of mold off the top of the cork before twisting in his corkscrew. There was no vintage on the bottle because no label can survive that humidity, so Chave announced its vintage, Hermitage *blanc,* 1952. Against the dark background, the deep golden color of the wine was stunning to the eye. The nose was old, thick, honeyed, alive, marvelous. Something about it, perhaps the sensation of immense depth, recalled those lordly bouquets of an old Yquem or an Alsatian *vendange tardive,* but the Hermitage seemed even more impressive for being dry. It dazzles without the advantage of sweetness or noble rot.

At harvest, the Hermitage hillside is a colorful scene bathed in a soft sunlight in which there is a suggestion of autumn's arrival. The vine's green foliage cascades from wooden stakes, but the impetuous growth of late spring and early summer has passed and the plant looks spent. The Syrah clusters are dark purple and so small, few, and far between you wonder (trying to get a foothold on the steep slope) at the effort that went into producing them. And then suddenly a bottle of Hermitage seems cheap.

Gérard Chave

and Hermitage

Because of the positioning of the hill, the view is spacious, bound by the distant Alps to the east, the Massif Central to the west, and to the south it always seems that if the sky were just a little clearer there would be a view all the way to the Mediterranean. And at the base of the hill there is the mighty Rhône executing an unusually graceful curve.

In 1986, Chave gathered his team of thirty harvesters on October 2, and they began picking the white grapes, which were not white at all. Some Marsanne grapes were golden, some almost purple, others dark and shriveled. The Marsanne was delicious eating right off the vine, and Chave said that he knows it will be a good vintage when he sees the pickers munching on grapes as they work.

Strangely enough, Chave's team was practically the only one on the hillside. Then I looked closer and noticed that the neighboring plots had already been stripped of their treasure.

"Almost everyone has finished harvesting," Chave said. He had a big grin. "They were afraid it might rain, afraid to gamble. Some of them finished eight days ago and we are just beginning. They won't have enough natural sugar in their grapes, so they will have to add sugar. Oh yes, even at Hermitage now they have granted us the right to chaptalize. It is scandalous. So these enologists tell everybody to harvest early in order to have more acidity and avoid the risk of rot. They tell them to pick early, that they can add the sugar later. Here, taste a green grape. You see, it has no flavor, no character. Now taste a golden one. See the difference? They want to make what I call a *vin technologique*. It is fruity, but they all taste the same whether they are from the Loire, the Rhône, or wherever. That is not what I want. Grapes are a fruit just like a pear or a peach. If they are ripe, they have a lot more flavor and aroma. People forget that a grape is a fruit. They would never eat a green peach, but they harvest green grapes. If they didn't chaptalize, some growers would have a white Hermitage at 11 degrees alcohol this year. We are harvesting ripe grapes which will produce a wine with 13 degrees alcohol! The flavor of the two wines will be totally different."

When I left, Chave was instructing his foreman to mix water into the harvesters' wine supply because at the end of the previous day one of them had stumbled and hit his head on a rock and an ambulance had to be called. They mulled over the subtle insurance question: was he still on the job, or was he on the way home *after* work? The worker had just finished washing his hands, the foreman said. Then he argued that if he diluted the wine some of the crew would be angry. "What about the guys who only take a sip from time to time? Are we going to penalize the moderate ones because of the two or three who overdo it?"

Chave said that the wine is too strong. He serves his harvesters Hermitage, a blend of the press wine, the wine from younger vines, and from the less successful *cuvées* that he does not want in his *assemblage*. "Hermitage is too strong to drink out in the hot sun."

It is an argument which must have a five-hundred-year history in the Chave family.

If Hermitage appears to have been created expressly for the vine, with only a few tucks and folds needed to perfect it, Côte Rôtie is obviously man's painstaking creation. The steep slopes are a sloppy patchwork of stone walls and terraces, often barely wide enough for a single row of vines. There are parts of the hill where the earth looks more like some jagged extraterrestrial metal than soil fit for cultivation, but the ancients tamed these slopes, and Côte Rôtie, along with Hermitage, is where the Syrah is capable of magnificence.

Syrah, serine, sarine, syrrah, sirah, syras, schiras, schirac, sirac. In 1868, after more than twenty centuries of winegrowing, someone noticed that the *serine* of Côte Rôtie and the *sirrah* of Hermitage were the same grape, an indication of how provincial this part of France was, and is. When I arrived in 1976, I was struck by how rustic the cellars and equipment remained, even though the Paris–Marseilles *autoroute* and railway line is never more than a few kilometers away.

Given the similarity between the wines of Côte Rôtie and

Hermitage, it is unbelievable that it took so long for someone
to deduce that they are born of the same parent vine. There is a
difference between the two wines, but describing that difference
has proven to be a problem. Gérard Chave says Côte Rôtie is less
heady than Hermitage, a statement that invites charges of chau-
vinism (or Chavinism) because the aroma of a well-vinified Côte
Rôtie from old vines grown upon the original roasted slope has
no peer in terms of headiness. There is a difference between these
two Syrahs, but to explain it I would have to dredge up notes
from a literature class years ago in which my professor tried to
simplify Nietzsche's distinction between Apollonian and Dionysian qualities. It went something like this:

Apollonian. Master of oneself, harmonious, a beauty that is
more formal, more architectural, as in the wine of Hermitage.

Dionysian. A wilder force, instinctive, immediate, a beauty
that is more passionate than cerebral, as in the wine of Côte
Rôtie.

In fact, were Côte Rôtie's carriage less regal, its aroma might
seem ostentatious. Only royalty can wear plumes and glittering
jewels and white fox robes and get away with it.

The village that hosts the Côte Rôtie spectacle is Ampuis.
Each wine village in France seems to boast Roman artifacts, but
when it comes to claims of antiquity, Ampuis is the undefeated
champion. Some wine books repeat the unproven story that Ampuis was the site of France's first vineyard. It is perhaps the name
of the place that prompts such nonsense. They say that the name
evolved from *ampelos,* Greek for "vine," proving that the Greeks
cultivated wine grapes at Ampuis even before the Romans showed
up. Well, why not?

But what about the theory that Ampuis comes from *empoisser,*
"to make sticky"? Plutarch wrote about the wine of the region
and called it a *vin empoissé,* or at least that is the French translation
of what he said. Some are convinced that the Romans added pitch
to their Côte Rôtie, which presumably would have made it sticky.
Pitch = *poix* in French, and it is not far from *em-poix* to Ampuis.
It is difficult to imagine anyone adulterating a Côte Rôtie with

pitch, but in our era, adulterating it with an overpowering smell of new oak seems to be considered acceptable behavior, so who knows?

Or, *am* can mean "around," and *puits*, which is pronounced exactly like *puis*, means "well." Following this theory, Ampuis means "around the well." To support this theory one can cite the Beaujolais village Amplepuis, meaning "generous well."

Or *am* might have been shortened over the centuries from *aimer*, meaning "to like" or "to love," or *aimable*, meaning "happy" or "lovable." Ampuis = the lovable well? I'll drink from that.

If *am* comes from *amoeba*, we may have a stagnant well.

Or *am* could have come from the Greek root *amph*, which can mean two hillsides or a rounded shape as in amphitheater.

The French word *puy* is also pronounced like *puis*, and means "mountain" or "height."

Then there is the theory that *puis* evolved from the Greek and Latin *podium*, which referred to the large wall that circled an amphitheater, on which were situated the seats of honor. This is not inconceivable if you visualize the stone walls which follow the rounded shape of the hillsides of Côte Rôtie; however, it does seem quite a drastic case of mispronunciation going from Ampodium to Ampuis.

Theories and legends also abound regarding the initial vine plantings. Many believe that the Syrah arrived via the Greeks, who had settled Marseilles (Massalia) at the mouth of the Rhône, and whose trade took them north via the river. There is no evidence of Greeks settling at Ampuis; however, Greek amphorae have been found downriver at Tain l'Hermitage. It is curious that the cultivation of the Syrah in Provence and in the southern Rhône is only a recent, twentieth-century occurrence, when it was imported from the northern Rhône with the farfetched idea of ennobling the southern wines. Had it worked its way north from Marseilles, would there not have been traces left in the south? While I have absolutely no historical foundation for supposing it, my nose tells me that the Syrah came from the east, via the Alps. A young Syrah has more in common with a young Nebbiolo from Piemonte than it does with a wine from the Marseilles region.

Terracing the hillsides of Ampuis could have taken centuries. It is doubtful that a Greek or Roman winemaker gazed up, nodded sagely, and decreed them the perfect site for Syrah. In the beginning the vines must have been planted at the bottom of the hill, where farming was easier and where there was plenty of water from the river nearby. And it must be remembered that the Rhône was not stationary. Only in the nineteenth century did man begin to control the course of the Rhône. Before, it changed course almost by whim, and a terrain that was farmed on the plain one year might have been submerged the next, another reason to cultivate the slopes. But when people began tasting wine from the roasted slope someone must have noticed that it produced finer wine, so the vineyards were expanded upward to meet the demand. All this is conjecture; perhaps the Creator installed the terraces on the sixth day in order to drink well on the seventh.

Constructing the stone walls served two purposes. It removed the large rocks from the soil, facilitating cultivation, and it prevented the remaining soil from washing down the hill in a rainstorm.

The walls are handmade, and some workers could not help expressing themselves by creating patterns as they labored. Therefore, some of the walls are random collections of stones, while others form eye-catching designs.

We know that in the seventh century Saint Eloi wrestled with a demon in the church at Ampuis, but as far as I can tell, and I am not the historical researcher needed here, the first documented statement, the first outright proof that there were vines at Ampuis, dates from A.D. 889. Before that, Côte Rôtie was always referred to as a *vin de Vienne,* or "wine of Vienne," the more important city a few kilometers north of Ampuis. An act dated "a Friday in the month of April in the second year after the death of Charlemagne" certifies that a certain Monsieur Rostaing and his wife, Andelmonde, donated to the church at Vienne two parcels of vineyard situated *"in villa Ampusio,"* reserving at the same time, however, their right to the actual fruit from those vines for the rest of their lifetime. Rather than leave the vineyard to some ne'er-do-well relative, they fixed it so the Good Lord would come into possession of some prime Côte Rôtie grapes just as He was deciding whether to send Rostaing and Andelmonde upward to paradise or down into the fiery pit.

Eleven centuries later, there is still a Rostaing with vines at Ampuis. I have neglected to ask him if he is a descendant of Rostaing and Andelmonde, because I cannot risk ruining such a perfect transition. Today's Rostaing, René Rostaing, was born in 1948 and vinified his first Côte Rôtie in 1970 at age twenty-two.

"In order to understand Côte Rôtie, you must climb up through the vineyards," he said one day. "Looking out the window of a car is not enough." He turned out to be a passionate guide who seems to know every nook and cranny, every stone's mineral composition and geological origin.

The different slopes of Côte Rôtie, such as the two most famous, Côte Blonde and Côte Brune, are separated by deep, stream-eroded ravines. According to Rostaing, the erosion over the millennia created dramatically diverse soils. "Ampuis is a small vineyard, one of France's smallest," he said. "We have less than three hundred acres planted in thirty different soils, and no more than a dozen acres share the same exact soil composition."

As one sees in Chave's cellar, different soils create different wines, especially when the plant is Syrah.

Hiking up his parcel of Côte Blonde, Rostaing said, "It is this siliceous base of chalk and quartz that gives Côte Blonde's wine its elegance and refinement. The Blonde is a wine that needs time. For the first few years it seems relatively muted, but with age it begins to express itself. It has a tannin that seems almost delicate, a tannin that is well-integrated into the wine. It has finesse."

We went back to his car in order to go have a look at La Landonne.

"La Landonne starts here, just beyond the creek," he said. "La Landonne is not part of the Côte Brune. I insist upon this point because the error has been repeated again and again. There are more slopes to Côte Rôtie than Brune and Blonde. Côte Brune and Blonde make up ten percent of Côte Rôtie and no more. This tendency to call the southern slopes Blonde and the northern Brune is an inaccurate simplification. From south to north you have Côte Mollard, Blonde, Brune, Moutonnes, Landonne, and Vieillière."

As we slipped and huffed and puffed our way up the stony incline, Rostaing shook his head sadly. "Look at this. La Landonne starts here, where there is nothing growing but weeds. Over here, a few vines. More weeds over there . . . La Landonne lies fifty percent fallow! Here is my parcel. Here is Rostaing's La Landonne! Three thousand square meters. Fifteen hundred bottles per year! The vines over there belong to my uncle, Marius Gentaz. He has five thousand square meters. It's steep, isn't it? He has old vines, at least sixty years old. See how they were trained? Beautiful vines! The soil here has more clay. There is very little quartz, so the wine it gives is more rustic, less elegant than Côte Blonde.

"My grandfather made wine here after World War I and sold it in barrel to the local café-bars. Five francs per liter. Côte Rôtie was the everyday wine for the people of Ampuis. You know, a glass while they played their game of *boules* outdoors in the square. Then, closer to World War II, life began to change, the cost of living began to increase. People wanted more comforts. Before, they would go fishing on Sundays, they wore the same clothes day after day, but later everyone had to own a car, then a second car, a new freezer, a vacation. Meanwhile, Côte Rôtie was selling no better. So what happened? The people decided it was not worth the effort to work the hillsides. They abandoned them. Half of La Landonne lies fallow, and it dates from that period. That was when they planted the flatlands below us, but they planted apricots because they were more profitable than selling Côte Rôtie. Apricots, lettuces, peas . . ."

The Roasted Slope

Later that day, Rostaing's uncle, Marius Gentaz, continued the story. A relaxed man in his sixties, dressed in the traditional French worker's blue coveralls, he said that some of those farmers on the plain had to sell their land to the government in the early 1960s when the Paris–Marseilles *autoroute* was built. Some used their money to buy vineyard land back on the slopes.

Many of the northern Rhône winemakers think that Gentaz is making the most typical, traditional Côte Rôtie of our day. I asked him what his secret is.

"In order to make a good Côte Rôtie," he said with unfeigned, almost naïve modesty, "the vines must be planted in the right place and you must bring in healthy grapes. And you cannot make great wine here with young vines. They must be fifteen to twenty years old before they begin to give a pretty wine."

I said surely there must be something in the vinification, some secret method to explain his wine's quality.

"Well, you've got to take good care of it, keep the barrels filled up to the top." (My apologies to any winemakers looking for the trick to making good Syrah!) Then Gentaz smiled and said, "You raise the wine the way it has to be raised. I haven't changed anything. I make my wine the way my father-in-law taught me, the way he made it eighty years ago. Exactly the same way!"

Fifty percent of La Landonne barren! And, according to René Rostaing, 60 percent of the wine harvested at Ampuis now comes from the plateau, which the ancients more appropriately devoted to corn and wheat. What a tragedy for one of the world's finest vineyards.

Ironically, in our time the very factor that might mean renewal for the original Côte Rôtie vineyards has an attendant risk, which is that it could alter so drastically the taste of Côte Rôtie as to render it unrecognizable to those who know the taste of the real thing. The various Côte Rôtie bottlings from Guigal, the *négociant* at Ampuis, dominate blind-tasting events, dominate the wine journals, newspapers, and magazines to a degree that has become dangerous. The public is very close to deciding a Côte Rôtie is by definition oaky and alcoholic, and the next step is the rejection of the traditional Côte Rôtie, which is not oaky or alcoholic.

By no means do I blame Guigal for this state of affairs. He has great commercial instincts and his oaky wines with their blistering alcoholic content are crowd pleasers. It requires talent to so enrapture the public and the critics. Ah, the critics. Never have I seen one single discouraging word about Guigal's Côte Rôtie, even though it is a very anonymous-tasting wine, easily mistaken for a big, oaky Gigondas or even a Bordeaux. I want my Côte Rôtie to taste like Côte Rôtie. This all reminds me of an acquaintance who always seemed to have a new girlfriend. His girlfriends all had two things in common: huge breasts. His choices might be pretty or not, intelligent or not, interesting or not. Nothing seemed to matter to him as long as the breasts were enormous. It was such an impractical way to assess the quality of a woman that it began to seem almost perverse. And I have an identical reaction to those who go gaga over an inky, oaky, monster wine that has, it might as well be by accident, a Côte Rôtie label. I cannot begin to communicate how profoundly the critics' embrace of such freak wines depresses me.

Why ask that a wine be jarring to the senses, a criterion that we do not apply to other arts like music or painting in which delicacy is valued, where shading, nuance, even silence or empty space can be considered remarkable. But keep an eye on the wine critics' ratings. If a wine is black, packs an alcoholic, tannic wallop, and smells like a lumberyard, it receives high points.

Traditional Côte Rôtie does not have a thick, heavy quality, as if it had been applied with a brush. A description from 1786 says Côte Rôtie is *"un vin flatteur et fort delicat"* (a seductive, highly delicate wine).

A later description says that Côte Rôtie is distinguished by *"la finesse de sa sève"* (the finesse of its sap) and its unique bouquet, which makes it "one of the most delicate and agreeable wines of France."

"The finesse of its *sève*." Consider the phrase. It is not bad at all. *Sève,* the sap or lifeblood of a plant, conveys an impression of vigor, of intensity. A Côte Rôtie is by no means light stuff; it is a substantial wine, but what is unusual is this saplike quality combined with a certain finesse, a certain delicacy. Top it off with that amazing perfume of Syrah fruit grown in this special *terroir* and you have a wine set apart from all others. Anyone can make a heavy, oaky wine. All you need is a new barrel and sugary (or sugared) grape juice. But a Côte Rôtie that tastes like Côte Rôtie can come only from the *terroir* of the roasted slope and from the traditional vinification developed over the centuries in the cellars of Ampuis.

How ironic that a heavy, oaky wine should be the object of such acclaim and desire that, thanks to it, the small Côte Rôtie growers are now obtaining a just price for their wine, and consequently land that had been abandoned is beginning to be replanted. I suppose I could be compared to a classical music fan who cannot stand the fact that the public is listening to Elvis or the Beatles instead of Haydn and Mozart, but I fear the day when the classic Côte Rôtie like that of Marius Gentaz disappears completely to be replaced by the Guigal recipe. In more and more cellars I see new oak barrels as the northern Rhône growers try to copy his success.

Beaujolais must be the most in-
spired invention in the history of wine. What a concept, downing
a newborn wine that has barely left the grape, a wine that retains
the cornucopian spirit of the harvest past. It even serves to remind
us of the first time man tasted fermented grape juice and decided
it was an accident of nature worth pursuing.

Who invented Beaujolais? We don't know, but some of the
revisionist winemakers who quite recently snuffed it out are very
well known indeed.

From Ampuis it is only about fifty minutes of life-threatening-

French-*autoroute*-madness to Lyons, where most of the Beaujolais produced used to be consumed. The cuisine of Lyons happens to be the kind that you eat with gusto, but it can stay with you. Waverly Root called it "liver-assaulting." Traditional Lyonnaise cuisine needs to be accompanied by cool draughts of the wine that was once Beaujolais. A heavy wine would have diminished the requisite appetite. It had to be a wine with a cutting edge of acidity to cope with the sausages and tripe and various other forms of pig. And it had to be light in alcohol because the cuisine of Lyons arouses a gargantuan thirst.

The Beaujolais vineyards commence just north of Lyons. When clients planning a trip to France ask my advice, I try to talk them into going to either Alsace or the Beaujolais. For the time being, demand and prices for Bordeaux and Burgundy make it difficult for tourists to get into the best cellars. The winemakers have more clients than wine, so they are not eager to pour samples to everyone who passes by. One year, one of my growers in Vosne-Romanée had one single barrel, twenty-five cases, of Richebourg, so it is easy to understand his reluctance to dip his thief into it.

In the Beaujolais there are cellars open for tasting wherever you look. And it is a prettier region than Bordeaux or the Côte d'Or. The Beaujolais offers vine-covered panoramas of undulating hills, winding country roads, forgotten hamlets built upon wine cellars, and unspoiled natives who like visitors. Beaujolais has everything a wine-loving tourist could desire except good wine.

When those who remember real Beaujolais describe it, they make my mouth water: a light, grapy, fizzy, tart, quaffable red wine. Bring on the *gras-double* (tripe with onions and parsley), the *boudin aux pommes* (blood sausages with baked apple), the *cervelas aux pistaches et truffes* (sausage stuffed with pistachio nuts and black truffles). With real Beaujolais, we can handle it.

Richard Olney remembers "a rush of green fruit . . ."

Jean-Baptiste Chaudet, Paris's leading wine merchant from the 1940s through the early 1970s, recalls in his autobiography *Marchand de Vin* a Beaujolais "very light in color, at times really pale, slightly aggressive, even a touch green, and rarely above

11 degrees alcohol. In those days, " Chaudet continues, "Beaujolais was still very good, which is not the case today because of extreme overproduction, less and less attention in the cellar, and above all because of this chaptalization, this addition of sugar to the must which allows them to raise the wine's alcoholic content up to 3 degrees. A chaptalized Beaujolais is recognizable because it is excessively supple. When the alcohol content rises above 12 degrees, it is no longer Beaujolais. Put a stop to chaptalization and the wine could become what it was before—young, light, and aggressive."

Compare Chaudet's descriptive adjectives with the following taken from Robert Parker's 1987 *Wine Buyer's Guide,* concerning today's Beaujolais: soft, lush, silky, full, fleshy, rich, supple, and so on. Mr. Parker is correct. His adjectives perfectly describe today's overchaptalized, overalcoholic Beaujolais.

One contemporary critic described the finest Beaujolais he had ever tasted as having a "sledgehammer-like feel on the palate," leading presumably to a smithereen-like finish?

In his autobiography Chaudet dropped the name of a Beaujolais producer he respected named Chauvet, so I looked him up, hoping to understand what had happened to the old-style Beaujolais and perhaps even to taste one. In Jules Chauvet I found a gracious, guileless man with a poetic streak that he seemed to want to repress, an eighty-year-old bachelor who is semiretired and who has no heirs to take over his small *négociant* firm.

Chauvet had just taken delivery of his 1986 Beaujolais-Villages and it was in barrels (a sight rare enough today in the Beaujolais) on the ground outdoors in his courtyard. We began tasting through them under a persistent drizzle. Chauvet would place the tip of his thief at the edge of the bunghole, raise his nose and eyebrows, and plunge the glass pipe down into the wine like a matador's coup de grace. Such an unlikely motion, barrel after barrel, from such a proper old fellow began to strike me as humorous, and I had to conceal a smile.

His Beaujolais was pale in color, with a light, pretty perfume. There were reminders of flowers, grapes, and fruits like peach and apricot. It was all quite delicate from start to finish, but lively all the same, and the flavor was elusive; more than anything, it *perfumed* the palate.

"It has 11 degrees alcohol," he said, "no chaptalization and no sulfur dioxide. You can drink it without getting vertigo."

Monsieur Chauvet has been in the Beaujolais business sixty years. I asked him what changes he has witnessed.

"In 1930 there was lower production, around forty hectoliters to the hectare, whereas now it is up to sixty and seventy. Well, it is rare to have both quantity and quality. They rhyme, but apart from that, they have nothing in common. And the soil is no longer cultivated. They simply add herbicides and fertilizers now. They poison the earth, instead of working it. For the moment, production is high, but the quality of the grape juice has fallen. One day soon, we shall see production drop, too, when the soil has been transformed by chemicals. That is a danger.

"And there is a difference today because everyone wants wines that are visually empty [*optiquement vide*]. We used to pay no attention to limpidity. I don't know how we got to this point, judging a wine by its limpidity. No one demands that fruit juice be clear. Why must wine be clear? I remember in 1930 with the great vintage of 1929, some Swiss clients bought some Fleurie in barrel, full of carbon dioxide gas, still on its lees. They rolled it into their restaurant in Switzerland, put it up on the counter, opened it up, stirred it up, turned the spigot, and served it like that. It was like red soup, but what a perfume! The Swiss were like that, they wanted the whole wine. Now you have to de-gas it, you know, take out the carbon dioxide, but when you do that, you also take out the wine's perfume. I wish we could convince the consumer to accept a fizzy wine with all its perfume intact. Have you noticed how everyone loves champagne, but they won't accept a bubbly Beaujolais?"

I asked Monsieur Chauvet what degree of alcohol Beaujolais had back in the thirties.

"In the little years, nine to ten degrees. In the hot years, twelve to thirteen degrees. I remember when my father delivered

Jules Chauvet

Beaujolais to Paris at nine degrees alcohol. People liked to consume healthy quantities of it."

"Why did things change?" I asked.

"We had two years, 1945 and 1947, when the wines were unusually rich in *natural* alcohol. Prices went up and afterward, *that* was Beaujolais, always thirteen to fourteen degrees. What a mistake! People here wanted to mimic the Burgundians and make big money. But Beaujolais is a simple wine. It is a beverage which must first of all calm one's thirst, but at fourteen degrees alcohol it is difficult to drink much of anything. We must come back to lighter Beaujolais for several reasons. Back in the old days, there was not so much automobile traffic, but nowadays everyone drives a car. How can you drink a wine at fourteen degrees and then drive home from a restaurant? That is not true Beaujolais. I say if you want something with lots of alcohol, drink whiskey."

I said I did not believe people consciously looked for high alcohol. But high alcohol equals full body, and by some twist of fate, people think full body is better than light body.

"Well, those people shouldn't drink Beaujolais. After all, wines with body are easy to find. They're everywhere. But a wine with perfume, that is what is difficult to find. If people would use their nose, learn how to smell again . . ."

And Monsieur Chauvet frowned, thrusting it all back on us, the buyers, the consumers.

And I am still searching for a rude, flirtatious little Beaujolais with a bit of a sting, because Monsieur Chauvet must now occupy himself with his health instead of his wine business. The last time I saw him he said, "I must warn you, I am receiving radiotherapy treatments at Lyons. I don't know if I will be here to receive you next spring. It is a cancer. They tell me that the treatments have stopped the progress, but we don't really know anything. We will know more in the spring. Or perhaps you will know, and I will not."

The Italians still make gay little thirst quenchers in the spirit of the Beaujolais of yesteryear, but I must admit that my clientele refuses to embrace them. Alas, the French have civilized the wine of Beaujolais, tried to disguise it as a society lady who wears cosmetics, phony scent, and costume jewelry. Whatever the vintage might give, whatever village it may be from, Brouilly, Saint-Amour, or Moulin-à-Vent, whichever, today's Beaujolais all turn out nearly alike in the end: it will be 13.5 degrees alcohol even if the grapes came in at 9 degrees natural sugar, which happens. The extra 4.5 degrees are obtained by chaptalization. It will have a limpid, slightly deep color even if it started with a cherrylike blush. It will have just enough acidity to keep it from tasting like mush, but will be almost as cloying because a little tartness might offend someone. It will have been degassed, of course, so that no one in a restaurant turns it back because they think it is fermenting in the bottle. Chaptalization and degassing leave it with a slightly thick, tongue-numbing texture. It will never throw a sediment. It will have a polite perfume, mildly fruitlike. Yes, sorry, the wine's natural, rambunctious fruitiness has been washed out by overproduction, masked by chaptalization, and brutalized by degassing and filtrations. Drink a carafe of the stuff (I do not like to call it Beaujolais) and your headache the next day will make you wish you *had* suffered a fatal accident on the way home from your restaurant. Alcohol, sulfur dioxide, prescription tannin, and I do not wish to know what else will be hammering at the inside of your skull. Your blood will feel thick, heavy . . . chaptalized. But Beaujolais should make you feel *light*-headed!

Here in the Beaujolais one sees that the nightmare can happen. A recipe, a formula, can take over an entire region. When old-timers like Chaudet and Chauvet are gone, even the memory of the old-style Beaujolais will have vanished.

When I see the wine writers taking the current formula Beaujolais seriously, treating it like wine, awarding points and stars, discussing the "banana" aroma, for example, I want to scream, *THESE ARE NOT LIVING WINES*. These are wine robots rolling off the assembly line, millions and millions of them.

Jean-Baptiste Chaudet wrote, "The day the consumer demands

a more natural product, the winemakers will be obliged to take up the methods of their ancestors." I agree that the consumer can influence quality. Winemakers began to filter and refilter their wines because of idiot complaints about sediment, which proves that consumers can change vinification practices, for better or worse.

Start by accepting Beaujolais as a gift of nature, with all that implies, including the cliché: *Don't look a gift horse in the mouth.* Value what nature gives, quirks and all. If ever you find a real Beaujolais, glory in its virtues, its immediacy, its spirit, instead of swirling and sniffing and seeking size and grandeur. Americans, comparative newcomers to fine wine, seem to look for a Great Experience every time they uncork a bottle.

Beaujolais should not be a civilized society lady; it is the one-night stand of wines.

Many consider the Beaujolais to be a part of Burgundy, but the way my mind sorts out and compartmentalizes things, Beaujolais is not even a blood relative to red Burgundy. Their soils, souls, and grape varieties are different. However, I consider the whites of the region, Mâcon, Saint-Veran, and Pouilly-Fuissé, to be proper white Burgundies. Here we have similar soils, the grape is Chardonnay, and the differences between the *appellations* are no more than passionately interesting questions of personality. Deciding whether to serve a Mâcon *blanc* or a Meursault is not a question of which is the best wine. It is an exercise in forming the most appropriate alliance between the wine and the plate it will accompany, or the environment in which it will be served. A Mâcon *blanc* should have certain traits and qualities which Meursault lacks, and vice versa.

The Mâcon *blanc* of my dreams has something gay, undemanding, and unsophisticated about it. It has a pale color. It is the whitest white Burgundy. Its aroma is, above all, fresh and direct, unhindered by sulfur dioxide, new oak, or oxidation. It smells of the countryside, of green pastures, or in riper years of springtime and wildflowers. The suggestion of chalk keeps it from seeming banal on the palate. It has a stimulating little sparkle without seeming bubbly. Mâcon *blanc* should be light-bodied, never above 12 percent alcohol, and it is even more useful a wine at 11 percent. It finishes crisply, which is not to say that it is thin or short on the palate, but it does not weigh on the palate. It leaves the palate freshened, the lips smacking.

Saint-Veran is rounder than Mâcon *blanc,* simpler than Pouilly-Fuissé. It will tolerate a bit of new oak. In fact, if production is kept to a reasonable quantity per acre and it is vinified in oak, a Saint-Veran can aspire to attract our attention while we enjoy downing it. Most important when trying to decide when to serve Saint-Veran is the fact that the size of one's swallow will be smaller than it is when drinking Mâcon, but larger in volume than with a Pouilly-Fuissé, so the cuisine must be considered in terms of the amount of thirst, the size of the swallow it will inspire. If it is refined cuisine best accompanied by contemplative sips, most Saint-Verans and Mâcons would be out of place.

Pouilly-Fuissé is the most difficult of the three Mâconnais whites to buy because both its price and one's expectations are higher. And it must be said that the Pouilly-Fuissé growers have been spoiled. It is too easy for them. No matter what they put behind a Pouilly-Fuissé label, it earns a good price. Sales are effortless. Consequently, most Pouilly-Fuissé are stretched in terms of yield per acre and then chaptalized to the point that they taste like fermented sugar and water. Most of them smell like greed to me.

Great Pouilly-Fuissé exists. Vintage plays a role in that it determines the wine's style: 1975 produced unctuous, botrytized wines; 1984 produced delicate, flinty Chardonnays that blossom at table with seafood.

The difference between a great Pouilly-Fuissé and a great white from the Côte d'Or like Puligny-Montrachet? Pouilly-Fuissé, the Mâconnais region, is that much nearer the south, the Mediterranean. The locals play *boules* and drink *pastis*. The rooftops are red-tiled. Pouilly-Fuissé has a looser, warmer, simpler spirit. It is less involved with itself than a wine from Puligny; it has less complicatedness.

The Mâconnais forms a perfect sort of *entrée* into the world of Burgundy, in terms of both wine and place. The first time I traveled to Burgundy, trailing along with another importer, we arrived by the old highway from Paris via Auxerre, Avallon, and Saulieu. We came around a curve and he turned off the highway onto a little road, and suddenly we were surrounded by vineyards. He stopped and pointed out his window, saying, "This is Le Montrachet." It was a dramatic way to arrive, but one could complain that it was a climactic way to arrive. After that, how much lessened was the impact of seeing the Meursault slopes for the first time, or Volnay, or Pommard, and so on?

It is more satisfying to experience Burgundy's Côte d'Or as you would order the wines at table, beginning with something simple like Mâcon and leading into the great growths. When you start at Mâcon and head north by the *route de vin* through the Côte Chalonnaise vineyards of Montagny and Mercurey, you have prepared yourself for that first magical glimpse of Le Montrachet. There is a perspective. Everything is more meaningful. Even today, after countless trips to Burgundy, my favorite route is to cut west from Mâcon to Cluny and then north on D-981 toward Chagny.

In Mâcon there is a restaurant that could be the perfect setting for enjoying the regional reds and whites. The Maison du Mâconnais is located right on the *route nationale,* across the highway from the Saône River. It is a big, crowded place with wooden tables and benches, a ringing clatter of knives and forks in action, and people taking joy in eating. The menu is admirably short, so you can be sure that your order was not microwaved. There is a generous *choucroute garnie,* or a *petit salé* with boiled potatoes and carrots, the sort of cuisine that requires a pot of mustard on the table. Here, of all places, one should be able to order a carafe of cool, crisp Mâcon *blanc,* or a light, spritzy Beaujolais *rouge* with which to irrigate the hearty, salty fare. Dining there once with a local wine *négociant,* I seemed to shock him by adding cold sparkling water to the thick, flat Beaujolais we had been served, but by the end of the meal he and his wife had resorted to the same improvised concoction in order to create something thirst-quenching.

Leaving Mâcon for Cluny, one is not far from the Pouilly-Fuissé vineyards and the landmark Roche de Solutré, a cliff famous in archaeological circles because of the traces of early man found there, including a massive pile of horse bones at its base. The ancients wilefully maneuvered wild horses up the gentle slope on the back side, then stampeded the poor beasts over the edge of the sheer cliff to slaughter them. Very French. And it is at Solutré that I ate rather well myself when I stayed year after year at the Relais de Solutré, a true country inn where I could obtain sausages grilled over coals with a side order of baked apple and a righteous glass of Saint-Veran or Saint-Amour. Now the inn has been purchased by one of those big-fish-eat-little-fish hotel chains and there, out in that beautiful countryside where one wakes up to roosters crowing and cows mooing, your morning jam arrives in a tacky little plastic container. I have yet to find a decent replacement for the Relais, although the Hôtel de Maritonnes across from the Deboeuf factory in Romanêche-Thorins still opens their guests' day with homemade jam in a clay pot.

The D-981 north from Cluny to Chagny is a little-traveled

On the Route de Vin.

Côte Chalonnaise

two-lane route which traverses idyllic farmland populated by the handsomest cows outside Switzerland, massive white beasts who munch the luxurious green herbage with an air of single-minded connoisseurship. The fields and occasional vineyards are broken into wild and cultivated parcels by hedgerows and stone walls, providing perfect hideaways for an off-the-road picnic. When traveling by car in France, sample the relaxing pleasures of roadside dining as the French themselves do. A picnic is so much more rewarding than the hazards of French fast-food stops. (Ours are gourmet treats in comparison.) Shop for provisions in one of the villages: some local sausages and prepared salad from a *charcuterie,* bread from a *boulangerie,* cheeses, plus an apple or pear from a fruit stand. When you see a winery sign, pick up a bottle of local wine, because once you're outside Paris, wineshops are rare. In the marketplace you are likely to encounter some memorable personalities instead of yet another impersonal waiter accustomed to serving tourists who will never return.

The city of Chalon-sur-Saône is the source of the name of this part of Burgundy, the Côte Chalonnaise. Like Bandol or Bordeaux, Chalon itself has no vines, but it was the commercial center, the port of departure for exporting wine from the hillsides of Montagny, Givry, Mercurey, and Rully. Today Chalon is not an important wine center, but the name sticks.

I retain a good share of wine-inspired souvenirs from the Côte Chalonnaise. I have found the cellars of those picturesque, unspoiled villages to be an excellent source of red and white Burgundy at fair prices. But when I think of the Chalonnais, hare and jackass also come to mind.

I think of jackass because of the years when I bought Rully *blanc* from Madame Niepce, a grandniece of Nicéphore Niepce, who is remembered in the encyclopedias as the man who invented photography. Madame Niepce had retired to the family estate and wine *domaine* at Rully after a notoriously wild life in Paris. She had enjoyed her share of champagne, probably from a silk slipper. She had lived it up, all right. Past extravagance showed on her face. Her clothes and her furniture were antiques, which showed taste and flair, but most vivid were the dried flowers everywhere, on every table, in every vase, up to the ceiling in each corner, and a bouquet of them, five feet across, centered on the dining-room table. Presumably there were only dried flowers because her pet jackass would have eaten them up had they been fresh. Her jackass had the run of the house. He was quite a lovely, caressable beast, but he had two flaws: he had to be let out for his toilet, and once outdoors he had an uncontrollable appetite for tender young grape leaves. Jackasses are not known for listening to reason, and finally the neighboring *vignerons* formed an angry association to ban his forays outside the house. Madame Niepce resisted ferociously. A free spirit, it pained her to be told what to do. However, the litter problem had she kept her jackass indoors would have been insurmountable. And after all, in Rully, wine interests are going to triumph over the civil rights of a jackass every time. She finally farmed out the jackass and replaced him with a shaggy dog of equal height and weight who displayed no gastronomic interest in grape leaves.

Hare springs to mind because of one of my own gastronomic experiences. I was staying at a friend's house which was so crowded that I ended up sleeping on a couch in the dining room. When I awoke, I was on my side facing the open kitchen doorway, and the first thing I beheld as one eye reluctantly opened was the cook holding a wriggling little rabbit upside down by its hind legs over a pot so the blood running from its cut throat could be saved for the sauce. This is the first step in preparing a Burgundian stew called *civet de lièvre*, or in this case *civet de lapin*, because rabbit was used instead of hare. It is a stew employing the animal's blood and liver in the sauce. Needless to say, it is a rich dish that makes an impression; some find the sauce too much. Once or twice in my life I had eaten it and liked it, particularly in late autumn when Burgundy turns icy and one's hands and feet will not warm up. I told the cook how sorry I was to have to miss her *civet,* but I had already made other plans.

First I had a stop near Buxy, where the Montagny vineyards

are located. After tasting, I was delighted to learn that the winemaker's wife had prepared a *civet de lièvre* for lunch. Too bad that her hare was dried out from overcooking. I enjoyed it nonetheless because outdoors it was wintry and wet, and at least her *civet* warmed me from the inside out.

That evening I drove farther south through a thick fog to Roanne, where I had the good fortune to dine in the kitchen of the Troisgros brothers' restaurant. It was fascinating, observing the battery of chefs in their white toques, highly organized, each with one specific task, everything handled with calm precision. Jean Troisgros announced that he had prepared something special for us that was not on the menu, *civet de lièvre*. His was not overcooked. Nor was his blood sauce the color of melted chocolate. The *civet* was actually quite fine in his version, but it is a hearty dish, no matter how delicate the cook's touch.

The next morning the sun came out and the dew-covered Côte Chalonnaise was radiantly beautiful. I drove up to Volnay in the Côte d'Or where I tasted with one of my producers. Then he invited me to select a vintage to uncork with lunch. We moved upstairs into the dining room and sat down to a huge platter of *civet de lièvre*.

My stomach spoke very clearly to me. "No," it said.

I picked up my silverware as eagerly as possible, tried to force my eyes aglow with delight, smiled greenly, and said, "Ooh, la la, I love *civet*," or something like that.

Alas, the poor hare had been horribly mistreated, first by the hunter who ended its life, then by Madame the cook, who had transformed its flesh into a dry, sawdustlike texture and its blood into a sauce as clotted as it was insipid. My system allowed three bites, three desperate swallows, then refused to consider anything more.

"You don't like it?" Madame asked, horrified.

With perspiration breaking out on my forehead and upper lip, I told them about my three *civets* within twenty-four hours, hopelessly attempting to excuse my . . . whatever is the opposite of appetite.

Her *civet* was lousy and she knew it and her husband knew it, but I could have smoothed everything over if only I could have taken a polite nibble every so often, but I could not even look at my plate. I thought to at least rub my bread in her sauce, go through the motions, but when I envisioned it I almost had to jump up from the table. I wore a smile and swirled a 1964 Volnay and tried not to see their forks rising to their mouths.

Once outside the limits of the Côte Chalonnaise, its Chardonnays from Montagny, Givry, Mercurey, Rully, or Bouzeron are regarded as substitute wines, uncorked when the occasion does not merit or the pocketbook does not permit an expensive Meursault, Puligny, or Chassagne. H. W. Yoxall, the English author, called the Chalonnais whites "acceptable," a choice of adjective that is not going to cause a buyers' stampede. In *The Wines of Burgundy*, which was for years the only book available in English about Burgundy, Yoxall wrote, "Their bottlings should be markedly less expensive than those of the Côte d'Or; otherwise they would not be worth importing—though they are pleasant for local drinking." Local drinking. If I read that in one more wine book, I may be arrested for the world's first corkscrew murder.

I have developed a soft spot for the wines of the Chalonnais, particularly the Montagny *blanc* and the Aligoté from Bouzeron. How many people might, like myself, finish by uncorking many more bottles of Chalonnais whites than the bigger, more serious whites of the Côte d'Or had they not been put off by Yoxall's snobbish, wrong-headed attitude. Montagny does not and should not try to taste like Meursault. It has its own charm, thank goodness.

The Parisian wine merchant Jean-Baptiste Chaudet confessed in his autobiography:

> In all sincerity I came to prefer [Chalonnais whites] to the *grand crus* because they are lighter, more ethereal, and easier to digest. I am, I must say, a big eater, and I like to drink well and quench my thirst. I perceived that during a meal it was

valuable to have this type of wine on the table, wines which do not oblige you to put on the brakes. Aside from that, the prices were more interesting. A low price does not mean that a wine is bad. And the opposite is equally true, an expensive wine is not necessarily better.

Chaudet was no wine snob, no status seeker. He liked to drink good wine, he had his preferences, and if they happened to be cheaper, so much the better.

How tempting Montagny sounds when described by the French writer Pierre Brejoux in *Les Vins de Bourgogne*: "Their golden green color, their fine bouquet, their taste of hazelnut, and their lightness, so appreciated in a white wine, make them seductive wines which go down easily and leave you clearheaded."

Wine buyers who end up agreeing with Brejoux and Chaudet have money to save and pleasures to discover. And while all my wine books claim that Montagny does not age well, in 1984 I had a 1966 that stole the show at a three-star dinner at the Lameloise Restaurant in nearby Chagny. The Chalonnais is full of such happy surprises.

Another white that is not purported to age with dignity is the Bourgogne Aligoté. Come to think of it, dignity and Aligoté are not normally mentioned in the same breath. To most wine buyers, Aligoté suggests a sharp, bare-boned wine that needs a shot of cassis syrup to flesh it out and make it palatable. One of my most embarrassing faux pas involved an Aligoté. In 1974 I tasted through the cellar of Aubert de Villaine in Bouzeron, the last wine village before one enters the Côte d'Or. I told him I had recently discovered an excellent *crème de cassis*, and with his Aligoté I would have the ingredients for a fine Kir to propose to my clients. His expression turned as sour as a bad Aligoté. It would be unfortunate, he informed me politely through clenched teeth, to obscure the quality of his Aligoté by pouring *crème de cassis* into it. Oops.

He was right, and thankfully he overlooked my naïveté. I have continued importing his Bourgogne Aligoté de Bouzeron ever since, and de Villaine has come up with some notable successes. One even aged well.

Traditionally, Aligoté was celebrated for its precociousness. The Burgundians drank all of it themselves, drawn right out of the barrel, while it was still full of gunk, funk, and fizz. It was the drink in the local bars, cafés, and bistros, the perfect accompaniment for regional specialties like parsleyed ham and garlicky snails. Aligoté is by no means a wine that is expected to last, much less improve in bottle, but in 1979 de Villaine came up with something special.

First, his grapes came from the stony Bouzeron slopes, the only village deemed worthy enough to broadcast its name on an Aligoté label. From a parcel of seventy-year-old vines he barrel-fermented the juice without chaptalization. It was bottled directly from the barrel, unfiltered. Nothing added, nothing taken out! Every last bottle was necessary to fill my fifty-case order. It was a striking wine, with depth, balance, and a delicious aroma reminiscent of fresh pear and pear skin.

I saved a few bottles just to see what might develop. Every time I opened one, rather than beginning to deteriorate, the wine continued to improve. In 1986 I served my last bottle of 1979 to de Villaine and his wife when they visited California. Some creature in my cellar had devoured the label, so the de Villaines could not see what it was they were tasting. I asked what they thought it might be. At first sniff Mme de Villaine, an excellent taster, said that it showed some of the aromatic richness of a white Hermitage! Her husband said no, it was not from the south, it was more Burgundian. It might be a Meursault, but no, there was that firmness, that structure, that stony aftertaste. It might be a Chablis . . . ?

It was still alive and really, well, quite grand in its way. A mere Aligoté. But if you are looking for great Burgundy, there is your recipe: a careful winemaker, old hillside vines, traditional vinification without excess chaptalization, then bottled unfiltered.

The recipe works for Pinot Noir, too. No grape is more sensitive to its vineyard site. In France, the Côte Chalonnaise is really the only place outside the Côte d'Or that produces worth-while Pinot Noir. Rully, Givry, and Mercurey have excellent *cuveés*, and Chalonnais reds labeled Bourgogne have the possibility to be more interesting than Bourgogne from the Côte d'Or itself, because most Côte d'Or Bourgogne is from flatland vines while Côte Chalonnaise bottlings are likely to be from hillsides. A Chalonnais Bourgogne *rouge* might be lighter in body, but it can be more expressive, with more personality, and these are certainly the world's most rewarding Pinot Noirs for the budget-conscious.

The fact remains, for the great growths of Burgundy one goes to the gentle slopes of the Côte d'Or, a long thin strip of vineyard that cannot supply the world with enough of its inimitable, incomparable nectar.

If I am pessimistic because of certain lamentable trends in the northern Rhône and genocide in the Beaujolais, where an entire race of wine has been snuffed out, I am an optimist about red Burgundy. Certainly, the odds are still against stumbling across a great bottle at the corner liquor store (even after you hand over a day's wages for it), but there is much more good Burgundy available to us now than there was fifteen years ago.

Good red Burgundy is the most captivating wine in the world. I have a friend who has a perfect cellar: dark, damp, and cold. While keeping corks nice and plump, the ample moisture also destroys wine labels, so he marks each bottle with chalk in order to keep track of what is what. Once he brought up a label-less bottle and announced that he had no idea what it contained, but if it turned out to be unpalatable, he would bring up something else. He decanted our mystery wine and poured it into our glasses. It was light ruby, with shimmering glints of this color and that. The bottle shape was Burgundian and so was its magical aroma, evoking a response like the first hearing of a Bach piece, that awe that something so extraordinary can exist, something man-made. Well, it drove us crazy, not knowing what we had in our glasses. Was it Côte de Beaune or Côte de Nuits? Vosne or Chambolle? Beaumonts or Malconsorts, or one of the Echézeaux? And if it was Beaumonts, who vinified it, and when? Only with Burgundy do the details matter so passionately . . . so *horribly* when you have a great one and there is no way to know what it is. Others have made beautiful Pinot Noirs, but none arouse the passions like a true Burgundy. And no other wine seems so French. California has produced some remarkable bottles, but California Pinot Noir is to Burgundy what the Empire State Building is to the Notre-Dame.

Now, the Burgundian as a character type is the most intricate in France, a type that ends by tying my mind up in knots. After I spend three weeks working in Burgundy, my composure is fragile; I feel like a bundle of mental twitches and glitches. However, upon arrival, I have noticed in myself an eager "leaping into the fray" attitude: *en garde,* thrust, parry, watch the rear, *touché!* Burgundy is a sort of testing ground. One cannot say anything or take anything said lightly. One's every word and gesture will be examined microscopically for the telling nuance. Even when a Burgundian asks with a warm smile, "How are you?" the antennae are out, the cerebral computer is plugged in, and even if you reply "Fine," your slightest inflection is noticed, inspected, measured, interpreted.

Aha, he looked away when he said he is fine. He could not look me in the eye. Is there something he does not want me to know, something he is hiding? He is not with his wife this time. Something may be bothering him about his marriage . . .

"And how is Madame?" he will ask you, hoping to bring out some further little morsel to gnaw on.

All this is fatiguing day after day, yet it is the nitty-gritty of doing business in Burgundy. They cannot help themselves. They would have an easier time trying to control their heartbeat.

Perhaps you just finished reading the *Herald Tribune* about the Bhopal catastrophe or a terrorist bombing in a crowded airport, so you answer absentmindedly, "What, oh yes, Madame is fine."

He seems gloomy about his wife. If his marriage is in trouble, what if there is a divorce? What if his alimony payments put him in a squeeze financially? He looks tired, older somehow. Maybe it is taking a toll on him psychologically. I remember the Duc de Framboise, who had a nervous breakdown when his wife deserted him for the Peugeot mechanic, and his creditors closed him down just like that. I'd better cut down his quantities this year, or, better yet, demand payment in advance.

So you must be constantly on guard lest your nuances be misinterpreted. Relaxing can be costly.

I always take a deep breath when I enter Burgundy. It is the most difficult wine to buy and its winemakers the most difficult to deal with. They are never happy. There is always too much rain or not enough, too much sun (rare, but I have heard the complaint) or not enough. I want to buy too much of one growth and not enough of another. I want to ship too soon or not soon enough, pay too early (rare, but I have heard the complaint) or too late. I want more wine than last year, or less. Or I arrive to taste when they should be out pruning their vines, and so on and on and on. It must be their horrid climate, rain, hail, fog, thunder, and lightning, frosts and snow, that makes them so ornery.

Making Burgundy, buying Burgundy, what agony: the

weather, the *petit* quantities, the prices, the vintages, the journalists assigning numbers to them as if they were grading term
papers, the mistaken notion that big is better, the infinite occasions for this most fragile of wines to be spoiled somehow
before it is uncorked. . . . Burgundy, source of the highest highs
and the most expensive depressions. If you do not believe me,
take a look at November 17, 1985, a day in the life of an importer
of small-*domaine* Burgundies:

I have three growers to see in Savigny-les-Beaune before lunch.
The first rendezvous is at 8:30 a.m. The morning is gray, frigid,
and gusty. Better wear two pair of wool socks; those cellar floors
are as cold as ice.

Monsieur L. has been a dependable supplier for years. His is
the most popular Savigny I import. He has a taste for new oak,
so he raises each and every vintage in new barrels. For me his
wine is too oaky, but that is my personal taste; his is good
wine and my clients adore it. His cellar is under his home and
you descend a steep stairway to enter it, bending your body
almost double lest you crack your noggin on the arched stone
doorway.

"*Attention à la tête*," he says. *Watch out for your head.* It sounds
so much like a recording, I wonder how many times in his life
he has repeated it as he leads his customers down to taste.

The *cave* is rectangular, with a gravel floor, crowded with
around thirty barrels along the walls and down the center. The
bright raw oak is stained purple here and there with splotches
of new wine.

He dips his thief into a barrel and draws out a taste of the
new vintage, 1985, just two months old. But wait, the 1985s
I have seen so far have been well colored. His is pale. I am even
more astonished by the aroma. There is little there except the
smell of new oak and something leafy or herbaceous. Where is
the wine smell?

"Have you changed something," I inquire, "something in your
vinification?"

He shakes his head no, but he won't look me in the eye and

I catch a glimpse of a mischievous smile replacing his normally dour expression.

"It is different this year," I say. "There is something, I am not sure what . . ."

"If I tell you what I changed, you will say that my wine tastes different," he says, "but I assure you, it is the same wine as always."

I smile and swirl and sniff. "What *is* different?" I ask in my friendly, just-one-of-the-guys voice.

"One sole difference. It was harvested by a mechanical harvester," he confesses proudly, as if he is the avant-garde. "I went in on one with three of my neighbors."

He proceeds to explain why. He is near retirement, growing tired of the work, and the team of harvesters each year is too much bother. You must feed them lunch every day, and then there is all the paperwork because you must treat each harvester as an honest-to-God employee, paying social security to the government, taking out insurance on every one of them even though they work for only one week . . . "And," he concludes, "no one can tell any difference in the wine."

There he is kidding himself. For the first time I leave his cellar without reserving a single barrel. It is a sad, terrible feeling, and the gray sky outside matches my mood. I know I will not see him again. A mechanical harvester! For Pinot Noir! At Savigny-les-Beaune! However, a twinge of my own future obsolescence shivers through my veins. More and more I feel as if what I am operating is not a business but a Preservation Society.

The next stop is a first-time, exploratory visit. After so many years, my first impression upon entering a cellar tells me a lot, and there are some promising signs here. My eyes light up when I spot an oak fermenter and an old oak press. Euphoria is dampened by the first wine tasted, a Bourgogne *blanc*, a barrel-fermented *cuvée* which already seems tired two months after birth. Then the winemaker offers a taste of the same wine out of stainless steel. It is fresh and tasty, and I feel a little flutter. I would buy this one.

§ *229* §

Next he pulls out a taste of Savigny *blanc*. I have always liked Savigny's white. While it never shows the nobility of a Puligny- or Chassagne-Montrachet, this is Burgundy from another angle, with the accent on its earthy, rustic soul. His is still fermenting, but it looks promising.

As the tasting proceeds, we change cellars again and again, up stairs and down, an underground tour of Savigny-les-Beaune.

His Savigny *villages* is full of sap and all in all, a very successful *cuvée*.

His 1985 *premier cru*, "Serpentières," is brash and wild, and I like it.

There is a fruity Savigny "Lavières," and, from a cellar about the size of my hotel room, a long, pretty Savigny "Les Verge-lesses" with extraordinary Pinot Noir fruit.

Then, for the first time in my career, I taste a Beaune "Le Genêt," from a tiny *premier cru* vineyard surrounded by "Clos du Roi," "Marconnets," and "Les Cents Vignes." Rounder than his Savignys, it is more dignified a wine with a velvety texture.

I feel better. *Au revoir* to Monsieur L. and his damnable har-vesting machine that cannot sort out the grapes from the grape leaves. Have I already found a replacement for his Savigny *rouge,* plus three different Savigny *premiers crus* and a seldom seen Beaune *premier cru,* not to mention the two whites?

What does he have for sale now, today?

"The 1983s are in bottle."

All right! The journalists have stirred up a hurricane force demand for the 1983 vintage. I have the clients if he has the wine.

He uncorks and pours his 1983 Savigny *rouge.* It is pale orange. There is no aroma. It seems to exhale only a pathetic sigh of fatigue.

His 1983 Savigny "Les Serpentières" tastes the same.

The 1983 Beaune "Le Gênet," exactly the same.

"Wait," I say, spirit deflated, "these seem so unlike your wines in barrel. What do you do when you bottle them?"

"I don't bottle them myself. I hired a bottling company from Beaune to do it."

More and more small growers, who previously sold their wine in barrel to *négociants*, have begun *"domaine* bottling," but lacking the equipment and know-how, they avail themselves of the services of mobile bottling vans, which back up to the cellar door and run their hoses down to where the wine is. Thus, they truthfully can say *mise au domaine* (bottled at the *domaine*), although *mise au camion* (bottled at the truck) would be more precise.

"They must have given them a pretty strong filtration. Were they as dark as your 1985s before the bottling?"

"The 1983? Almost black. They do two filtrations, one by *kieselguhr* [diatomaceous earth] for the larger particles, then by sterile membrane for security."

"Security?"

"To guarantee nothing will go bad in the bottle."

It is difficult not to burst out laughing. Talk about *bad in the bottle*! There we stand, surrounded by stacks and stacks of cartons of his pale, feeble, thoroughly deceased 1983s. I sense that he knows his '83s have been trashed, but he says nothing, hoping I might buy them anyway. I tell him there is no need to pull more corks, that I have seen enough. I advise him to bottle his beautiful 1985s himself; why not ask one of the old-timers in the village how the bottling used to be done before the enologist-entrepreneurs arrived, selling security from the back of a van.

The Pichenot brothers' cellar will be the last stop in Savigny before I break for lunch and head north into the Côte de Nuits. Before they began bottling for me, they sold all their production to *négociants*. They work two *premier cru* vineyards, "En Grevains" and "Les Serpentières," both on the Pernand/Corton side of the village. Usually I ask them to blend the two together, because the blend seems more complete than either one alone. Each year they put a small percentage into new barrels, so I am able to season my blend with what I consider to be the proper proportion of new oak. I like the way their wine smells, the expansiveness of it, the solid Pinot quality, some earthiness, a little reminder of the barnyard, a hint of black pepper, its candid, rustic charm. Too much oak would mask that flawless expression of Savigny-les-Beaune's unique *goût de terroir*.

The Pichenot brothers are in their fifties, two bachelors who never left home, who still live with their widowed mother. The two have developed the same mannerisms, the same expressions. They are farmers, down-home types. In the United States, some might call them yokels. Beaune is only five kilometers away, but I have the impression that a trip to Beaune is an event, and that they know little of the world outside their cellar and their rows of vines.

Their 1985 is succulent. I am especially enthused by "Les Serpentières."

"Oh, listen," they seem to say in unison, "if you bring in grapes like that, you can't make shit."

Having always loved the vineyard name, "Les Serpentières," which goes back to at least the thirteenth century, I ask if they know its origin.

"There are a lot of vipers there."

"Not really. There in the vineyard?"

"It's true. Just ten days ago a young woman was bitten and spent a day in the hospital."

Their 1985 "Serpentières" will not bite. It is fleshy, velvety, and altogether delicious, with that Savigny blend of berry and earth. Before genius and technology set in, everyone in Burgundy made their wine pretty much like the Pichenot brothers do. They are not creators of new techniques. Their "secret": a low yield, grapes as healthy as possible, vinified in wood, the wine not put through wild gyrations of temperature or clarification, aged in barrel underground where it is moist and cold, bottled unfiltered when the moon says it is time. Above all, baby it along while following tradition.

The traditional vinification of each French wine region, each *terroir,* allowed the *terroir* to speak in the wine. Modern techniques

The Brothers Pichenot.

Savigny-les-Beaune

destroy or mask this originality in the name of security. Instead of a winemaker making his wine as he learned from his family, nowadays it is more often than not an enologist who makes the decisions. How did these people who received passing grades in chemistry classes gain control over the taste of our wine? Few of them know how to taste, or care how a wine tastes, as long as the analysis is correct. And most of them sell products to correct wines that do not conform to their laboratory "ideal," which seems to be a conflict of interest, like a physician prescribing drugs who also happens to be a pharmacist. They feel secure with a sterile wine. I say if it is sterile it is not wine. Let us come up with another name for those grape-based drinks. Wine is alive.

Both Pichenots wear an "aw, shucks" expression while I praise their 1985. Then I say that I would like to increase my order over last year's. Both begin kicking at the gravel cellar floor and shaking their heads distressfully, saying, *"Ooh la la, ça? Ay yi yi."*

"Is there a problem?" I ask.

It turns out that the *négociants* took a strong stand on the 1985s, meaning they ordered a lot, early, at high prices. Two months after the harvest, only three barrels (nine hundred bottles) of Pichenot Savigny-les-Beaune remain unsold. I practically go through the vaulted stone ceiling, but all my anger and arguments are in vain. They are not businessmen, and they are accustomed to selling to the first buyer who wants their wine. In their opinion, I arrived too late, and that is all there is to it.

In fact, the transition from selling in barrel to selling in bottle is not a simple matter for the growers, and the Pichenots remain uncomfortable with the idea, because by selling their 1985 to a *négociant* they will receive payment in three parts, the total by June 1986. Selling in bottle, they must raise the wine sixteen months in barrel, bottle and label it, and they will not be paid until January 1988. Even though they receive more money for the wine in bottle than they would by the barrel, it is a difficult economic and psychological transition for a small farmer to make.

* * *

After lunch I drive up to Gevrey-Chambertin to the Domaine G., anxious to retaste his 1983 Gevrey-Chambertin, one of the most memorable young Burgundies in my experience. I had already presold every last bottle of my reservation in advance. In the offer to my clients I wrote:

> Domaine G. has old vines, the so-called Pinot *fin* as opposed to the new clonal selections that are taking over the Burgundy vineyards. It is a small dark grape with concentrated flavors. Whereas Château d'Yquem goes to great lengths to select only rotten grapes, G. painstakingly sorts his out by hand to include only the healthiest berries. They are vinified in the old style, fined with egg whites *if necessary,* and bottled unfiltered. His 1983 is almost black, quite tannic, with enormous potential. The nose is thick, dramatic, beautiful.

Even though G.'s is a *village* Gevrey, all the factors combine to produce a wine that is a match for most of the *grand cru* Chambertins I have tasted.

We begin with his 1985, which consists of about a dozen barrels, marked by a *V* in chalk along a pretty, mold-covered stone wall. As we taste I inquire, "What does the V signify?"

"*Vendu.*"

"*Vendu?*"

"*Oui, vendu.*"

Vendu means "sold." I count down the row of barrels. "They are not all sold?" My brain will not accept the inevitable Vs right down to the last barrel.

"Yes, I received an excellent offer from a consortium of bankers from Holland, Belgium, Germany, and Switzerland."

My life is not complicated enough. Now I must compete for wine with a bankers' consortium. "You saved nothing for me?"

He is a young fellow, slightly nervous, but without a shadow of compunction on his stony face.

"I would have liked to, but I did not know when you would

come, or if you would buy, and they put the money on the table, a fabulous price, so I had to take it."

We taste his 1984s. I had reserved four barrels. It is a lovely piece of work, light and fine, discreetly chaptalized to 12 degrees instead of the 13 degrees and 13.5 degrees that weighed down so many 1984s. The Gevrey *terroir* is very clearly expressed in the delicate aroma. But the difference between selling a 1984 and a 1985 . . . The wine journalists had decided 1984s were not worth buying, so it would be necessary to find those clients who do not believe everything they read and who have a palate fine enough and independent enough to appreciate the delicate beauty of the 1984s. In other words, 1984 would be hard work, while the 1985s would sell themselves. I tell G. that I will take an equal number of barrels of 1984 and 1985.

"But there are no more 1985s," he says.

"Then we will forget 1984 and taste that 1983."

He uncorks it and pours out a rosé-colored thing. *Déjà vu!* I sit staring at my glass as he sniffs at his. I feel as if I am going to lose control and whirl right into outer space.

"What have you done?" I ask.

"Done?"

"This is not the wine I ordered."

"It is, this is the 1983." He turns the bottle to show me the vintage on the label.

"Where is the color? It was black."

"It was recently bottled. The color will come back."

"It will not change back from rosé to black. Where did it go?" I take a sniff. Zero. "Where is the aroma?"

"It will come back."

I take a taste. Zero. "Where is the flavor? The body? This is not the wine I reserved."

He explains that he hired a bottling company from Beaune to bottle his 1983!

"But why? Your own bottlings have always been impeccable. Never a problem."

"No, I did have a problem," he says with an air of serious

concern. "You know that I bottled each barrel by hand, separately, and that there will always be differences from one barrel to another. Well, a restaurant reordered my 1982, then they called to complain that it had a different taste than the first batch. So, they returned the wine to me. I realized that it is better to have uniformity from bottle to bottle. I had to solve the problem. By assembling all the barrels before bottling, I could solve the problem, but I do not own a vat large enough in which to do it. Someone recommended this bottling company in Beaune. I called and they had the equipment necessary to ensure that all the bottles are the same, so I had them bottle it."

"You allowed them to ruin your wine because one client complained?" I begin thinking of the people who preordered the wine at home based upon my recommendation, thinking of them uncorking and pouring this pitiful stuff out into their glasses. Sadly I say, "I cannot buy this wine. It is no longer the wine that I reserved."

He draws himself up proudly and says, "That's all right, the bottling company offered to buy it at two francs per bottle more than the price I gave you. You will be doing me a favor if you don't take it."

"The bottling company is buying wine?"

"Yes, they do a lot of export."

I leave, composing a letter of apology in my mind that will accompany the refund I shall have to send to my clients, and hating the thought of what happened to that extraordinary Gevrey-Chambertin. The filter sopped up one of the finest red Burgundies produced in 1983. Domaine G. has an exceptional vineyard, but the winemaker lacks the one essential trait that separates a great winemaker from the rest, pride in what pours from his bottles.

From Gevrey-Chambertin to Morey-Saint-Denis and the Domaine Ponsot is a two-minute passage through some of Burgundy's most sacred ground: Mazis, Clos de Bèze, Chapelle and Griotte, Le Chambertin, Charmes and Latricières, Combottes, and then, without a break in the sweep of vineyard, Clos de la

Roche. After Bandol or Côte Rôtie, the terrain here is far from dramatic, the slope rather gentle, manifesting no outward evidence at all of the resonant splendor of the wines man has learned to inveigle from it year after year, century after century.

For decades the Domaine Ponsot has been producing some of Burgundy's finest bottles, and has been shipping to the United States since Frank Schoonmaker purchased some 1934 Clos de la Roche.

With Jean-Marie Ponsot I need not launch into my antifiltration routine. Here is a Pinot Noir master who believes in tradition, all the while keeping an eye on new techniques, experimenting before judging them pro or con, and the results he obtained by filtration did not impress him.

"Filtration dries out a wine," he told me during one conversation. "It takes out some of the substance and flavor and a part of the perfume. True, you gain clarity, limpidity, but you lose flavor and taste. That's what I found!"

His son, Laurent Ponsot, added that one should not look only at techniques of vinification to explain quality. They would not have the same wine if their yield per hectare were not one of the lowest in Burgundy, twenty-one hectoliters per hectare in 1985, only eighteen in 1983!

Today turns out to be the wrong day for a visit. When we enter his cellar, there is an overwhelming odor of fuel oil. During the night a canister of the stuff, which is used for home-heating systems, developed a leak and the smell remains in the air, making it impossible to taste even when we take a glass out into the street. Tasting wine is really smelling wine; the primary function of the palate is to register balance. Now the fuel oil has temporarily obliterated our sense of smell, which means that I shall have to return another day to the Domaine Ponsot, and that for once I will be on time to a day's final appointment.

Henri Jayer lives five minutes away, in a modest, rather modern house just off the *route nationale* in Vosne-Romanée. Jayer does everything himself, including the work in the vines, so he always prefers that we do our tasting and business after sundown, when he can no longer accomplish anything outdoors. He shakes my hand at the cellar door and we discuss the mass of low black clouds overhead. We can smell the rainfall threatening in the air. Discussing the weather is not small talk to a *vigneron*. It will decide the quality of the product of an entire year's labor as well as how he spends his time working: rain means cellar chores, dry means vineyard duty.

At Vosne-Romanée in the 1980s, after Domaine de la Romanée-Conti, the attention of the wine world has been directed at Henri Jayer and his minuscule production of *premiers* and *grands crus*. He carries his newfound fame with confidence and without pretension. In conversation, one is struck by Jayer's candor and wisdom, and his wines express the same personality. It is difficult to believe that Jayer is in his late sixties. I would have guessed mid-fifties. He will point to his bald head as proof of his age, but his skin is not wrinkled and his eyes remain bright and youthful.

Henri Jayer is one of wine's most lucid intellects, and I often become so engrossed by our conversation that I neglect to keep track of the wines we are tasting. When he criticizes today's *"vins standards"* or *"vins techniques,"* he finds in me a receptive audience. He says that fewer and fewer winemakers are willing to take the risks it requires to make wine in the traditional way, and he warns that enology is replacing the artistic side of winemaking.

"Once upon a time," he says, "not so long ago, the *négociants* would taste the wine for sale. If it was good, they took it; if not, they left it. Now it is an analysis that says: there is such and such a level of acidity, such and such a level of volatility, the malolactic fermentation is finished or not. That is how they buy now. It is no longer based on taste, which is sad.

"We tend to count too much on science, where, before, people gave importance to natural things. One thing is certain, the ancients were not dumb, and if they established a tradition it was because of their experience. They tried to eliminate unfavorable elements and preserve what worked best.

"Now there is no longer that shared experience. No one talks together in the vineyard. That changes everything. We used to know each other well. We used to walk to work together through the vineyards. At 7 a.m., we were out in the vines. At nine, we all shared a snack. Someone brought some sausage, a little cheese, a bottle of wine. We discussed everything. Why does this plant give smaller grapes than that one? Why are his leaves green and healthy and his yellow? Now we pass each other in our cars on the way to work. We honk. In the vineyard we are up on our tractors, which make so much noise no one can talk.

"It is the modern world and the wine has changed with it. Today's average quality is perhaps superior, I'm not sure, but we do not reach the summits that we used to.

"The Pinot Noir is the most beautiful grape variety which exists, and if everyone envies us for it, that tells you something. Unfortunately for the others, the Pinot made its home here in Burgundy, and this is where it expresses itself best. It is a delicate little beast, the Pinot; it needs sunshine but not too much, rainfall but not too much. It is complex, all this, but it is here that the Pinot found the microclimate that suits it best. Above all, Pinot Noir means Burgundy. They make Pinot Noir elsewhere, but it is not the same.

"Black is not the color of Burgundy. You must be able to see through a glass of it. The Pinot has a pretty robe, glistening and shimmering like a cat's eyes, sparkling like a diamond. It is a wine that enchants with its perfume. It must be fine and elegant, which does not exclude a solid structure. For me, a perfect Pinot is an alliance between great finesse and a tannin present but not dominant.

"What I love here in Burgundy is the diversity of styles from one cellar to another. But we are losing that diversity with these *vins standards*. They are perfect, perfectly neutral, worthless. Oh, a lot of the restaurants like them because they won't receive any complaints. No compliments, no complaints. But the day we have nothing but *vins standards* we are going to be bored stiff."

After two hours talking and tasting, I am ready to leave, having reserved the maximum quantities available to me of Jayer's 1983 vintage:

15 cases Nuits-Saint-Georges "Les Meurgers"
10 cases Vosne-Romanée "Cros Parantoux"
10 cases Vosne-Romanée "Les Brûlées"
15 cases Vosne-Romanée "Les Beaumonts"
25 cases Echézeaux
 2 cases Richebourg

Shaking hands goodbye, he looks slightly embarrassed, like someone who screwed up a wine by forgetting to top up the barrel. Then he announces his future retirement from winemaking. I feel like someone whose heart suddenly forgets to beat.

"I'm sixty-five years old," he says. "Everyone has to quit some-day . . ."

"You look younger than I do," I say.

"If you look at the life expectancy in France, on the average of course, I have seven more years to live. So I think it is time for me to stop and profit a little from my work."

"What will you do? You'll be bored."

"Isn't it better to quit while holding your head up high than to wait too long and get sacked?" he asks, smiling. "Don't worry, there will be some '85s, some '86s. I still have some time to go."

Driving back to my hotel room in Beaune, eager for nothing more fancy than to prop my feet up on the furnace because two pair of wool socks could not withstand the cellar chill, I ask myself what was accomplished during the day. Seventy-five cases of Savigny-les-Beaune, seventy-seven cases assorted Jayer, one producer lost to the dread mechanical harvester, another to the Beaune bottler, and the prospect of a future without the wines of Henri Jayer. At this rate, I will not be flying home first-class.

Certainly, not every day is equally insufferable as November 17, 1985, but working Burgundy is a sacred chore, with its fair share of idiots and whores and incomparable satisfactions. After fifteen years, my Burgundy list is only thirty growers long, and that includes the Côte d'Or, Chalonnais, and Mâconnais vineyards. Unearthing its rare gems there is a reward that does not show up on the profit-and-loss sheet.

Jayer spoke about wine having an artistic side. Some dismiss the notion of wine as art, but if we can simplify such an endlessly disputed subject as aesthetics, we might agree that creating a thing of beauty is a legitimate artistic goal. People like Jayer are trying to create something beautiful, beautiful to the eye, the smell, the taste, the intellect, the spirit. Isak Dinesen went so far as to say, "There are many ways to the recognition of truth, and Burgundy is one of them."

From behind the sales counter I see firsthand how people buy red Burgundy, and I find some of the tactics puzzling.

When I was growing up in California during the fifties, automobiles were the indicators of income and status. If you could afford a new one every year, you bought one. If you could afford a Pontiac, you did not buy a Chevy. If you could afford a Buick, you were not in a Pontiac. And if your pocketbook permitted, you drove a Cadillac, because it was the top of the line, what people aimed for. Red Burgundy is not like that. Even if one can afford Chambertin every night, that would be wrong-headed and self-defeating because of other pleasures missed.

Nor is red Burgundy, even with its *grands crus* and *premiers crus,* like airline seating's first, business, and economy class. First class is more comfortable than economy. If you can afford it, fly in comfort. Burgundy is more like music. Is a Wagner opera better than a Mozart divertimento? "Better for what?" is the only sensible answer. Is Chambertin better than Savigny-les-Beaune? Better for what? Whose Savigny, whose Chambertin? Because it is very possible that a good vintner's Savigny will be even grander than a lousy vintner's Chambertin. What plate will your Burgundy accompany? What is the occasion, the setting? In Burgundy, you cannot talk about a "best" wine. Such an ideal bottle that all the others are trying to imitate does not exist. Every bottle does not want to be the same. Diversity is one of the qualities that make Burgundy glorious.

The truth is, you cannot know in advance if it will be a Savigny or a Chambertin, for example, which will linger in your memory after it is gone. Wine's pleasures may be transitory in the sense that the wine is consumed, but the memory of it can endure. For me, a Pommard 1964 stands out above all the other wines that I enjoyed during a certain period of my life. Over a number of years, I must have gone through three or four cases of it. A Pommard, even though certain wine critics have not been kind.

ANTHONY HANSON : "I avoid Pommard like the plague."
HUGH JOHNSON : ". . . the least wonderful and the best known of the villages of Burgundy."
H. W. YOXALL : ". . . pleasant drinks without much authority . . . light in body . . . not very exciting . . ."

As I say, you cannot know in advance which red Burgundy will zing your strings, and the critics' taste will not always follow your own.

Then how should one enter the complex world of red Burgundy? I would advise a full case, twelve bottles of a single wine, a Savigny or Pernand, a Mercurey or Rully, something like that. Go through the case, bottle by bottle, before moving on to another. Unless it is flawed of course, do not judge it one way or another. Rather, listen to it, see what it has to say, get to know it. Next try one of the *premier cru* vineyards from Volnay or Pommard, Chambolle or Nuits for example, always listening to the wine instead of imposing upon it your own preconceptions. What does the Volnay *premier cru* say that the Savigny did not, and vice versa. Next splurge on some bottles of a *grand cru* like Clos de la Roche, Echézeaux, or one of the Chambertins, and see what it has to say. Afterward you will be in a position to taste a bottle of Burgundy and enjoy it for what it is, with an open mind, looking for pleasure instead of a numerical rating.

§ 243 §

Then I suggest sampling releases from various Burgundian *domaines*. Do some research. Try to ascertain if your wine merchant stocks natural Burgundies that have been shipped and stored properly. When you find a grower whose wine pleases you, stock a few bottles to drink over several years, and continue to put down his wine in each vintage. Remember, even the winemaker is never certain how each vintage will evolve (the vintage charts continue to undervalue 1972 red Burgundies, a vintage that produced some of my favorites), and a talented winemaker will come up with something worth tasting every year. Do not spread yourself too thin, trying to get a bit of everything. Concentrate on the great talents year after year and your pleasure of the wines will be deepened and more intimate.

Stock more of the lesser *appellations* than you do the great growths, because they are more useful, more frequently appropriate.

Do not demand thick, heavy Burgundy. More often than not, this is a sign of overchaptalization. Instead, look for personality, aroma, lucidity, finesse, wonder, and magic.

The Côte d'Or is largely, almost exclusively, planted in Pinot Noir until you arrive at Meursault, Puligny, and Chassagne, today's great white Burgundy villages. Here are the Chardonnays that launched a thousand Chardonnays, which all the wine-producing countries of the world desire to emulate.

A mere century ago these whites were even rarer because large portions of Puligny and Chassagne were planted in red grapes. One old French text contains the remarkable statement:

> If one makes an exception of the vineyards producing the great white wines of Montrachet and Bâtard-Montrachet, one finds at Chassagne only a few plots planted here and there in Chardonnay. Above all, the Pinot Noir is cultivated there and from time immemorial it is the red wines which have created the reputation of this excellent *terroir*. (!)

Try telling that to today's wine snobs who treat red Chassagne like some kind of bastard wine that has no right to exist.

In the old records of the Marquis de Laguiche one finds the stupefying stipulation that "one gives one bottle of Chassagne 'Morgeots' *rouge* for two bottles of Le Montrachet." (!!) Nowadays I question whether a dozen *rouge* would earn you one Montrachet. Is wine fad-prone?

Puligny-Montrachet "Pucelles," "Clavaillon," "Caillerets," and "Blagny" were producing red Burgundy. In 1855 J. Lavalle wrote that the reds of Puligny could equal the best of the Côte de Beaune. Now Puligny is so lily-white that one cannot find a bottle of red to judge for oneself.

Strangely enough, Puligny-Montrachet today is probably the hippest name of the three notorious white-Burgundy villages, and yet I have found many more successful *cuvées* at Meursault, not because of a superior *terroir,* but because of matters of vinification. *Domaine* bottling is very recent at Puligny due to its water table, which does not permit the growers to dig deep enough to construct subterranean cellars. Consequently, their wines had to be sold off in barrel to the *négociants* before warm weather came along each spring and harmed the wines. Does this explain why few growers at Puligny have mastered the art of bottling? Puligny *blanc* is said to be more tender, more civilized than Meursault or Chassagne, but to me it too often seems more bland than tender, as if the men in white lab coats had once more intruded at bottling time.

By contrast, Meursault has a healthy tradition of small-grower, estate-bottled wines. The town is built upon a warren of wine cellars. It is easier to find Meursaults intact in bottle, undiminished by the bottling process, than it is at Puligny.

Meursault has been kind to me over the years. I have worked with a number of proud growers, each with his distinctive style, each with plots of vineyard in several different sections of the slope, so that Meursault has become in my mind a mosaic of friendly faces, cellars, and wines.

It would be difficult to explain to someone who has never

tasted the wines just how enchanting Burgundy's diversity can be. At Meursault, producing classic, definitive Meursaults, you find such extreme opposites as Bernard Michelot and François Jobard. I mean, you taste their two wines and both taste like Meursault, they could not be anything else, and yet the two wines are as different as the two growers' personalities.

Bernard Michelot is short, husky, and expansive. François Jobard is short, lean, skull-faced.

When he conducts a tasting, Michelot plays to the crowd with a smile as ready as Ronald Reagan's. Jobard has that Jimmy Carter–like discomfort around people.

Michelot is irrepressible and uninhibited. Once I arrived to hear him describe his bypass surgery in dramatic detail, including a show-stopping finale when he yanked up his shirt to reveal the fresh scar. Jobard would be the last person to pull up his shirt in public. Given his reticence, I cannot imagine him even mentioning surgery were he to undergo it.

Michelot is a Souza march, or one of those blasting, blaring, Burgundian hunting-horn fanfares. Jobard is a string quartet, fastidious, meticulous, alert to every nuance, prickling under the skin.

The two cellars are contrasts as well. Meursault is small, population 1,750, but its narrow streets wind this way and that so unpredictably that one is easily lost and confused. But Michelot's cellar is on Meursault's main street, easy to spot, and he can usually be found underground in the midst of old mold-covered bottles, pouring tastes for visitors. If you arrive soon after the harvest, it is not unusual to descend into a comfortable warmth, because Michelot has equipped his cellar with a heating system, enabling him to speed up the alcoholic and malolactic fermentations when he desires.

An appointment must be fixed with Jobard. If not, he will be out in his vineyard with his wife, working the vines. His cellar is under their home at the end of a hard-to-find dead-end street. His is the coldest cellar I have experienced in the Côte d'Or, which must explain why his wines develop so slowly. The tem-

Bernard Michelot's cellar

perature slows down everything. He has about the same proportion of new oak as Michelot, but Michelot's Meursaults taste oakier, so warmth must boost oak extraction.

Michelot knows what he wants from his Meursaults, and his vinification imprints them with the Michelot style. As soon as they have zipped through their two fermentations, they taste good and they taste Michelot.

With François Jobard you have the impression that he is waiting, allowing each wine to reveal itself unhurriedly as it develops in that icy *cave,* and he is reluctant to interfere or to influence it. There are always stubborn *cuvées* that will not finish their fermentation, but he is not going to beat them into shape. Of course, just as in raising children, Jobard's vigilant fastidiousness and patient noninterference shape the personality of his wine as much as Michelot's take-charge approach does his.

One of Jobard's most memorable wines is his 1984 Meursault-Blagny. A wine of limpid brilliance, the nose is pure, classic Meursault, and a whiff of it takes me right back to the village and Jobard's cellar; there is peach skin, stone, freshly crushed grape skins, toast, and hazelnut. A wine with a haunting, exquisite beauty, it is a marvel of grace and finesse. It will evolve very slowly over the years, retaining a freshness of aroma that is part of the Jobard trademark.

Of the tens of thousands of wines I have tasted, Michelot produced one of a handful that remain vividly alive in my memory. During one of my initial trips to France, in 1974 or 1975, I was dining at Le Vieux Moulin out past Savigny-les-Beaune in Bouilland. In those days the chef offered a hot rabbit terrine in a pastry crust with a black truffle sauce. I recall the waiter (who, strangely enough, resembled François Jobard) because he glowed with approval when I ordered the terrine, as if thereby I had exhibited unexpected, even miraculous discernment, and when I asked for the Michelot 1971 Meursault "Genevrières," I thought the waiter was going to orgasm with delight at the sheer genius of my selection. I often think back to that waiter with his beaming eyes and his rare talent. How many waiters (waitpersons, we call them in Berkeley) know how to make a guest feel wise, discrim-inating, comfortable, and even a bit self-congratulatory? He ar-rived with the bottle and poured a taste for my approval. Even the color was flamboyant: deep, thick gold, with elusive sparks of chartreuse. The aroma was almost visible rising from the glass: ripe, spicy Chardonnay fruit, a good bit of botrytis, loads of toast and vanilla. On the palate: glycerined, bursting at the seams with richness and flavor. When the steaming terrine arrived with its perfume of black truffle, it all created a gourmet's version of *bliss consciousness*.

Two wines, both Meursault, but they were so different thanks to the vintages, the austere soil of Blagny as opposed to that of Genevrières, the cellar environment, the vinification, and the personality of each winemaker.

François Jobard is also the source of one of wine's insoluble mysteries. He makes the one wine I have encountered that does not travel well, even under temperature-controlled conditions. And it is red! Why does his Blagny *blanc* arrive tasting exactly as it does in Meursault, while his Blagny *rouge* is irreparably fatigued? When I taste it there I want it, not for the commerce, because who out there is dying for a red called Blagny anyway? I love the wine enough to want it in my own cellar to enjoy from time to time at home. The wine has a dark tone, but there is not much coloring material. It has an intense fragrance somewhat reminiscent of forest berries, somewhat like an Alsatian *eau de vie* from raspberries. It is so ethereal and fine, and so apart from any other Pinot Noir in my experience. Is this one more proof that the Pinot is the most delicate, fragile, impressionable grape variety in existence?

While Meursault has provided the warmest memories, the white Burgundy that raises the hair on my back, that arouses passions ranging from teeth-gnashing outrage to utmost euphoria, is not even from the Côte d'Or. It is Chablis, northernmost Chablis, the yellow to golden-green wine from the gray, forgettable village of the same name, which has over two thousand inhabitants yet still manages to seem smaller than Meursault.

Halfway between Beaune and Paris, Chablis is surrounded by little burgs with names like Villy, Milly, Mussy, Bouilly, Joigny,

Maligny, Irancy, Nitry, Chitry, and Ervy. On the road, when you begin noticing all the y's, you know you are in the neighborhood of Chablis. Why it is not Chably, no one can tell me. None of the others has entered into the world vocabulary, but Chablis means something in many tongues. None of the others gave birth to an inimitable wine, so inimitable that Chablis itself has trouble begetting lucid versions of itself.

I worked to turn up a wine worthy of the fabled name Chablis, worked my palate to the quick in that bleak, drizzly, stone-cold village. Perhaps because its wine was too sour to the German taste, their bombers practically destroyed Chablis in June 1940, and I think its citizens still have not forgiven the rest of the world for that misfortune. I would like to announce to the people of Chablis that I had nothing to do with that bombing, that I was unborn, and that we Americans in general were gearing up to jump into the fray.

Aside from bombing runs and the local little cheese biscuits called *gougères,* wine is the only reason to go to Chablis. Otherwise, watch out for cold sheets, questionable *quenelles,* and frostbite.

Bitter? Yes, I am bitter. Loving Chablis is like falling in love with a frigid floozy. You begin to wonder if the rewards are worth the heartbreak and deception. And the *vignerons* there are bitter. They are bitter because of the frost and hailstorms that terrorize their grapevines. Imagine watching the fruits of your year's labor destroyed in an evening. In his late-sixties book about Burgundy, Pierre Brejoux wrote that the harvest from the steepest Chablis slopes is destroyed two out of three years, and often the catastrophe is spread wider, as in 1957, when one single hectoliter (133 bottles) of *grand cru* Chablis was declared. Between 1955 and 1961, frost struck every year except 1958.

I can hardly complain about my first visit in 1974. Dinner included a heart-pounding flirtation with an adorable young kitchen maid and a bottle of 1929 Le Clos with cheeses. The following day I stumbled upon and purchased some impeccable 1973 *grand cru* Bougros and Preuses. This is not only easy, it's fun, I thought, but then I returned two, sometimes three times per year, always to drive away empty-handed. The drought lasted seven years.

Well, of course, it is bloody simple to buy Chablis. My local supermarket sells "Chablis" by the jug, made in California. Or pay a visit to one of the big shipper houses in Beaune. You would think there was a river of the stuff. Hugh Johnson wrote about Chablis: "Every day, as much wine is drunk under its name as it often produces in a whole harvest." No, thanks, I was determined to buy Chablis from grapes grown in Chablis's stony Kimmeridgean limestone and clay. I wanted it raised in wood as my initial purchase in 1974 had been, and I wanted it bottled alive.

Before World War I, the *vignerons* at Chablis were also *tonneliers,* or coopers. Everyone made their own *feuillettes,* the small 132-liter barrels that were favored at Chablis, more than likely because in those icy cellars, where everything is slowed down, more wine-to-wood contact was desirable than farther south at Meursault or Puligny. The wine was sold in barrel; in other words, when a buyer bought Chablis, he bought the wine and its container. Thus, the growers were *obliged* to put their wine into new oak each vintage. New oak brought its special tannin and all sorts of other qualities to the raw wine, including greater potential for aging. Then the roller-coaster prices Chablis suffers finally make it financially impractical for the growers to afford new barrels every year. One grower claims seeing some years when the barrel was more costly than the wine in it.

How can one be for or against new oak for Chablis? One likes the flavor or not. What is undeniable is that Chablis *premiers* and *grands crus* profit from a passage in oak, old or new, be it *feuillette,* barrel, or the larger-sized *demi-muid.* Yet today it is rare to see an oak container at Chablis unless the winemaker has placed one on display outside his cellar to let passersby know that he has wine for sale. Modern vinification, which has almost taken over, employing 100 percent glass-lined or stainless-steel tanks, can produce good wine. There is a freshness to it that is not bad.

But I have never tasted one that possessed the depth of character, the profoundness, if you will, of the old style, which is aged in wood. Chablis, from that rough soil and climate, needs that respiration, that exchange with the atmosphere that glass and stainless cannot provide. Barrel aging refines the wine while slowly liberating its character. Even when well done, the new vinification in tanks inhibits this evolution toward a certain kind of maturity, resulting in a good rather than a great wine.

When it is badly done . . . ah, here is where the gnashing of teeth comes in. Chablis that tastes like Chablis is so hard to find even in the cellars of Chablis that I have trouble working up any sympathy for the French howls of noble outrage when they begin raving about our supermarket jugs of *Chablis* and even *Pink Chablis*. I know their indignation is justified, that Chablis is a place-name, that it is not fair to allow a vulgar *vin ordinaire* to parade about sporting the name of a truly noble growth whose reputation has been honored for centuries, blah, blah, blah . . . Agreed! On the other hand, criticism, like charity, begins at home, or should. By the time many bottles roll off the bottling lines at Chablis, the grapes might as well have come from Fresno, because cellar after cellar turns out the same anonymous-tasting plonk. No *goût de terroir*, no Chablis character, and little wine flavor left to them. The poor juice undergoes flash this or flash that, heat here and drop it below zero there, dose it with a hit of this and a hit of that, pump it up, down, and sideways through this filter and then through that, inject a stinky cloud of sulfur dioxide just to be extra-safe, insert the cork, *eh voilà!* it is in bottle and on the market three months after the harvest, calling itself wine and wearing a Chablis label. And they want us to worry about *Pink Chablis?*

If anyone has wondered why I did not simply return to the producer of my 1973 Bougros and Preuses, I did, and it was quite like my Sancerre experience. I found the old fellow's son in charge and nary a barrel left in sight. He had *improved* the vinification. He was in the process of gathering together the most extensive collection of filter devices I have ever seen.

§ *253* §

Then one year I visited a grower named Dauvissat, and I was swept away by what I tasted in barrel. I bought a few bottles to sample later, but when I uncorked them, by some inexplicable fluke, they had an off-taste. Or more likely, my taste was off. Based on those two or three bottles, I did not return to Dauvissat's cellar and I have kicked myself ever since. I order Dauvissat's Chablis whenever I see it, because it satisfies my notion of real Chablis.

But finally I did find what I was looking for and I found it at Taillevent, the gastronomic palace in Paris that possesses such a lovely wine list, including ancient vintages. Always on the look-out for a good Chablis, I spotted a 1976 Montée de Tonnerre from François Raveneau, and I knew as soon as I drew in its perfume that it was his that I wanted to import. Here was Chablis to rival the world's finest Chardonnays.

The next day I was to drive south from Paris, so it would be an easy detour to Chablis. I telephoned François Raveneau. His phone rang and rang. Then, just as I was about to give up, a rather steely voice responded: *J'écoute!* which means "I'm listening!"

I gave him my name and business and told him I tasted his wine at . . .

"I am not a factory. I don't export. I have nothing to sell." Click.

My left ear shattered from frostbite, I pondered taking up another line of work.

The next time in France, though, I rang him up again, "just to drop by, say *Bonjour,* see your cellar, taste the new vintage . . . ?"

No. He was too busy and there was no wine for sale. But he did say *Au revoir* before clicking off.

Six months later I received an excited phone call from Rebecca Wasserman, an American living and working in Burgundy. She announced breathlessly that she had visited Raveneau.

"You *what?* How did you manage *that?*"

She was exporting certain products for Jean Troisgros, the three-star restaurateur who bought Raveneau Chablis regularly

François Raveneau.

Chablis

for his wine list. Jean Troisgros invited her along to taste in Raveneau's cellar with him.

Well, after that, it was really very simple for me to get into Raveneau's cellar, too. When she called him to request an appointment for me, how could a Frenchman refuse a woman, a woman who was also an associate of Jean Troisgros? It would have been not only uncavalier but an insult to French gastronomy as well.

But, Raveneau told her firmly, the visit would be a visit to taste only! He had nothing for sale.

I invited Hubert de Montille from Volnay along with me, one of the illustrious names in Burgundian winemaking, who is also a successful attorney-at-law, an altogether persuasive combination, I hoped.

While de Montille and I tasted and enthused about the wines, Raveneau seemed impatient, cold, and aloof. Then I confronted him with the matter of a few cases of wine for the United States. He turned me off sharply. Too much paperwork. His wines were too fragile to ship. They were all sold, anyway! I turned away, mumbling and gnawing my glass of Chablis.

By the time we left, de Montille and Raveneau were gabbling so rapidly and I was enveloped in such a fog of despair that I could not keep up with their French. Did I say goodbye? In the car I swore that I never wanted to see or hear the word Chablis again. "I give up!"

"Didn't you understand?" de Montille asked. "At the end he said he will save three or four cartons for you from his next vintage!"

But that, I knew, would not be the end of it, and what Raveneau had said in a moment of warmth toward the irresistible Hubert de Montille might not be remembered a year later when I returned to Chablis alone.

Then I had an additional bit of luck. I was dining at the Champagne house of Billecart-Salmon, and Monsieur Billecart brought up a magnum of Le Clos, *François Raveneau!*

"Do you know Monsieur Raveneau?" I asked.

"Yes, quite well. We trade bottles from time to time."

"You could do me a great favor . . ."

Later Monsieur Billecart reported that Raveneau remained strongly against shipping overseas because his is a natural wine which undergoes no treatment whatsoever to stabilize it.

When I saw Raveneau again, I stated my case: that I take unusual pains in the transport of my wines, that his Chablis would be safe in a refrigerated container, that I buy other completely natural wines and have experienced no problems.

"All right," he growled, "but if one bottle spoils, I don't even want to hear about it."

And that is how, with a little help from Taillevent, Rebecca Wasserman, Jean Troisgros, Hubert de Montille, and Jean-Roland Billecart, I bought three hundred bottles of 1979 Chablis Le Clos.

If the nerve-jangling freeway that circles Paris, the *périphérique,* is not too jammed (*bouché,* or corked, as they say in Provence), Charles de Gaulle Airport can be less than a two-hour drive from Chablis. The last time I left France, I stayed the night in a Chablis hotel and shared a brunch of Chablis and oysters with the Raveneau family the next morning. Chablis with oysters is a stimulating combination which goes back at least to the tenth century, if the dating of this poetic fragment is correct:

§ *258* §

Chablis is so good with oysters
that I'm tempted to leave these cloisters
and find true love whe'ere I'm apt to.

Oysters washed down with a crisp, minerally Chablis invigorate the spirit. I felt good. The empty feeling that comes after weeks on the road was gone. I was excited and happy to be heading home. The *autoroute* was empty, the air was crisp and clear through my open window, traffic on the *périphérique* moved along at a wondrously sane pace, and my flight departed on time. Twelve hours later I was home in California, where my wife had some smoked salmon and a chilled half-bottle of Bandol rosé prepared for me, along with other long-awaited comforts of home. By far, it was the easiest departure and arrival I have experienced.

Life on the road. No one envies a traveling salesman. What am I if not a traveling buyer? Still, mine is a beckoning road whereupon my morning might be spent in a château with Count so-and-so and the afternoon in an earthen, wine-stained cellar under a farmhouse. Yet life on the road, even on the wine route, provides plenty of occasions to sing a traveling man's blues. There was the time I walked through the gates of a winery property near Beaune. I was on time for the rendezvous and the sign on the gate said ENTRÉE, so I entered. Instantly I found myself surrounded by five snarling dogs. Except for a near crash-landing, I have never been more terrified. The smallest of the five, a German shepherd, snapped a morsel out of my rear end. I made no purchases; the wines were dogs, too.

Second verse of my blues: hotel and restaurant disasters have been numerous. For example, the empty hotels during the winter season whose proprietors are too stingy to turn on the heat or hot water for one single guest, or that hotel on the beach near the Spanish border when the night was too hot to leave the windows closed, but once they were opened, a massive gathering of bloodthirsty mosquitoes turned the ceiling black. Bzzzz. The hotelkeeper offered me a bug bomb the size of a fire extinguisher, and I sat there trying to choose between slow death by insecticide poisoning or sacrificing myself drop by drop as nourishment for a mosquito orgy. I slept, sort of, in my car.

Once I had booked an early-morning flight home and I felt a desperate need for a relaxing night's sleep before departure, so I decided to skip downtown Paris. I checked the Michelin guide and found a hotel/restaurant recommended in a speck-sized village about twenty minutes from the airport. It was freezing out, so I sat in bed with a mystery novel while I waited for the dinner hour. Then the lights blinked off, which is not that unusual in France, but as I waited for them to blink back on, I began to notice the chill invading my room. I felt my way through darkened corridors to the lobby, where I was informed that the gas and electric workers were on strike, didn't I read the local papers, and no one knew when they would throw the switch back on. I lay under the covers in the dark and noticed what seemed like a rumble of thunder. My hotel was situated in the center of town, where the main highway narrowed, dipped, and took a sharp turn a few steps outside the door. A nonstop convoy of truckers had to brake, navigate the curve, then step heavily on the gas to accelerate out of the dip. In addition to the constant throb and rumble, the trucks also deposited a fog of diesel fumes, which collected in the basin where my hotel sat. The odor was nearly unbearable. The hotel's restaurant must have had a generator, because when I entered, it was brightly lit. The table settings were garishly ritzy with candelabra, several wineglasses, and lots of glittering silverware around the plates, all the meaningless accouterments that are necessary to obtain a listing in the *Guide Michelin*. I was the only diner. The waiter recommended the *andouillette* with mustard sauce. An *andouillette* is a tripe sausage. It can be delicious and sounded French enough to be an appropriate farewell dinner. Three or four bites were all I could force down, but they were enough to provoke relentless waves of nausea thirty minutes after I left the table. I was awake all night, shivering in the dark, gagging on diesel exhaust, and retasting that excuse for an *andouillette*. The next morning, weak and trembling, I barely made my flight.

Hotel disasters, food poisonings, auto breakdowns, airline horrors, so go the lyrics to a traveling man's blues.

After my last tour, taking off directly from Raveneau's table, I believe I finally found the best departure formula. Then, settling into my seat on the 747, I spent a couple of hours catching up on the American wine press. My office had forwarded a batch of recent publications to me.

I learned that a French insurance group had purchased Château Pichon Baron, a second growth in Pauillac, for a reported $45 million. What is an insurance group doing in the wine business? And if they have $45 million extra hanging around, why did they not refund it or lower their rates?

I learned that fifty percent of the Médoc is now harvested by machines. Man becomes more and more alienated from the means of wine production.

I read about a California politician's proposal that a special tax on wine provide funding for extra crime fighters. Why wine lovers were singled out to shoulder the burden was left unexplained, but is it not that in America wine is perceived as sinful? Too euphoric, perhaps. We sinners who enjoy wine are expected to foot the bill for the sinners who rape, loot, and murder.

Another article reported a wine auction in the Napa Valley where a six-pack wine cooler brought $2,800.

Then I read about a "Chardonnay shoot-out"! Château Wyatt Earp vs. Domaine Bat Masterson?

American wine critics were sounding the intellectual shallows, passionately debating numerical ratings for wine. The level of their debate: which is better, a 20- or 100-point scoring system? Not one critic suggested the possibility that scoring wine by numbers is inappropriate, that numerical ratings lead consumers away from a realistic, meaningful appreciation of fine wine.

The wine that I liked enough to consume more often than any other during 1987, Domaine Tempier's 1983 Bandol *rouge*, scored a measly 78 points in *The Wine Spectator*. So much for my palate! But consider the pleasure I would have missed had I followed the numbers instead of my own taste.

One wine writer claimed to have improved Paul Draper's 1980 Ridge Geyserville Zinfandel by freezing it, pouring off some of the alcohol (which separates out and remains liquid), then thawing out the wine in a microwave, thereby, according to the journalist, improving the wine's balance.

Another writer attacked the notion that wine improves with age. It is a myth, the propaganda of wine producers, the lore of "wine snobs"! That may be the least profound statement I have ever read about wine.

Then I read about California legislation that would require a pictograph of a pregnant woman and a giant wineglass with a slash through it on each wine label. Remember, I was on my way home from a country that regards wine as beneficial to health, where our French doctor advised my pregnant wife, "Of course you do not want to drink five liters a day, but a glass of wine with lunch and dinner will be good for you." In fact, the wine press was full of news about possible cigarette-style health warnings and ingredient labeling on wine bottles. Never mind that throughout history man has recognized that wine is nourishing and healthy—not unhealthy, not even neutral, but *healthy*. Thomas Jefferson and Jesus Christ advocated wine for medicinal purposes. Top those sources! But once again, at the drop of a hat, we reject the experience and wisdom of our ancestors. Now we place our faith in a new deity, statistics, and we look to them for eternal life. However, the do-gooders select their statistics carefully. In fact, there are statistics which indicate that the traditional Mediterranean diet built around grains, olives, and wine lowers the incidence of heart disease, stroke, stress, and certain cancers, but strangely enough, those statistics are not legally permitted on wine labels. Statistics also support Thomas Jefferson's assertion that wine-drinking populations suffer less alcoholism than others.

I am afraid the day is near when Mouton-Rothschild's beautiful artists' label and all the rest will be marred by misguided, nonsensical health warnings. I wish wine could be a constitutionally protected form of expression, to keep it out of the hands of pressure groups, politicians, hysterical moralists, and joyenders. We risk screwing up what is actually a very complex, delicate thing. The more rules and regulations there are, the less chance there will be to import those two or three barrels of handcrafted natural wine. The advantage will belong to the factory operations, with their thousands of cases of processed wine and their well-equipped office staffs which will permit them to cope with costly, time-consuming, bureaucratic requirements. In the wine world, bureaucracy begets standardized wine.

Colette wrote that "wine makes the true savor of the earth intelligible to man." And Nikos Kazantzakis wrote: "When you drank it, you felt as if you were in communion with the blood of the earth itself." Compare their almost mystical respect for wine to the claptrap I had been reading.

I was returning home to another country. The fragrant, humid cellars seemed so distant once I was buckled into my seat on the 747. I recalled the men and the women I had met. Their rare potions. Soon the ships would sail and deliver the goods I had purchased. I had to wonder if my treasures would be frozen and microwaved, entered in shoot-outs, assigned simplistic numerical scores, drunk up too early because maturity is merely a wine snob's myth. Would they be subjected to a sin tax? Would they be treated as a toxic substance?

Real wine is more than an alcoholic beverage. When you taste one from a noble *terroir* that is well made, that is intact and alive, you think here is a gift of nature, the fruit of the vine eked out of our earth, ripened by our sun, fashioned by man.

Once I took an afternoon off from wine tasting in Tuscany to visit a little museum in Florence where two recently discovered Greek statues were on display. The larger-than-life statues had a manlike shape and a heart-stopping, godlike presence. How had man created something so powerfully exquisite? Wine can produce the same reaction, but unlike music, literature, or visual arts, a great wine does not require a creative genius. A farmer working his piece of earth can produce something inspiring and profound.

There is so much contained in a glass of good wine. It is a gift of nature that tastes of man's foibles, his sense of the beautiful, his idealism and virtuosity.

Index